Buddhism in Indian Literature

Buddhism
in
Indian Literature

Edited by

NARENDRA K. DASH

INDIAN INSTITUTE OF ADVANCED STUDY
Shimla

ARYAN BOOKS INTERNATIONAL
New Delhi

BUDDHISM IN INDIAN LITERATURE

ISBN-81-7305-308-1

First published in **2007** by

INDIAN INSTITUTE OF ADVANCED STUDY
Rashtrapati Nivas, Shimla-171 005

and

ARYAN BOOKS INTERNATIONAL
Pooja Apartments, 4B, Ansari Road, New Delhi-110 002 (India)
Tel.: 23287589, 23255799; Fax: 91-11-23270385
E-mail : aryanbooks@vsnl.com

Computer Typeset and Printed in India at
ABI Prints & Publishing Co., New Delhi

Preface

The present volume contains the research papers presented in the National Seminar on 'Buddhism in Indian Literature' which was organised at Visva-Bharati, Santiniketan in collaboration with the Indian Institute of Advanced Study, Shimla to highlight the influence of Buddhist thoughts and religion on Indian literature, both ancient and modern. Twenty-three scholars from different parts of the country presented papers in the Seminar. The inaugural address by Swami Prabhananda Maharaj of the Ramakrishna Mission Institute of Culture, Kolkata and the keynote address by Professor Biswanath Banerjee, President, The Asiatic Society, Kolkata have also been included in this volume. Professor S.K. Pathak and Professor D.K. Barua's writings on modern Bhoti literature and pre-modern Bengali literature respectively are unique addition to this volume. We have also included considerable papers on the influence of Buddhism on Rabindra literature in particular and other Bengali literature in general written by prominent critics of the present time. Papers on the influence of Buddhism on the Oriya literature, the Tamil literature, the Telugu literature, the Hindi literature, the Sanskrit literature, the Urdu literature, the Marathi literature and Indian Poetry in English enrich this volume. Besides, two other papers, one on 'Buddhist samgha in early Indian texts' by Professor Pranabananda Jash, and the other on 'Recent works in Bengali on Buddhist Metaphysics and Pramāṇa Śāstras' by Professor Rita Gupta have also been incorporated in this volume.

I hope that these papers would eminently enlighten the researchers in furthering their interest in Buddhist Studies.

Contents

List of Contributors

Dr. Narendra Kumar Dash
Head, Department of Indo-Tibetan Studies, Visva-Bharati, Santiniketan-731 235.

Swami Prabhananda
President, Ramakrishan Mission Institute of Culture, Gole Park, Kolkata-700 029.

Prof. Biswanath Banerjee
President, The Asiatic Society, Park Street, Kolkata-700 164.

Prof. Suniti K. Pathak
Avanpalli, Birbhum, Santiniketan-731 235.

Prof. Dipak Kumar Barua
Government Housing Estate, Block No. L/1, Flat No. 1, 40/1, R.N. Choudhary Road (Tangra Road), Kolkata-700 015.

Prof. Sumita Chakrabarty
Krishnachuda Apartments, Ibhrahimpur Road, Jadavpur, Kolkata.

Prof. Biplab Chakrabarty
Flat No. 202, Archan Apartment, Baguaiati, Chawal Patty, P.O. Deshbandhu Nagar, Kolkata-700 059.

Dr. Sabuj Kali Sen (Mitra)
Department of Philosophy & Comparative Religion, Visva-Bharati, Santiniketan-731 235.

Prof. Bhabatosh Datta
Ratan Palli, Daily Bread Road, Santiniketan-731 235.

Prof. Pranabananda Jash
Department of A.I.H.C. & A., Visva-Bharati, Santiniketan-731 235.

Prof. Bijayananda Kar
House No. AM-26, VSS Nagar, Bhubaneswar-751 007 (Orissa).

Dr. Manoranjan Pradhan
Department of Oriya, Visva-Bharati, Santiniketan-731 235.

Prof. C. Muthiah
Department of Tamil, Visva-Bharati, Santiniketan-731 235.

Prof. Bela Bhattacharya
39 C, Palm Avenue, Kolkata-700 019.

Dr. (Mrs.) J. Sitaramamma
Associate Professor, Centre of Mahayana Buddhist Studies, Nagarjuna Universtiy, Nagarjuna Nagar, Guntur-522 510 (A.P.).

Prof. Angraj Choudhary
Vipassana Research Institute, Dhammagiri, Igatpuri, Nasik-422 403 (Maharashtra).

Dr. Bimalendra Kumar
Department of Pali & Buddhist Studies, Faculty of Arts, Banaras Hindu University, Varanasi-221 005 (U.P.).

Prof. Kalpika Mukherjee
Department of Sanskrit, Visva-Bharati, Santiniketan-731 235.

Prof. Aziz Haider
Kashi Vidya Peeth, Varanasi-221 002.

Prof. Sirajuddin Ahmed
Rabindra Professor, Tripura University, Agartala-799 004 (Tripura).

Dr. Rita Gupta
Department of Philosophy & Comparative Religion, Visva-Bharati, Santiniketan-731 235.

Prof. Niranjan Mohanty
Department of English, Visva-Bharati, Santiniketan-731 235.

Dr. Vimalakirtti
21, Subhash Nagar, Hingna Road, Nagpur-440 002.

Introduction

An intellectual inquisitiveness into the tenets and ideals of Buddhism grew strong in Bengal in the mid-nineteenth century AD leading to diverse scholarly research and in-depth studies of Buddhism, and culminating in the learned publications. Maharshi Debendranath Tagore, the father of the poet Rabindranath Tagore, was attracted towards the high and liberal ideals of Buddhism. Maharshi (1817-1905) along with his second son Satyendranath (1842-1923) and Keshab Chandra Sen (1838-1884) went to Ceylon in 1859 and witnessed the actual modes of functioning of Buddhism as a living religious force for the people. Keshab Chandra Sen was moved by the deep devotion and dedication of the Buddhists to their religion. Such a reverential stance of the people created in him a sense of love and respect for Buddhism because of which his whole family developed an abiding interest in this religion. His younger brother Krishnabehari Sen engaged himself in Buddhist studies and his *Asokacarita* (1892) was the first work in Bengali written on a theme related to Buddhism. Sunita Devi, the eldest daughter of Keshab Chandra, wrote *The Life of Princess Yasodhara* in 1929. Aghoranath, a disciple of Keshab Chandra composed his famous work *Sakyamuni-carit O Nirvana Tattva* in 1882, based on intensive research. This book of Aghoranath inspired many Bengali intellectuals and gradually many new books were published on the Buddha and his religion. The *Buddhadeva carit O Bauddhadharmer-Samksipta Vivaran* of Krishna Kumar Mitra was published in 1883 where the author proves that the Buddha was not a non-believer of God. Satyendranath, the eldest brother of Rabindranath Tagore wrote his book *Bauddhadharma* and it was published in 1901. This book makes a faithful study of the principles and teachings of the Buddha, highlighting the history and philosophy of Buddhism.

The establishment of the Mahabodhi Society in 1891 and the Bengal Buddhist Association in 1892 were also responsible for the revival of Buddhism and dissemination of certain aspects of Buddhist culture in Bengal. Raja Rajendralala Mitra (1822-1891), the first Indian president of the Royal Asiatic Society, was devoted to writing many books on Buddhism. Mention may be made of the *Buddhagaya, the Hermitage of Sakyamuni* and the *Sanskrit Buddhist Literature of Nepal* which inspired Rabindranath Tagore and many other Bengali writers.

The Indologist Ramdas Sen's *Modern Buddhistic Researches* (1870) and *Buddhadeva* (1891) also influenced Bengali intellectuals so far as Buddhism was concerned. Bankim Chandra Chattopadhyaya's *Samya* (1897) mentions that the first person who preached and practised equality in Indian society was Buddhadeva. Akshayakumar Dutta (1820-86), the editor of the *Tattvabodhini Patrika,* has dealt with Buddhism in the second part of his work entitled *Bharatavarsiya Upasak Sampradaya.* The name of Hara Prasad Shastri cannot be forgotten in the context of his contribution to the Buddhist studies.

Rabindranath Tagore was responsible for introducing Buddhism in modern Bengali literature, even though the poet Nabin Chandra Sen (1847-1909) composed his poetic work *Amitabha* (1895) on the life and philosophy of the Buddha. Nabin Chandra, following Arnold, depicted the life of the Buddha from his birth to his attainment of *parinirvana.* Rabindranath's poetic compositions like *Srestha Bhiksha* (1897), *Mastaka Bikraya* (1897), *Pujarini* (1899), *Abhisar* (1899), *Parisodh* (1899), *Samanya Kshati* (1899), *Mulyaprapti* (1899), *Sapamocana* (1931) and Satyendranath Datta's *Susveta* (1882-1922), *Ghum-Gumphay, Buddhapurnima* and the *Buddhabarana* also pay reverential homage to Lord Buddha. Besides, Bejoy Chandra Majumdar (1861-1942) in his poems celebrated many aspects of Buddhism. In *Yajnabhasma* and the *Pancakamala,* the collections of poems contain episodes from the life of the Buddha and some descriptions of the glories of Buddhist India. It may not be out of context to mention that Majumdar has translated the Pali text *Therigatha* into Bengali.

Among the prominent Bengali plays the *Buddhadeva Carita* (1887) of Girishchandra Ghosh happens to be first of its kind which deals with the outward events, inner struggles and final triumph of Siddhartha's life. His second play *Ashoka* (1911) depicts the transformation of *Candashoka* to *Dharmashoka.* Incorporating Buddha's concept of universal love and non-violence, Rabindranath has excelled in writing plays. Even if *Valmiki-pratibha* and *Visarjana* have not adopted any Buddhist stories, Buddhist idols inspired the poet to compose those dramas. *Malini* (1896), *Raja* (1910), *Acalayatana* (1912), *Natir Puja, Candalika* (1939), *Shyama* (1939), *Muktir Dak* (1923), *Rajpuri* (1925), and *Ashoka* (1933) have been composed on the basis of the Buddhist legends, *Jatakas* or *Avadanas.*

The Assamese language flourished under the neo-Vaishnavite psyche fighting against the ritualistic practices of the Tantras and the

Brahmanical scriptures between 14th and 16th centuries. During this time Buddha was canonized and taken as an incarnation of Vishnu in the Vaishnav literature, viz.,

Buddharupe veda pantha kari chhanna/
Vananaya sasre muhiacha sarbajana//

It means "in the form of the Buddha, you destroyed the Vedic way, only to lure people with false logic".

The *Light of Asia* of Edwin Arnold was translated into Assamese by Ananda Baruah, which tempted the Assamese writers to grow interest in the subject. Buddhist themes are also available in the writings of Madhabdev Sarma, Gopinath Bardoloi, Surya Kumar Bhuyan and Megharam Pathok. The translation of *Milinda Panho* (Dhirendranath Das), the *Dhammapada* (Upen Lekharu), *Bhikshu Pattimoksa, Datha Vamsa* by Sasanavamsa Bhikkshu and *Acariya Dhammapada* created much interest in Buddhism among the laity in Assam. The *Saddhama Siksa* of *Sasanavamsa* contains prayers and songs sung by the laity.

The *Buddhagaya* of Bidya Kanta Bora is a significant example of continuing interest in Buddhism in the contemporary period. B.K. Barua and Atul Chandra Hazarika also rendered the *Jataka* stories in different versions in Assamese. Buddhist thought is also reflected in the poems of Nilomoni Pukkan.

The kind-hearted, innocent and poor people of Orissa not only accepted Buddhism, the intellectuals made the propagator an incarnation of Vishnu. Indrabhuti, a royal sage of Orissa in the 7th century AD, who was the original exponent of *Vajrayana*, a Tantric school of Mahayana system, gave a new identity to the Hindu deity Jagannath, bringing together the two faiths of Buddhism and Brahmanism, viz.,

pranipatya jagannatham sarvajinavara rcitam/
sarvabuddhamayam siddhi vyapinam gaganopamam//

The fifteenth-century Oriya poet Sarala Das accepted the *mahasukha* concept of the Sahajayanists and gave a Vaishnavite colour to this Tantric term in his *Mahabharata*. To him, the stream of milk that flows from the *Kadamba* tree will give *mahasukha* to the *bhaktas*. Again, the same poet refers to various Buddhist technical concepts like *sunya, sahajasadhana* and *dharma* which suggest that Sarala Das was considerably influenced by Buddhism. The *Sahaja* concept of the Mahayanists influenced almost all the literary personalities of Orissa in the medieval period.

In the modern period, Fakir Mohan Senapati (1843-1918) composed his *Buddhavatarakavya* (1909) with the objective of social reforms. This composition on the Buddha's life led to the emergence of Fakir Mohan as a novelist and a prose writer. Two other poets of this period, Radhanath Ray (1848-1908) and Madhusudan Rao (1853-1912) used the Buddhist ideas in their compositions for the socio-religious progress. We find in the poems *Mahayatra* (1997) and *Darabara* (1897) of Radhanath Ray many Buddhist concepts. In *Mahayatra,* he stresses that *kali* begins from *kama* (lust) and in *Darabara,* he argues that in the eyes of *dharma* there is no difference between the trees below and those on the hill-top. If we see the world being seated on the hill of *dharma,* we will find everything as equal and the world dancing around us.

The Sabuja poet Baikunthanath Pattanaik (1904-1978) has used the message of the Buddha in his writings like *Amba Palir Utkantha* and *Bhikshu.* Another noted poet of Sabuja Movement, Mayadhara Mansingh (1915-1973) seems to have been influenced by the Buddha and his philosophical ideas. In his *Buddhavani* he celebrates Lord Buddha's greatness:

> Oh! Buddha, you are pure;
> You are the greatest *siddha*;
> The world is looking for you today.

This long poem displays a sensitive response to nature and a patriotic recollection of the country's past and combines these with a semi-mystical perception of an unknown force of life.

Thus the Oriya novels, dramas, short stories, epics and poems contained Buddhist themes. The Buddhist culture, philosophy and religion influenced the literary personalities who had considerable influence on the society.

The modern Hindi writers like Ramachandra Sukla, Jaisankar Prasad, Maithilisaran Gupta, Mahadevi Verma, Sohanlal Dwivedi, Chatursen Sastri, Ramakumar Verma, Mohan Rakesh, Chandragupta Vidyalankara, Rahul Sankrtyayana, Nagarjuna and Bhadant Ananda Kausalyayan were influenced by Buddhist thoughts and philosophy. For our interest, we mention some of the literary works along with the names of the writers, where we find expression of some Buddhist thoughts and ideas:

	Title	Author	Type
1.	*Buddhacarita*	Ramachandra Sukla	Poetry (translation)
2.	*Yasodhara*	Maithilisaran Gupta	Poetry
3.	*Kunal*	Sohanlal Dwivedi	Poetry
4.	*Ajatasatru*	Jaisankar Prasad	Drama
5.	*Chandragupta*	"	"
6.	*Skandagupta*	"	"
7.	*Visakha*	"	"
8.	*Rajasri*	"	"
9.	*Samrat Kaniska*	"	"
10.	*Carumitra*	Ram Kumar Verma	"
11.	*Ashoka*	Chandra Gupta Vidyalankar	"
12.	*Leharon ke Rajhamsa*	Mohan Rakesh	"
13.	*Vaisali ki Nagarvadhu*	Chatursen Sastri	Novel
14.	*Bodhivrksa Ki Chhayamen*	"	"
15.	*Simha Senapati*	Rahul Samkrityayana	"
16.	*Jai Yaudheya*	"	"
17.	*Vismrut Yatri*	"	"
18.	*Iravati*	Jaisankar Prasad	"

The works like *Buddhacarita, Yasodhara, Bodhivrksa ki Chhayamen* and *Leharon ke Rajhamsa* drew the themes directly from the life of the Buddha. The *Buddhacarita* is a translation of the famous English poetical work *The Light of Asia* by Edwin Arnold. The work of Chatursen Sastri, *Under the shade of Bodhi tree,* contains the story of the Buddha, Ashoka and Harshavardhana. The author of this work seems to have consulted the Buddhist scriptures, the *Jatakas* and some other works of ancient Buddhist writers. The work not only speaks about the important events in the life of the Buddha from his childhood to his attaining *nirvana* but also quotes from the canonical literature.

The *Vaisali ki Nagarvudhu, Simha Senapati* and the *Ajatasatru* are basically historical works in Hindi. In the novel of Chatursen Sastri, Amrapali is the central character. The author has narrated the story of the Buddha's acceptance of Amrapali's invitation to a feast and her gift of a large mango-grove for constructing a *Vihara.*

Though Jainism flourished in Gujarat and Rajasthan, still in the literature of these two states we find many compositions with Buddhist themes. The Buddha has been recognized as an *avatara* in many devotional songs of Rajasthan. Poet Hari Das and Isar Das have included Lord Buddha in the list of 24 *avataras.* Isar Das suggests that the Buddha came to this earth to preach the concept of kindness or *daya,* viz.,

namo bhava-bodh bhayo bhagavan/
namo grahi jiva-daya urgyan //

Poet Kanhaiya Lal Sethia depicts Lord Buddha as the prince of peace. Poet Satya Prakash Joshi has also narrated the importance of peace in his epic *Radha.* The poet Chandra Prakash Dewal in his poem *Prahas sonor* describes the teaching of non-violence of Buddhism. The praise of Lord Buddha in the sonorous metrical verse of *Dingal* style is an impressive piece of Rajasthani poetry:

juddha vratisu jagat me raham bhav bhaye ruddha/
suddha karan nar-samajh ne pragate buddh-prabuddh//

The Light of Asia by Edwin Arnold was translated into Gujarati by Narsimharao Divetia. The Gujarati title of his work is *Buddhacarita.* The novel *Sarasvaticandra* of Govardhanram was composed with Buddhist themes and thoughts. The play *Sanghamitra* of Nhanalal depicts the last days of King Ashoka, when he insists Mahendra and Sanghamitra to propagate the message of Lord Buddha.

During the Gandhian age of modern Gujarati literature, the Buddha's life and teachings received greater attention of the people at large. Two great Gujarati poets of this age, Umashankar Joshi and Sundaram were influenced by the philosophy and personality of Lord Buddha. Joshi's *Visvashanti* teaches the importance of universal love and tolerance. Another poem by the same author, *Barne Barne Buddha,* sings of war and conflict-ridden humanity longing for peace and love, and praying for the arrival of a Gandhi, a Buddha, at every doorstep. Sundaram or Tribhuvandas Luhar's poem *Buddhana Cakshu* uses the theme of the Buddha's compassion for the poor and the depressed. In his poem *Trimurti,* he highlights the relevance of Buddhist ideals in the context of the modern Indian environment. The poems like *Buddha* of B.K. Thakor, *Tadguna* of Narsimharao, *Yasodhara* of Nathalal Dave, *Sulocanu Locandan* of Sunderjee Betai, *Buddhanu Punaragamana* of Krishnalal Shridharani, *Abhisra* of Zaverchand Meghani and *Parajayanijit* and *Chhellipuja* of Prahlad Parekh speak of Buddhist themes and values.

A biography of the Buddha was also composed in Gujarati, entitled *Buddha-caritramrit* by Valjibhai Desai. The same author is also credited with *Bodhicaryavatar*, which combines the biography of the Buddha with a brief introduction to his teachings. Dharmananda Damodar Kosambi published a Gujarati version of the *Dhammapada* and the *Dhammapada Navnit*. Bholabhai Patel also translated the Bengali story composed by Jyotindra Datta into Gujarati under the title *Buddhanu nirvan*.

After the publication of the book *Buddha Dharma ani Sangha* of Dharmanand Kosambi, an active interest in Buddhism was aroused among the Marathi writers. Of course, three more works in Marathi were composed before Dharmanand that are related to the Buddha or Buddhism. These are: a) *Buddha Dharmaca Sansthapak Sakyamuni Gautam Yace Caritra* (1883) by Vasudev Lakshman Athavale; b) *Sri-Jagadguru Gautamabuddha Caritra athava Mahabhiniskraman* (1894) by Govind Narayan Kane; and c) *Gautama Buddha Caritra* (1898) by Krishnarao Keluskar. Dharmanand's work portrays the Buddha's personality as exhibiting a dynamic fusion of sacrifice, endurance, control, peace, non-violence and universal love. It also expounds the three steps of *Sila, Samadhi* and *Prajna* in the Buddhist *Dhamma* and analytically elucidates the significance, nature and importance of *samgha*.

The short story writers like V.S. Khandekar, C.V. Joshi, Cintamani, Madhav Keshab Katdare, V.S. Gurjar and many others have used the Buddhist themes in their literary compositions. However, Buddhism was widely accepted in Maharashtra by Dr. Ambedkar and his followers. Ambedkar's work, *The Buddha and his Dhamma* (1974) supports Kosambi's claim that Buddha's *pravrajya* was the result of a deeply thought, well-planned and determined decision. He left the society with the consent of his wife without yielding to the pressure of his weeping parents.

Shankarrao Kharat, a follower of Ambedkar, composed his novel *Manusakici hak* in 1957. The *dalit* life is nicely depicted in this novel. A *dalit* is driven out of the village when he goes against the tradition or convention. Then the *dalit* accepts Lord Buddha and steps forward towards revolution. Thus the whole atmosphere becomes surcharged with *Buddham saranam gacchami*. The *Muktisangram* of H.G. Bansode is also written with a similar story. Thus the Buddha and his teachings influenced the *dalit* literature of Maharashtra and the *dalit* writers firmly believe that Buddha, Jotiba Phule and

Ambedkar are the only persons who have severely attacked the casteism.

Among the Dravidian languages, the *Buddhacarita* (1902) was composed in Telugu by poets Divakarla Sastri and Cellapilla Venkatasastri and this is the first Telugu composition with a Buddhist theme. In 1904, G.Y. Doraswamiah published his prose work *Gautama-Buddha-Caritra.* The first biographical work of the Buddha in Telugu is the *Siddhartha-Caritra* of Cilakamarti Lakshmi Narasimham. The modern Telugu writers have used the Buddhist themes in their poetry, dramas, novels, short stories and translations with great joy. Many Telugu translators have translated of philosophical and religious works of Buddhist thinkers in the 20th century AD. The translations of the *Madhyamika Vimsati, Mula-madhyamika-karikalu, Vigraha Vyavartani, Bhavasamkranti sutravrtti, Pratityasamutpada hrdayam, Ratnavali* and the *Vajrachedika* are important works in the Buddhist philosophical literature.

The *Buddha Gita* (1943) of Vedula Suryanarayan Sarma, the *Kathalu-gathalu* (1947) of Veluri Sivarama Sastri, the *Pragi yoti* (1959) of Ramachandra Reddy, the *Premanjali* (1968) of Vadlamudi Siddhaiah Kavi and the *Sujata* (1976) of the same author are some of the poetical works where we find considerable influence of Buddhist themes.

The prose compositions of Pemmaraju Venkatachalapai Rao (*Gautama Buddhamuni Jivitamu*), D.B. Krishnaiah (*Buddha Puranamu*), Ratnakara Balaraju (*Buddha Yugamu*), K.V. Ramana Reddy (*Padmpuja*) and Tirumala Ramachandra (*Dharmadiksa*) contain Buddhist themes and stories.

In modern Tamil literature, we find the influence of Buddhism only after the foundation of the Theosophical Society in Madras. The Madras branch of the Mahabodhi Society was also established in the year 1899. These two social organizations are responsible for the revival of Buddhism in South India. Of course, a little before, Yalappanam Ci. Vai. Tamotaram Pillai published the Buddhist grammatical work *Viracoliyam* of Puttamittirar in 1881 and U. Ve. Caminata Aiyar edited the Tamil epic *Manimekhalai* in 1898. The *Jataka* stories and the *Dhammapada* have also been translated into Tamil.

The *Manimekhalai* have influenced the creative writers of the modern Tamil literature. We find the influence of the epic on the saint Ramalinka Cuvamikal (1825-1874) who propagated the ideals of *Canmarkkam* (right path) and *Jivakarunyam* (compassion) in his poems. Venkatachalam Pillai's *Manimekhalai Natakam* (1949) is nothing but the dramatized form of the epic *Manimekhalai.*

In 1938 Cuttananta Parati published the drama *Buddhar Karunai* based on the life and teachings of the Buddha. Towards the last part of the 20th century, Cuntaran Canmukanar composed a long poem of epic with 30 chapters entitled *Kautama Puttar Kappiyam* (1986) on the life of the Buddha. The novel *Kettatellam Potum* (1971) of Ra. Cu. Nallaperumal is the only work in Tamil dealing with the spiritual development of Siddhartha into the Buddha. This novel narrates in detail the activities of Siddhartha after he left the palace and before becoming the Buddha. Ku. Pa. Rajagopalan in his short stories like *Lrulilitruntu* and *Mahabodam* has taken the plot from Buddhist stories. In the *Mahabodam,* he narrates the episode of Sujata who fed the Buddha with *payas.* The writer depicts that this is a great moment when the master realized the limitations of painful meditations and learned the path of love and compassion from Sujata, which he preached to the world.

Scholars opine that Buddhism influenced the social and spiritual life of Kerala from 3rd century BC. Though there was a fight between Hinduism and Buddhism, and the Saivites captured the Buddhist monasteries, Buddhism continued to prevail in the social and cultural life of Kerala. In modern period the social reform movement was mainly responsible for the reflection of Buddhist themes in Malayalam literature. The *Light of Asia* was translated into Malayalam by Nalapattu Narayana Menon and drew attention of the intellectuals of Kerala. The *Buddhadharmam* seems to be the first comprehensive account in Malayalam on the theory and practice of Buddhism.

Kumaran Asan, a well-known Malayalam poet, had great respect for the Buddha. Therefore, towards his last days he composed a *Buddha caritam* on the basis of the *Light of Asia.* However, he could not complete the work. His compositions like *Candala Bhiksuki, Karuna* and *Durabastha* seemed to be influenced by Buddhism. In *Durabastha,* the poet raised his voice against casteism and the heroine Savitri, who being a Namboodiri girl marries a *Pulaya* boy, Cattan. In *Candala Bhiksuki,* he fights against caste oppression and untouchability. The story of this work is taken from the *Essence of Buddhism* of Lakshmi Narasu. The Buddhist story of Vasavadatta seems to be served as the basis of the plot of *Karuna* of Kumaran Asan.

The influence of Buddhist themes is also considerably found on the Kashmiri literature. The religion of the Buddha made its way to Kashmir much before Ashoka. The *Mahavamsa* suggests that Madhiantika converted Yakhsa Pandita and a Naga to Buddhism in the first instance. However, during the time of Rin-Chen-Zan-po, this religion was firmly rooted in this region. Like other Indian literature, the literature of Kashmir was also influenced by the facts, stories and other themes related to the Buddha and his religion and philosophy.

A close study on the subject suggests that the Kashmiri literature was developed in Buddhist lore. The 14th-century poet Lal Ded and his immediate successor Nund Risi (1377-1442) seem to be highly influenced by Buddhism. Lal Ded, the lady poet of Kashmir, argues that Buddhism keeps us away from two extremes, i.e., the life of ease and luxury and the life of rigorous asceticism. Nund Risi not only preached love, non-violence, compassion and universal brotherhood, but also led a pious life. His first long poem *Buddha-carita* is found in some *Risi-nama.*

Modern literary figures like Master Zinda Kaul, Motilal Kemmu, Avtar Krishan Rehbar, Motilal Sagi, Dina Nath Nadim, Ariandev Majboor and Abdul Ahad Azad used Buddhist themes in their compositions in the modern period.

The play *Tsay* of Motilal Kemmu is an important literary work in Kashmiri literature. The subject of the play is avoidance of war. Embodying protest against war and its repercussions, the writer has borrowed freely from the history of Buddhism and other Buddhist themes. The hero of the play, Saravajna Mitra, was a Kashmiri by birth and a teacher of the famous University of Taxila.

The short story *Nirvana* of Avtar Krishan Rehbar teaches that the concept of *Nirvana* has lost its meaning for the present-day man who goes running after wealth and other sensual pleasures. Motilal Sagi has translated a good number of *Jataka* stories into Kashmiri. One of his poems *Mrgvan* also dealt with the subject of attainment of enlightenment of the Buddha.

Thus, Buddhism was very much alive in Indian minds and therefore, the modern writers from each corner of this country have taken the Buddhist themes for their own compositions. In the modern period, the Theosophical Society and the Mahabodhi Society of India worked for the revival of Buddhism and the *Light of Asia* played a vital role in influencing modern writers to use Buddhist themes in their poems, plays and stories. The translation of Buddhist works into regional languages also was started with full effort only after the composition of Arnold's work. Buddhism disappeared as a distinct religion in India for historical reasons after giving rise to all that is best in our culture. This religion had given to us an art and a literature of which we are still proud. It may not be an injustice if we opine that because of this religion, India is known as a holy land in the world. Therefore, Dr. P.C. Bagchi rightly remarked in his book *India and Central Asia*: "No scheme of cultural reconstruction of India can afford to neglect the study of Buddhist civilization. An Asiatic Academy which will centre round Buddhist studies in all its phases, Chinese, Tibetan, Mongolian, Manchurian, Korean, Japanese, Siamese, Anamites, Cambodian, Burmese and Ceylonese can render the greatest service to the cause of humanity by bringing about a profound cultural understanding between the races of three quarters of Asia."

Considering the influence of Buddhist themes on the Indian literature, the Department of Indo-Tibetan and Buddhist studies, Visva-Bharati proposed the Indian Institute of Advanced Study, Shimla, to hold a National Seminar on the subject to explore the unknown and unexplored areas where there is considerable influence of Buddhist themes. The Indian Institute of Advanced Study kindly accepted our proposal and provided necessary funds to materialize the proposal. We are also grateful to some reputed and erudite scholars in this field. The department is highly obliged to Swami Prabhananda of Ramakrishna Mission Institute of Culture, Professor V.C. Srivastava, Director, Indian Institute of Advanced Study, Professor V. Venkatachalam and Professor Biswanath Banerjee, President, The Asiatic Society, for their kind presence at the inaugural session of the Seminar.

Lastly, I am thankful to the authorities of the Indian Institute of Advanced Study, Shimla, for their kind help to publish the proceedings of the National Seminar in a book form for the benefit of the academic world.

Santiniketan NARENDRA K. DASH

1

Buddhism in Indian Literature

Swami Prabhananda

Though the subject "Buddhism in Indian Literature" is very interesting and thought provoking, I consider myself unequal to the task. I do not claim expertise on any aspect of this multi-faceted subject. However, this talk has given me a unique opportunity to express my feelings as an admirer of the great Buddha and his teachings and also to pay my tribute to the vast literature that has grown from them.

Indian literature today means the literature produced in the Indian languages, beginning with Vedic Sanskrit in the hoary past to the literature written by Indians in English, Hindi, and other regional languages. Substance and form inter-penetrate and mingle in any literary composition. Here we are concerned more with the substance called Buddhism in the context of Indian literature.

There abides something more subtle than just a chemistry of language and substance in a piece of literature, and herein one discovers the genius of India, a genius that flows quietly and steadily, in spite of the almost imperceptible changes through the years and the ethos of the different epochs. Naturally, therefore, Indian literature glorifying Buddhism will be somewhat distinct and different from literature of other countries wherein Buddhism has flourished.

Buddhism was once popular and very influential in India. The probable reason for this can be given by quoting Mahatma Gandhi, who once observed, "Buddha's teachings like his heart was all-expanding and all-embracing, and so it has survived his body and swept across the face of the earth."[1]

Buddhist literature centring round the Buddha and Buddhism is vast, and it is extant in different languages. Logically, as Buddha was such a world-renowned and historical figure, the major portion of the Buddhist literature should have been devoted to him, but it is not so. Strangely enough, there is no complete historical biography of Gautama, the Buddha in the early Buddhist scriptures. The doctrines ascribed to the Buddha are better known than the details of his life, except for a few works, such as *Malankara Watthu,* written in Pali perhaps about two thousand years after the Buddha himself; an older life sketch of the Buddha, called the *Jataka,* written in Pali in the fifth century and covering the first thirty-six years of his life; two Sanskrit poems, the *Buddha Carita* and the *Lalita Vistara,* written in the early part of this era–there is no biography as such. Of all the so-called life stories, the most popular is the beautiful English poem entitled *The Light of Asia,* written by Sir Edwin Arnold. Nevertheless, one cannot deny the tremendous influence of the Buddha and his teachings even today. Swami Vivekananda was a great admirer of Lord Buddha. Once, in response to a query whether he was a Buddhist, he observed:

"I am the servant of the servants of the servants of the Buddha. Who was there ever like him? The Lord—who never performed one action for himself—with a heart that embraced the whole world! So full of pity that he—the prince and the monk—would give his life to save a little goat! So loving that he sacrificed himself to the hunger of a tigress—to the hospitality of a pariah and blessed him! And he came into my room when I was a boy and I fell at his feet! For I knew it was the Lord Himself!"[2]

In the words of Swami Vivekananda, "Jesus Christ was a Jew, and Shakya Muni was a Hindu. The Jews rejected Jesus Christ, but the Hindus have accepted Shakya Muni as God and worship him.... Shakya Muni came not to destroy, but he was the fulfilment, the logical conclusion, the logical development of the religion of the Hindus." In the same lecture Swami Vivekananda pointed out that the separation between the Buddhists and the Brahmins was the cause of the downfall of India.[3] In a wider perspective Buddha was but a rebel child of Hinduism as was pointed out by Swami Vivekanand.

The following perceptive comments from the pen of the great thinker Rabindranath Tagore gives some insight into the spirit of Buddhist literature, as also the continued popularity of the Buddha and his enlightenment, popularly called "bodhi". He wrote: "So when a man lives the life of *avidya* he is confined within his own self. It is a spiritual sleep; his consciousness is not fully awake to the highest reality that surrounds him, therefore, he knows not the reality of his own soul. When he attains bodhi, i.e., the awakenment from the sleep of self to the perfection of consciousness, he becomes the Buddha.... The emancipation of our physical nature is in attaining health, of our social being in attaining goodness, and of our self in attaining love. This last is what the Buddha describes as extinction—the extinction of selfishness. This is the function of love, and it does not lead to darkness but to illumination. This is the attainment of bodhi, or the true awakening, it is the revealing in us of the infinite joy by the light of love."

This opens up the hope of light for every man. Man can attain "bodhi"; he can become a Buddha. The great Buddha inspires every one of us to become *Atmadipa* (a light to oneself), and to help others to light their lamps in order to remove the darkness of sorrow that enshrouds humanity.

T.W. Rhys Davids once observed: "Gotama was born and brought up, and lived and died a Hindu. His teaching, far-reaching and original as it was, and really subversive of the religion of the day, was Indian throughout. Without the intellectual work of his predecessors his own work, however original, would have been impossible. He was no doubt the greatest of them all."[4] Buddhism was no doubt swallowed by the powerful and traditional Hindu religion, yet its true history remains an unexplained mystery. However, Buddhism was very much Indian in content and spirit. Though Buddhism as a cult did not survive, it survived in literature. Then, through its contact with the West, there was widespread interest in Buddhism in the 19th century.

After his enlightenment, Gautama Buddha converted five recluses to his new doctrine at Sarnath, near Varanasi, and in three months' time the number of his followers rose to sixty persons. Though diametrically opposed to the dominant creed of the Brahmins, his teachings spread rapidly but peacefully unlike the Christian and Mohammedan teachings. This created a golden chapter in human history.

After the Buddha's death, Buddhist councils were convened to ascertain the authenticity and priority of the available teachings of the Buddha. The third council, held more than two hundred years after the Buddha's *parinirvana*, settled the Buddhist canonical literature and grouped it under three divisions (*Tripitaka*): (a) the *Vinaya Pitaka* (the rules for the conduct of the order), (b) the *Sutta*

Pitaka (doctrines of the order), and (c) the *Abhidhamma Pitaka* (higher subtleties of the doctrine). *Tripitaka* means three *pitakas** or baskets.

The *Vinaya Pitaka* contains rules of discipline for the guidance of the Buddhist Sangha and precepts for regulating the daily life of monks and nuns. The *Sutta Pitaka* is a collection of the doctrinal expositions, large and small. It is the primary source for the teachings of the Buddha and his earliest disciples. The *Abhidhamma Pitaka* consists of seven books, usually known as the *Sattapakaranas.* According to the Pali tradition, this is what the Buddha first preached to the *tavatimsa* gods, and subsequently to Sariputta. The contents do not form a systematic philosophy, but are a special treatment of the *Dhamma* as found in the *Sutta Pitaka.* The *Dhammapada* is an anthology containing 423 verses, divided into 26 *vaggas* (chapters). The Buddhists believe that they are the very words of the Great Teacher. Its main objective is to impart moral teachings to the common man. It is the most popular Buddhist treatise and has been translated into various languages of Asia and Europe.

Most Buddhist sects had their own version of the *Pitakas.* With the exception of the Pali *Pitakas* of *Sthaviravādins,* these have not survived in entirety. In most schools of Mahajans their place was largely taken by later texts, mostly composed in the early part of the Christian Era. These were in Sanskrit in India, though in other parts of Asia preference was in local vernacular.

Many of the manuscripts of the Buddhist literature, originally written in Pali, Buddhist Sanskrit, and pure Sanskrit were lost, but they were preserved in Tibetan and Chinese translations. The whole of the old Buddhist literature consists of collections of sermons, conversations, sayings, songs, narratives, and rules of the countries in which it exerted influence. Buddhism also underwent many transformations in its migrations from its home country to Sri Lanka, China and Japan.

Apart from the original canonical literature in Pali, there are also a large number of later Pali works. The *Milindapanha* is the oldest and most famous, containing the dialogue between King Milinda and the venerable monk Nagasena. Besides, works on rhetorics and metrics and lexicons constitute a vast and varied literature in Pali.

* *Pitaka* means basket. The long strips of prepared palm-leaf on which the text were written were originally stored in baskets.

Most of them are the works of the monks of Sri Lanka. Buddhist literature was further enriched by a galaxy of eminent scholars such as Asvaghosa, Nagarjuna, etc. who wrote in pure Sanskrit. In fact, most of the works of the Buddhist literature that were incorporated into the mainstream of Buddhist thought and culture "stand unparalleled for their sublime thought, super-intellectual treatment and unique literary excellences", observed Anukul Chandra Banerjee.[5]

In this connection, A.L. Basham's observation seems to be quite interesting. It pinpoints a new dimension of Buddhist thoughts. He writes, "The basic proposition of the great body of literature are not metaphysical, but psychological. Sorrow, suffering, dissatisfaction, and the manifold unpleasantness, which are referred to by the word *dhukha* are inherent in life as it is ordinarily lived; they can only be eliminated by giving up 'thirst' (tanha), often translated 'craving', which includes personal ambition, desire, longing, and selfishness of all kinds."[6]

To appreciate the relative importance of Pali texts, and Sanskrit and semi-Sanskrit texts, we shall do well to refer to Maurice Winternitz's *A History of Indian Literature.* There he writes, "If we had only the Pali texts and nothing besides, we would certainly form merely a one-sided idea of Buddhism. On the other hand, if only the Sanskrit and semi-Sanskrit Buddhist texts and none of the Pali canon had come down to us, we should have an entirely distorted picture of Buddhism and only a scanty notion of the original teaching and personality of Buddha."[7] The Sanskrit Buddhist literature of Nepal and the Chinese and Tibetan translation from the Sanskrit constituted a lot. Reviewing the panorama of the Buddhist Literature Winternitz concluded observing, "Whatever our views of the new Buddhist movement may be, we cannot but admire the vitality of Buddhism and of the works of the Buddhist literature, which have ever and again inspired the minds of thinkers and poets of all nations, and still continue to do so."[8]

The tremendous impact of Buddhism on ancient Indian literature remains almost unrecognized among scholars. We can get some idea of this influence from the following comments penned by the great scholar Dr. Surendranath Dasgupta. He observed: "Most of the highest teachings of the *Puranas* can be read word for word in the Buddhist scriptures which preceded them. Many of the myths and stories of the *Puranas* too owe their origin to the *Jatakas* and

Avadanas. The whole of Patanjali's *Yogasutra* with *Vyasabhasya* does not seem to be anything more than a Hindu version of the Buddhist Yoga." He further noted: "I yield to none in my profound respect for the great teacher Sankara, but a careful analysis of his writings demonstrates indisputably that he largely borrowed his doctrine, his phraseology, his dialectics and his method of approach from Buddhism. Not only Sankara, but many of his followers like Sriharsa, Anandajnana and others who have constructed the Vedanta into a rational system of philosophy deliberately followed the footprints of Nagarjuna and other Buddhist writers."[9]

The vastness of the influence of Buddhism over a period of two thousand years is awe-inspiring. We may recall T.W. Rhys David's remark that: "The history of Buddhism is the history of more than half the people in the world for more than two thousand years."[10] None can deny that Buddhism has left some indelible marks on the social and cultural life of the people in different parts of India. However, his teaching was Indian throughout. And Buddhism is essentially an Indian system.

With the passage of time the original colour of Buddhism became diversified into various shades, and consequently the Buddhist literature too became diversified. This diversity was largely the combined result of geographical diffusion and cultural adaptations. Wherever, Buddhism was introduced, it became an integral part of the local culture "partly by adapting to local beliefs and cults and partly by absorbing them into its own system. The absence of a central doctrinal authority like the Catholic church, the relation of the Buddhist Order with the temporal power, social stratification within the clergy, royal patronage, and other such characteristics of Buddhism itself were also factors that stimulated diversification" and this in turn, cast its shadow on the Buddhist literature in different regions and in different languages.

Buddhist scriptures have for many centuries been translated into a great variety of regional languages. So also, original writings appeared in many of these languages. The literature in these languages was influenced by geographical diffusion as well as ongoing regional differentiation, and thus came up great diversity in the literature produced presenting Buddha and his great sublime teachings. It happened in different periods of history at different pace. No doubt, Buddhism in different Indian regional languages is a vast subject.

During the 19th century, Buddhism's contact with the West gave it a much-needed fillip, as also a new lease of life in India. The increasing interest of European scholars stirred the hearts of Indian intellectuals. According to some scholars, Migeltuwalte Gunanande's dynamic role in the famous debate at Panadura in August 1873 drew the attention of outside scholars and created a stir. Then, after Col. Olcott's and Madame Blavatsky's visit to India and Ceylon in 1880, the Theosophical Society helped in the revival of Buddhism. With the help of Maha Theras, Col. Olcott established the Buddhist Theosophical Society on June 17, 1880 in Colombo. But Anagarika Dharmapala's founding of the Mahabodhi Society in 1891 proved to be a singular contribution to the revival of Buddhism within India as well as outside India. The society took upon itself the publication of Buddhist literature in English and Indian vernaculars. Also about this time Sir Edwin Arnold's poem *The Light of Asia* appeared. Its wide influence on modern Indian languages was remarkable. Almost all major Indian languages have renderings or adaptations of it.

The impact of the Buddhist crusade against orthodoxy, against the static caste system and the privileges associated with it, as well as against ritualistic worship and other things was felt in different regions of India during the third century, and it naturally left its mark on the literature of the regional languages. Thereafter decline set in, and Buddhism was, for all practical purposes, banished from the land of its birth. Then after a lull of many centuries Buddhist literature re-surfaced, first in the regional languages of India. From this time on there was a resurgence of Buddhism in different Indian languages. Visva-Bharati's contributions to the enrichment of Buddhistic studies also deserve special mention. More recently, a new wave of Buddhism's revival swept over India under the leadership of Bhimrao Ramji Ambedkar.

We shall briefly mention here, by way of illustration, what happened in South India. This is based on the *Encyclopaedia of Indian Literature.*

In Kannada: There are several works in Kannada propagating Jainism in Karnataka, but we do not find any significant growth of Buddhist literature in Kannada. In fact, Buddhism died in Karnataka in the 12th century.

In Malayalam: Buddhism reached Kerala during the reign of Ashoka, and *viharas* sprang up in places like Karunagapally, Karthikappally, Trichur, Takazhi, etc.

Kumaran Asan's work *Sreebuddhacharitam* is a free rendering of

Edwin Arnold's *The Light of Asia* (1879) into Malayalam. Then Asan's two other poems, *Karuna* and *Chandala Bhikshuki*, are based on Buddhistic doctrine. Nalappat Narayana Menon's translation of *The Light of Asia* entitled *Pourastyadeepam* is an important work. Asvaghosa's *Buddhacharitam*, the *Jataka* stories, etc. were also translated.

In Tamil: Buddhism was popular in the Tamil Nadu region between the 5th and the 7th centuries, but by the 14th century it had almost disappeared. Kanchipuram, Pattinam, Madurai, Nagapattinam, Thanjavur, Kanchi, etc. were the important seats of Buddhistic settlements.

Bimbisara Gathi is a Buddhistic work which was lost. *Siddhartattohai* and *Tiruppatikam* are on Buddhistic doctrine. Then *Virasoliyam* is a Tamil grammatical treatise by a Buddhist scholar.

The Buddhist stress on annihilation of desire has been powerfully expressed by Tiruvalluvar in the *Tirukkural*. The greatness of renunciation and the instability of worldly affections and attachments have all been highlighted in this famous Tamil treatise. Naturally, some scholars felt tempted to see parallels with Buddhism in Tiruvalluvar's thought.

Silappadikaram (2nd century AD) contains a few references to Buddhism. *Manimekalai* is a Buddhist epic and a record of Buddhist thoughts and ideas. However, except in a few works of literature, Buddhism has practically disappeared from Tamil Nadu.

In Telugu: As Andhra patronized Buddhism, there has been a rich crop of Buddhist literature, even during the modern period. The twin poets Tirapati and Venkata Kavulu compiled the life of Buddha in verse form in the *Buddhacharita*. Their pupils Pingali and Katuri Kavulu wrote *Saundaranandam* in verse, depicting the story of the "Bodhisattva". Edwin Arnold's *The Light of Asia* was translated into Telugu verse under the title *Pragjyoti*. Then *Samagamam, Karuna Sindhuvu, Mahabodhi, Dharma Gita,* etc. are all Telugu translations of important Sanskrit Buddhist works.

No doubt the Buddha and his teachings continued to be a major theme inspiring Indian literature for many centuries, even when Buddhism reached its greatest state of decline. Among the various kinds of transformations that Buddhism was subjected to, the most significant, was that later Buddhist leaders were obliged to hold forth the Buddha himself as almost the equivalent of a deity. Thus, Buddhism itself contradicted the belief that a person can hold to the great moral principles enunciated by Buddhism for the attainment of *nirvana* without resorting to some form of devotion, as practiced in other religions. Finally, as things stand today, it is Buddha the man, rather than Buddhism based on his teachings, that continue to exert a benign influence on the Indian mind.

NOTES

1. P.N. Chopra (ed.), *Contribution of Buddhism to World Civilization and Culture,* Preface.
2. *The Complete Works of Swami Vivekananda* (Calcutta: Advaita Ashrama), IX: 349.
3. *Ibid.*, I: 21, 23.
4. T.W. Rhys Davids, *The History and Literature of Buddhism,* p. 76.
5. *The Cultural Heritage of India* (Calcutta: The Ramakrishna Mission Institute of Culture), V: 208.
6. A.L. Basham, *The Wonder that was India,* 3rd revised edn., p. 268.
7. Maurice Winternitz, *A History of Indian Literature,* Vol. II: p. 20.
8. *Ibid.*, p. 423.
9. P.N. Chopra (ed.), *op. cit.*, p. 77-8.
10. T.W. Rhys Davids, *op. cit.*, p. 268.

2

Buddhist Themes in Indian Literature

Biswanath Banerjee

I have been asked by the co-ordinator of the Seminar to deliver the keynote address today. I am aware of my limitations and I am afraid it is not only difficult but almost beyond my capacity to do justice to this assignment. I have no knowledge of even the most important literatures and am unable to give any idea about how, or if at all, Buddhism has been viewed or discussed or referred to in most of them. Nevertheless, I may be permitted to suggest or indicate some lines of discussion in which distinguished scholars will participate and give us positive ideas concerning today's theme.

It is no use reiterating the importance of Buddhism and its contribution to Indian life and thought. That Buddha's words exercised a potent influence on the culture of India over the centuries cannot be denied and it is expected that at least the literatures in the major languages of India received inspiration in some way or other from the Buddha and his teachings in their literary and philosophical treatment. We may examine the relationship of Buddhism with a particular literature and see how it reacted to Buddhism and Buddhist principles in the different periods of its history. It will also be an important point of discussion to know how the Buddha's words were received in the society and by the common people as reflected in the literary works. We would also like to be enlightened if the Buddha's words and ideas gave rise to any particular band of writers, composers or thought-leaders in different languages, and in what ways. Pali is generally acclaimed as the repository of the original sayings of the Buddha, and learned scholars wrote a large number of original texts elaborating and enunciating the thesis and principles of Buddhism in Pali. Recent researches have proved beyond doubt that the sacred canon in Sanskrit is as much old as the Pali canon and in certain cases Sanskrit preserves the oldest forms of some portions at least. The Master wanted his teachings to reach every corner of the society and desired his immediate disciples to instruct the people in their respective languages. It is to be kept in mind, however, that anything in Pali relates to Buddhism but whatever is Buddhism is not only in Pali, Sanskrit has a much more share in serving the cause of Buddhism.

In ancient and medieval times, Sanskrit functioned as a significant medium for the propagation of Buddhism, and we have a vast Buddhist literature in Sanskrit. *Lalitavistara, Mahavastu* and the like are excellent specimens of Buddha-biography in Sanskrit but the most important and valuable writing in Sanskrit on the subject in the earliest days is the *Buddhacarita* by Asvaghosa. The poem is unique of its kind as the earliest specimen of a *sargavandho mahakarya.* His *Saundarananda Kavya* is also an excellent piece of poem though it cannot equal the merit of the earlier one. Fragments received in Central Asia of a dramatic composition entitled *Sariputra Prakarana* is the earliest specimen of its kind in Sanskrit. I am not here to indulge in the depiction of the merit of these works but to only add that these works of Asvaghosa paved the way for the development of epic poetry and dramatic writings in Sanskrit. Asvaghosa has been a poet by nature and deeply religious by conviction. We may refer to the *Jatakamala* by Aryasura, dated about the 4th century AD, and the vast Avadana literature including the *Bodhisattvavadana-kalpalata* by Ksemendra, the Kashmirian polymath, as having purely Buddhist subjects of varied nature and contents. Gems of philosophical texts by Asanga, Vasubandhu, Dharmakirti, Santideva and other Buddhist masterminds are all in Sanskrit.

Besides these original Buddhist texts in Sanskrit, we have many instances of either referring to the Buddha or the Buddhists in a number of Sanskrit works, and not always in an appreciative attitude. Examples are so numerous that we cannot but restrict ourselves to only a few of them. The Buddha has been invoked in the *Garudapurana* as an incarnation of Vishnu for the protection of the world from the sinners. In the *Varahapurana,* the Buddha is adored as the god of beauty. The *Krtyaratnakara,* a Dharmasastra text, says that the *Sakya-dharma* was preached by Vishnu in the form of Buddha. Jayadeva, the composer of the *Gita-govindam,* in the *Dasavatarasutra,* sings of Kesava as having assumed the body of the Buddha. Not only these earlier texts but a Sanskrit text of the Kalacakra school of the medieval times refers to the Buddha as an incarnation. The *Kathasaritsagara* of Somadev, and the *Vetalapancavimsatika* are considered by discerning critics as having Buddhist traits. Sriharsa in his great epic poem praises Buddha's self-control and graceful forgiveness and has a very significant reference to the Buddhist goddess Tara, whereas competent authorities think that the poetician Bhamaha has made good use of Buddhist doctrines in his treatment in chapter V of his famous text on poetics. There are many other instances of appreciating references to Buddhism in ancient and medieval Sanskrit texts, but scoffing or pejorative references to the Buddha and Buddhism are no less wanting in Sanskrit literature or philosophical texts.

To Yajnavalkya the sight of a yellow-robed monk is a bad augury and the same sentiment is expressed in Sudraka's *Mrcchakatika.* In the *Bhagavata,* the religion of the Buddha is stated as an *upadharma.* Sulapani, the *Smrti* digest-writer, thinks the sight of a Buddhist a sin worthy of expiation and the *Caitanyacaritamrta* of Krsndasa Kaviraja makes the Buddhists as equal with the Mlecchas. The *Mattavilasa,* a dramatic work of the 7th century, has a Buddhist monk quoting scriptures to justify his addiction to wine and women and the *Bhagavadajjukiya* shows people flocking to Buddhist Order to earn easy bread and comforts only at the cost of shaving the hair. Dandin refers to nuns as go-betweens with a Buddhist lady as the chief procuress in the *Dasakumara.* In the *Malavikagnimitra* of Kalidasa and in the *Malati Madhava* of Bhavabhuti, Buddhists are represented with disparaging conduct. The *Prabodhacandrodaya* of Krsnamisra ridicules the Buddhists and Jains as atheistic groups. Ksemendra in his *Narmamala* speaks of a Buddhist nun as the traditional go-between; and *Caturbhani,* the *Latakamelaka,* etc. refer to the evil conduct of the Buddhists in no uncertain manner. We cannot but mention the view of the great logician Gangesopadhyaya that he has made an attempt in his work to deliver men from the darkness created by the Buddhists and the title of Udayana's text *Bauddhadhikkara* speaks of the author's hostile bias.

Moral laxity particularly during the time of Tantra Buddhism certainly caused a downfall of Buddhism from its high pedestal of authority and reverential appreciation but the *Saddharma* did continue to persist in an inherent manner in the life and thought of not only the people of India but also a large number of Asiatic peoples.

Next to Sanskrit I would like to make a treatment of the theme in Bengali literature for obvious reasons and for this I crave the indulgence of the audience. When one speaks of Bengali literature, the name of Gurudeva comes to the foremost. Gurudeva has declared that in his estimate Gautama, the Buddha, is the greatest figure in human history. We are struck with admiring wonder when we know that he had a strangely pleasing sensation when he for the first time stood before the bright image of the *all-compassionate one* in the Buddha temple at Bodhgaya. He could not but prostrate himself before the image beaming with loving friendship and compassion. In his inimitable style Gurudeva has invoked a new descent of the Buddha for saving humanity with his nectar-like message. Gurudeva has been the greatest exponent of Buddha and his teachings in Bengali literature. The poet has excelled in writing plays and poems on Buddhist themes, and the values cherished by the Buddha and Buddhism come out in his compositions in a brilliant manner. He imbibed the spirit of the Buddha's gospel and this is reflected in his numerous writings—essays, poems, dramas, symbolic plays, dance-dramas and songs. In many of his poems and dance-dramas he has used the Buddhist themes derived from the Avadanas. The spirit of loving friendship or *Maitribhavana* inspired the poet so much that again and again he dealt with the idea in many of his writings. Buddhism disapproves of dealing violence with violence, enmity with enmity, or anger with anger. *Na hi verena verani sammantidha kudacanam, averena ca sammanti esa dhammo sanantano* not at any time does enmity end with enmity, it is removed through non-enmity, this is the eternal law. Again, *akkodhena jine kodham asadhum sadhuna jine, jine kadariyam danena saccenalikavadinam.* (Anger to be overcome by non-anger, evil to be defeated by good). The character of Dhananjay Vairagi in the drama *Muktadhara* appears to have given a human treatment to this Buddhist spirit. Dhananjay is a symbol of the non-violent spirit; Dhananjay observes, waves cannot be subdued by a strike at them, they can be overcome by keeping the steer of the boat unshaked. The Buddha has taught that an individual is his own saviour; all internal impurities have to be removed by one's own latent power. The poet asks himself when he would be able to see him in fullness within himself. It has been thought in many quarters that the Buddha's religion made people weak and dispirited, but Tagore believed that it was not the intention of the Master to teach indifference to worldly affairs by inaction or propagate message of love and loving friendship through a feeble voice. He declares: *sannyasir je mantra manuske rikta kare, nagna kare, manuser jaubanke pa̱nigu kare, manabcittake nana dike kharba kare, e se mantra naya. e jarajirna krsapran brddher bani naya, er madhye paripurna pran, biryaban jaubaner prabhab.* The Buddha's message is not that idea of a hermit which makes man destitute, renders the youth paralysed, cripples the spirit of humanity in many ways, it is not the message of an old and infirm but herein is found the spirit of life in full, a vigorous youth. This vigorous youth and life-spirit in Buddhism inspired our poets to the fullest. We propose to stop here from citing instances of Gurudeva's treatment of Buddhist themes as that may carry us to an enormous extent.

Bankim Chandra Chattopadhyay, the greatest writer in Bengali in the nineteenth century who gave us the immortal *Vande Mataram,* evinces a great respect for the Buddha at many places in his writings. In his essay on Equality (*Samya*) he holds Buddha as the first person who has taught *equality* to Indian society. In his essay on Samkhya philosophy, Bankim has expressed his opinion that the most glorious chapter of Indian history was the one thousand years that was under the influence of Buddhism. Akshay Kumar Datta, a great educationist and journalist, deals elaborately with Buddha and Buddhism in his great work on the religious seats of India *Bharatavarsiya Upasak Sampradaya.* The family of the great Brahmo leader Keshab Chandra Sen had an abiding interest in the religion of the Buddha. *Asokacarita* of Krisnabihari Sen, the younger brother of Keshab Chandra, seems to be the author of the first ever book in Bengali written on Ashoka. Keshab Chandra's daughter Suniti Devi's work entitled *The Life of Princess Yasodhara* speaks of her interest in Buddhism. Satyendranath Tagore, the first Indian I.C.S. and an elder brother of Rabindranath, has to his credit a book entitled *Bauddhadharma.* Rathindranath, the son of the poet, translated the *Buddhacarit* into Bengali. Poets like Nabin Chandra Sen, Satyendranath Dutta, and Bejoy Chandra Majumdar are some of the great ones who composed poems with inspiration from Buddhist themes. The great dramatist of Bengal of the nineteenth century, Girischandra Ghosh showed his devotion to the Buddha in his *Buddhadevcarit.* The drama has been called a *Devanatak* inasmuch as the Buddha is a *deva* or god to the dramatist. In another drama *Ashoka* we find Girischandra depicting the transformation of the violent Ashoka to the virtuous one (Candasoka to Dharmasoka). Haraprasad Shastri, the great scholar of Buddhist studies, has to his credit a novel like *Kancanamala* based on the Avadana story of Kunala. Last but not the least, we may mention the writings of Swami Vivekananda in whose opinion the character of the Buddha is the greatest in the world. In *Devavani*, Swamiji writes that it was the Buddha who for the first time placed before the world a code of morality complete in itself and always worked undaunted for the good of all.

Writers in almost all Indian languages have always felt an inspiring influence of the Buddha and Buddhism and their reactions have been reflected in respective literatures. Distinguished scholars present here will enlighten us on the subject. We have quite a good number of poets and writers in Hindi who have enriched Hindi literature with their literary works on Buddhist themes. The *Buddhacarit* by Ramchandra Shukla is an excellent rendering in Hindi of Edwin Arnold's *The Light of Asia*, a poetical work in English. We have in Hindi poetical works, dramas and novels with Buddhist themes pertaining mainly to the life of the Buddha, the time of the Buddha, later developments in Buddhism, Buddhist philosophical ideas, etc. Indicating perhaps the idea that there is a woman behind the success of all great men, Maithilisaran Gupta composed his poem *Yasodhara* in praise of Siddhartha's spouse. *Vaisali ki Nagaravadhu*, a novel by Acarya Catursen Sastri, has Amrapali as the principal character to expose the cruel custom in ancient India that women of unparallel beauty should not marry and lead a tragic, shameful life of a courtesan. The drama *Lehro ke Rajhans* by Mohan Rakesh is based on a story in which Sundari, the young wife of Nanda, the cousin of Siddhartha, boasts of her control over the husband and thinks that Siddhartha became the Buddha owing to the inefficiency of Yasodhara as a wife. She is confident that her husband would never leave her to join the group of monks under the Buddha. Interesting situations follow to make the husband confused about his decision. Sohanlal Dwivedi, Jaishankar Prasad, Ramkumar Varma, Rahul Samkrityayan are some of the other writers working on Buddhist themes in Hindi. Andhra Pradesh has an important bearing historically on the development of Buddhism and Telugu, the language of the area, has an ancient history. The first Telugu poetical composition, *Buddhacarita* with a Buddhist theme was written by Tirupati D. Sastri and C. Venkatasastri known as twin poets in 1902. The work appears to have been based on Asvaghosa's *Buddhacarit* and Edwin Arnold's work mentioned above. *Gautama Buddha caritra* by G.Y. Doraswamiah is a prose work in Telugu written in 1904 and *Siddhartha caritra* by C. Lakshmi Narasimham published in 1905 is perhaps the first biography of the Buddha in Telugu. There have been a good number of Telugu translations of standard Buddhist literary, legendary as well as philosophical works since the beginning of the twentieth century. Rabindranath's Bengali works based on Buddhist themes and Rahul Samkrityayan's Hindi writings have been translated into Telugu. *Jataka* stories with the ideals of peace, compassion and sacrifice caught the imagination of Telugu writers who have contributed a number of works in propagating these ideals. The Avadana story of Upagupta and Vasavadatta has been the theme of *Mumuksuvu*, *Ragavina* and poems of Rabindranath rendered into Telugu. The drama *Ksemabhiksu* explains the theory of impermanence or *Ksanikavada* of Buddhism. As it appears Telugu literature is somewhat rich with works on Buddhist themes primarily written in modern times.

Orissa is an important state with significant spiritual, religious, social and cultural history. It is the land that caused a change in the nature of the Mauryan king Ashoka. Orissa and for that matter Oriya literature having works with Buddhist themes has been mainly concerned with later Buddhism and allied cults. Before the fifteenth century the Buddha came to be regarded as an incarnation of Vishnu and several sects of Buddhism prevailed in Orissa. After Sarata Das, the Pancasakha poets, Bhima Bhai appears Fakir Mohan, the first poet of the modern period who composed the *Buddhavatara-kavya* depicting the life and teachings of the Buddha with its main emphasis on social reforms. Baikunthanath Pattarnayak, a modern poet of the Sabuja literary movement, makes an exposition of the Buddha's exhortations to his disciples to wander for the benefit of many in his poems like *Amba*, *Bhiksu*, etc. Mayadhar Mansingh is also a noted poet of the Sabuja Movement inspired by the message of the Buddha and in his *Buddhavani* he has sought shelter under the Buddha.

We have already covered much of our time and it is almost an impossible task even to touch the literary history of other Indian languages making use of Buddhist themes. The task I prefer to leave to the treatment of experts present here.

To conclude I utter the words of the great Master conveying the well-being of all sentient beings: *sabbe satta bhavantu sukhitatta.*

3

Buddhist Perspective in the Modern Bhotia Literature

Suniti K. Pathak

Although the Bhotias in India belong to ethnic common identity of being a Mongoloid group, their religious identity is not similar. Among them, the Muslims and the Christians maintain a spirit of cultural integration with co-existence. In other words, the Bhotias of Indian Himalayas hold a pluralistic culture scenario.

According to the geological account, the Himalayas are the youngest of mountain ranges in Euro-Asia. Obviously, the immigration of different peoples of the neighbouring regions makes the Himalayan inhabitants ethnically varied and distinguishable from each other. Until the development of present-day motorable roads and other communicative facilities, the Himalayans were separated and handicapped in many respect. Since the spread of English education by the Christian missionaries and other educationists, the Bhotias and the other Himalayan communities have become close to the rest of the Indians residing in the plains. Now, the political awareness and socio-cultural integration all over the country make the Himalayans closer. So, new trends in their cultural growth among the Himalayan peoples in general and the Bhotias in particular, demarcate from what they were in the pre-Independence period by the thirties of the last century.

The present paper attempts to deal with the modern Bhotia literature, which represents their bifurcation in life-style and prospective approach. For the last five decades or more, an unprecedented awareness for respective linguistic identity has generated among the Himalayan inhabitants whether they hold written scripts or not. Those who have written scripts to distinguish themselves from the others are almost in cheers of spiritual awakening. In that respect the government of Sikkim has experimented a novel stance by declaring six state languages with equal scope for march and advancement. Among them, Bhotia, locally named *Dajongka*, is one. On account of different ethnic groups among the Indo-Tibetans settled in different regions of Indian Himalayas from Kameng district of Arunachal Pradesh upto Ladakh inclusive of the Syok river valley of POK (Pak-occupied Kashmir), Bhotia has many regional names. Despite that, their linguistic genus is common, i.e., Tibetan, though it has multiple dialects. The authors of modern times follow the Tibetan scripts and the Tibetan dictions unhesitatingly although they tend to compose their writings indigenously in most cases. It is to mention that the Tibetan scripts are out of the Indian Brahmi-originated design, which Pandit Rahul Sankrityayana had shown vividly. The Tibetan classic dictions are of Sanskritic inflexional structure morphologically, in spite of its monosyllabic genesis having a tendency of agglutination.

As regards the growth of modern Bhotia literature in the Indian Himalayas, the social interactions with the neighbouring inhabitants belonging to each region are to be taken into account. For instance, the Mons, the Serdukpens, the Khambas, the Membas interact socially and culturally with the Adis, the Deflas and many others in Arunachal Pradesh. The Bhotias of West Bengal are familiar with the Nepali, Gurung, Newaris, etc. Similarly, the Dukpa Bhutias and the Dajong pas are culturally akin to the Rong, the Mon and the Nepali of Sikkim including the Rai, Limbu, etc. Again, the Marcha and the Tolcha have cultural affinity with other communities of Pithorgarh district and those of Uttar Kashi in Uttaranchal. In Ladakh, a complex-cultural scenario becomes colourful when the Bodi enjoys the festive days with others for brotherhood and family kinship in many cases. Such interactions make the Himalayan Khunu, Lahuli, Spettian Bhotia family complex consolidated. Mutual exchange of socio-economic requirements with due regards to each other make the Himalayan people culturally integrated as a whole through centuries uninterruptedly.

II

Now let us examine how far their life-style and their approaches to the threefold prosperity *phun sum tshogs*, wealth, gain and spirituality are depicted in their modern Bhotia literature. As the Bhotias are descendants of the Bod pa, *bhautta-jana* in Sanskrit, the major emphasis is laid on spiritual accessibility to enrich with an adjustment of the worldly gain, which is the basis of the Buddha's teachings, "Those, by good deeds, cover up the evil deeds done already, they illuminate this world, like the moon freed from clouds.

yassa pāpam katam kammam kusalena pidhīyati /
so imam lokam pabhāseti abbhā mutto va candimā //

(Dhammapada 13.7)

Tibetan rendering in *Chos kyi tsigs su bcad pa* ed. C.R. Lama, Sarnath, 1982:

gang zhig sdig pa't las byas pa /
dge bas 'gebgs par byed pa de /
sprin bral nyi ma zla ba ltar /
'jig rten'di na kun tu gsal //

The core of the above saying enkindles the lamp within what is *attadipo bhava*: Be thy self illuminated.

For the last few decades, several periodicals and popular writings have come out in different regions, where the Bhotias are advanced in education with mental ability for having their creative literature. Tibet Mirror Press at Kalimpong under the leadership of G. Tharchin started *Yul chog so so'i gsar 'gyur me long* in 1925. That continued for about three decades continuously. Again *Krung dbyang gsar 'gyur* was published in Trung-yang Press as the mouthpiece of Tibetan-speaking population from Calcutta since the pre-Independence days. N. Zimpa has edited the *Bod mi'irtsa don* from Darjeeling.

The Sikkim official authorities from Gangtok had *Yar rgya gong 'phal*, in Hindi *Pragati* is now discontinued. But the '*bras lgongs bya marta*' from "Bras gzhing dril sgrags las khung" (Public Relation Office) Gangtok deserves a mention.

In this connection, the immigrant Tibetans have taken a bold step to publish several newspapers and periodicals in Tibetan to promote solidarity among the Tibetan and the Bhotia-speaking population in India, and that at the international level. Resultantly, *Rang dbang* from Freedom Press, Darjeeling later changed its name to *Bod mi'i rang dbang* Freedom. Also, the *pha yul bod kyi thus'bab* from Dharmshala, Himachal Pradesh are important periodicals.

A bi-monthly issue from the Jammu and Kashmir Government Academy of Art, Culture and Language, *Dzammu Kasmira gyi bzo shes rig dang skad kyi slob sde a ka da mi, gle la dwags*, focusses multiple dimensions of the Ladakhi-speaking inhabitants who area in the region since the eleventh century AD.

In this regard, the Bhotias of Darjeeling, Kalimpong and Pedang including the Dajongpas of Sikkim interact with the Nepali prose—authors, poets, and novelists who have accepted modernism at par with the literary creative mannerism of the nineteenth century in the Indian regional contemporary literature, in general, and Bengali, in particular. Also, the Hindi literature as well as the Nepali literature have developed simultaneously in the twentieth century and that prompts the Bhotia literature to welcome the new ideas. Among them, three trends are observed, such as:

i) Outbursts of their psychic ethos in sorrow or joyous emotions with aesthetic creativity in literary compositions of meters or in prose or in both. Short stories, through realistic picturesque in presentation are of high aesthetic value to focus the individual life and the social environs.
ii) Secular writings relating to social, political, regional topics concerned are generally composed in prose writings like essays or stories, etc.
iii) Traditional thematic mannerism for creative writings in verses or in narrative prose forms having a lien to Buddhism refers to their religious identity.

The paper aims to focus on the last trend briefly. Besides that, some specimens of their indigenous folk songs are also referred here.

Generally, an author with traditional base of education prefers to begin a composition with salutation. Blo bzang dngos grubs begins his recollection of the cultural close-up of India with Tibet (Rang dbang gsar shog, 9,1964).

rgyal bstan/yongs kyi/mnga' bdag/gangs ri'i mgon/
mgon di'i/gsang gsum/mdzad pa'i/gzhing gi/mtha'/
mtha 'dag rgyal bas brdzed kyi mi lang na/
nga gzhon tshur mthong bzang la smos ci' tshad//
'on kyang dad pa'i chu gter' gog med du/
'phyur bas mgon po gang gi gsang gsum la//
mos dang than cig snyin pa'i yul 'ga dag /
snyig kha'i ngos su zum zhang lan brgyar bsngags//

"What else is to say and to see when the Jina's teachings become saviour of the mountain of snow and those are deep, sublime and secret. Despite that, irresisting stream-like devotion flows over to the protector and bough-like reverence unmeasured is submitted in folded hands to praise the smiling-faced one for hundred times."

An authentic biography of Shakyamuni based on twelve accomplishments in *thanka* paintings is composed by Acarya Samtan Gyatso Lepcha. His work is entitled *Sangs rgyas bcom ldan 'das kyi mdzad rnam gaal bar bkod pa thar lam gsal ba'i sgron me (clear lamp of the path of liberation)*, 1998. Twelve *thankas* deal with topics like:

1. The Bodhisattva's descending from *Tusita dga ldan*
2. Entrance in his mother's womb
3. Birth of the Bodhisattva
4. Accomplishment in Bodhi
5. Bodhisattva's indulgence with Yasodhara *sa'tsho ma*
6. Renunciation
7. Penance
8. Incidents at Vajrasana towards the path of enlightenment
9. *Maravijaya* subduing the evils
10. Attainment of the Bodhi
11. Turning of the wheel of the Truth, *Dharma cakrapravartana*
12. His demise—*Mahaparinirvana*

Samten Gyatso Lepeha's work gives the important narratives from Bodhisattva Sarvasiddhartha and Shakyamuni, the Buddha.

Besides the biographical works, by the Bhotia authors, some translations of the Indian authors on the Buddhist thought in prose, verse and drama have been contributed. For instance, Angrup Lahuli rendered Rabindranath Tagore's *Gitanjali Glu thal sbyor ba* published by Tibet House, New Delhi. Prior to that, the author prepared a collection of select poems of Tagore *snyan ngag bsdus pa* and published them from Sahitya Akademi, New Delhi, 1961. The said collection contains many poems composed by Tagore on Buddhist themes and narratives. In the periodical *Yar rgya gong 'phel* several translated materials on Buddhist themes from Oriya and other Indian languages were published. Among the Indian drama Rabindranath Tagore's *Natir Pujā, A Courtesan's worship* and his essay book *Buddhadeva* deserve mention.

Some historical works referring to the Buddhist monasteries in the Himalayas may come in purview. Tashi Tshering's history of the Kyi monastery in Spiti entitled *spyi ti dkyil dgon nor bu dge 'phel gyi byung ba brjod pa'i rab byed' phags nor bdun idan* is not only an account of the growth of Buddhism in the Western Indian Himalayas, but also a critical perspective on the doctrine of Tibetan Buddhism through changes. Similarly, *Rta pho dgng snying gi byung rab lo rgyus mdor sdus* narrates the historical account of Tabo monastery in Spiti, which was founded in the 10th century AD.

Also Sa phud Thub bstan dpal ldan's *La dwags* (1982) deals thoroughly with the Buddhist monasteries in Ladakh, Buddhist literary works and the Buddhist doctrine. A brief account of the spread and development of Tibetan Buddhism in Ladakh has been traced out. The Ladakhi author mentions the following salient features: 1. Important incidents in Shakyamuni Buddha's life. 2. Ashoka's narratives. 3. Contributions of the Indian Buddhists in Tibet from the 8th century AD like *Danashila, Vishunddha-simha,* etc. from Kashmira. 4. Atisha Dipankara's *Bodhipatha-pradipa,* which had been a guide for the Buddhists. 5. Interaction between the Indian Pandits and Tibetan scholars to develop Indian Buddhism in Tibet. 6. Different teachers of major lineages in Tibetan Buddhism like *Bka' rgyud,* especially *Karma bka' rgyud, Bri khung bka rgyud.* The *Sa-(s) kya* lineage and thereafter the *Dge lugs pa* teachers established themselves in Ladakh with their respective monasteries. The fourth chapter captioned *dgon pa khag gi chags rabs* mentions religious activities of the important monasteries together with the works contributed by the eminent monastic leaders of different monasteries (chapter 5). Another Ladakhi historian Tashi rab rgyas of our days followed the foot-tract of Father Gergan (Senior) in writing the impact of Buddhism in Ladakh. Both the historians covered the socio-political history of Ladakh up till the 26th century AD.

As referred above, the series of *shes rab zom* from Ladakh Akademi present many essays on the Buddhistic themes, such as the Buddha and Doctrine *ston pa dang bstan pa* by Blo bzang tshe dbang (1990, *Lo gsar gyi deb,* pp. 196) on Ambedkar by Tshering Tashi (*Shes rab zamm* 1990, p.121-130) in prose.

Among the Bhotias, dance, music and songs are popular. In their songs, devotion to the Buddha and reverence to the recluses' lama (*bla ma*) are occasionally observed. A Ladakhi song *alchi chos bskor* (pilgrimage to Alci) runs thus:

Ya ru la ma by the right side
By the left, the left wing of army chief.
Our fatherland is thus prosperous,

Let it sound all over
Dragon roar of the *Dharma*;
Alchi being propitious
Dragon roar of the *Dharma*
Let it sound all over.
On the dry tree,
Let flowers grow extensive
Let descents grow in number
Be our wishful prayer *monlam*.
While to *tsa bas*
Monlam wishing prayer
Let prosperity with happiness
Come down in order with no misery.

The Ladakhi text is:

/gyas phyogs gyas kyi bla ma /
/ gyon phyogs gyon gyi dpon po /
/ gyan phyogs gyas kyi bla ma /
/ gyon phyogs gyon gyi dpon po /
/pha yul skyid po'i ngang nas /
/ chos kyi 'brug sgra kun Idir red /
/Al lci skyid po'i ngang nas /
/ chos kyi 'brug sgra kun ldir red /
/ shing skam la lo 'dab rgyas shig /
/ nga tshos btabs pa yi smon lam /
/ bu rgyud mtha' nas rgyas shig /
/ lo tsa sba tabs pa yi smon lam /
/ bde skyid phun gsum tshogs pa yi/
/ zag med rten 'brel sgrigs shig /
/ bde skid phun gsum tshags pa yi /
/ zag med rten 'brel sgrigs shig //

la dwags kyi yul qlu, Jammu Kashmir gyi bzo/
shes rig dang skad kyi slob sde/ a ka da mi /

gle La dwags, Folk songs of Ladakh, vol 12, 1992, working eds. Dge thub bstan dpal ldan sa phud,Tshe ring nor bu mar rtse, Dge Tshe ring Chos 'phel. Chief Editor Ngag dbang tshe ring shag po. (LDSRZ).

APPENDIX-A

Some important works on Buddhism in the Bhotia literature by the authors (A.) of the Indian Himalayas are given below:

Prose

A. Dngos grub gar zha pa (Angrup Lahauli) *chos kyi lo rgyus thog zangs dkar dang gar zha mkha' 'gro'i gling gi 'brel ba* (Account of Zankar and Gazha Khando ling) HCSP 2000-32.

A. Bka' chen Ye shes ngos grub (LDSRZ 1978, pp.14-23)

Rin po che Blo bzang tshul Khrims chos 'phel gyi rtsom (Contributions of Lossang tsulthim chosphel Rinpoche).

A. 'Jam dbyangs rgyal mtshan

Lha chen dpal gyi mgon (oalgon) LDSRZ 1985, No.1(c), pp. 1-7.

Sa pan gyi rol mo'i bstan bcos (Shastra of Saskya Pandita's joy) LDSRZ 1979, pp. 35-43.

A. Mkan po Dkon mchog bstan 'dzin (LDSRZ 1982) *Gyung drung dgon pa* (Yungtung monastery).

A. Bka' chen Blo bzang bzad pa (LDSRZ 1979, no. 2)

Stod byang sems shes rab bzang po (Bodhisattva Prajnabhadra of Stod) monastery. *Mchod rten ka ni ka* Kaṇnikā Caitya, (Shrine of Kaṇikā) LDSRZ 1981, pp. 1-13. Khrig se'i dgon pa tshul khrims rnam daggling LDSRZ 1982.

A. Blo bzang rig 'dzin *Sdug bsngal spong thabs* (Means of eradicating the suffering) LDSRZ 1985, no. 2, pp. 33-40.

A. Tshering norbu *Mani dang mani thang* (Mani and Manithang)LDSRZ 1985, No.1(e), pp. 8-29.

A. Geshe Ye shes don grub, *Rten' brel* Dependent origination) LDSRZ 1984, no. 3, pp. 17-20.

A. Geshe Orgyan dgra'dul: *Sangs rgyas dang khong gi chos* (The Buddha and his Dharma) LDSRZ 1990, Nos. 3&4, pp. 69-82.

A. Rdo brug chu bzang rin po che:

Guru Padma 'byung gnas kyi ngo sprod. (An Introduction to Guru Padmasambhava) Bibliotheca Sikkim Himalayica SRIT, 1996.

A. La chen sgom rinpoche:

Sleb spon chen po 'i bka' drin rjes dran gyi rnam thar mdo bsdus (An abridged account of great teacher Padmasambhava) (ibid.).

A. Mkhan po Bde chen rdo rje:

Guru Padmasambhava'i mdzad rnam rgya mtsho'i chu things ma (drops of Ocean of Guru Padmasambhava's works) (ibid.).

A. Mkhan po lha tshering:

Slob dpon chen pos bsil ldan gangs ri'i gongs 'dir bkrim che tshul gyi mdzad bsdus (Blessed contributions of Great Acarya in this snow-cold region) (ibid.).

A. Sar sgrub Gdung' dzin Rin po che:

Orgyan sangs rgyas gnyis pa'i 'khrungs dkar dus chen khyad par can zhig yin pa'i lo rgyus (An account of splendour on the advent of the second Uddiyana Buddha).

BIOGRAPHICAL

A. Bkrashis rab rgyas Dge bshes Ye shes don grub: (Geshe Yeshe dondub) LDBRL 1980 (c) 36-42. Grub chen thang shon rgyal po dang mana pa'i sral (Mahasiddha Thang tougyapo) LDSRZ 1982(e) 1-18

ii) A.Bkra shis mcho mo: *Grub thab stag tshang ras chen Ngag dbang rgya mcho* (Mahasiddha Ngawang gyatsho) LDSRZ 1982, Vol. 2, pp. 90-100.

SCIENTIFIC KNOWLEDGE

A. Gesh Ngawang gyatsho Gnags rin po che (Himalayas) LDSRZ, 1991(c), 31-39.

A. *Bkrashis rab rgyas Sa Yen rig pa* (Science) LDSRZ, 1979(c), 26-34. Dkar nag rtis kyi 'byung tshul (Origin of white and black account) 1985, No.3, LDSRZ, pp. 1-10.

LINGUISTICS/GRAMMAR

A Sod nams phun tshogs LDSRZ 1991(C), pp. 1-10.

'Brogs pa'i skad kyi 'byung khungs (Source of Dag pa Language)
A. Blo bzang tshe dbang LDSRZ 1983, Vol. I, pp. 36-47.
La dwags kyi skad shes rig (Ladakhi Language and Culture)

HANDICRAFTS AND INDUSTRY

A.'Chi med rnam rgyal *Bzo bo rig pa* (Science of arts) LDSRZ 1991(e), pp. 57-70.
A.Tshering Wangdu *Ri mo'i rnam bzhag* (Art of painting) LDSRZ 1991(e), 13/5-6, pp. 45-54. Ladwags Kyi mkhar rvams Kyi rtsig bzo *A. Dgshe Thub bstan dpal ldan.* (Art of walls in Ladakhi forts).

BHOTIA SHORT STORIES

A. Geshe Tse dbang rig 'dzin.
Mdza 'bo bu mo'i gtam rgyud (Girl friend)LDSRZ 1981, pp. 100ff.
Ngan 'gro'i lam (Wrong path) LDSRZ 1980, 109F.
Norbu dang bu don grub (Nor bu and Dondub) LDSRZ 1985 (ss)51F.
Nor bradab (Covetusus wealth) LDSRZ 1990, Vol. I-II, pp. 67-81.
A. Geshe Tshe ring chapel (Tshe ring chos 'phel)
Bsam pa sngon la ma brtan na 'gyod pa rting na. LDSRZ 1992(ss), pp. 74-82.
A. Gishe Kencho phande (dkon michug phan bde)
Dung sgsa (*sankha*, conchshell) LDSRZ 1980, Vol. I.
A. Geshe Tubtan paldan (dge bshes Thub bstan dpal ldan)
Dga 'phel bu'i gtam rgyud (Gaphe's son). LDSRZ 1979 (ss)114F.
Tshon dpon brnab can (Covetons merchant) LDSRZ 1991, pp. 61-68.
A. Rin chen don dub
Me tog sgrol ma (personal name Metbdolma, Kusumitara) LDSRZ (1979), Vol.2(ss), 93F.
A.Geshe Tshe dbang rig 'dzin (LDSRZ 1980, Vol. 2, pp. 36-42) *Ro ngos grub can gyi sgrung* (A story of dead Ngodubcan).
A. Tshering Narbu A yu: *Sgrung gtam* (An essay dealing with technic and aesthetics) LDSRZ 1990, 5-6, p. 14-23.
A special number of LDSRZ dealing with short stories and their 'mannerism of presentation contains many learned papers by authors like Tubtan pal dan, Lossang tsondu, Tshewang darje, Tshering Tashi, Tshering Norbu Ayn, etc.

DRAMALET, DANCE AND MUSIC

A. Geshe Tubtan paldan (dge bshes thub dpal ldan)
Rin chen bzang po (a biographical account of famous personality Rin chen bzang po) LDSRZ 1991, Annual publication, pp. 86-115.
A. Thering norbu Mar Tse
Mi rlam bar do (Mid life in dream) LDSRZ 1992(d), pp. 83-100.
Ladakhi Annual publication of LDSRZ 1989 contains eleven articles on Dances and Music in which Ven. Geshe Ngawang gyatsho Tshewang rigzin, Kon cho nam gyal, Tshering tashi jigme dorje and Madam Tashi tshome, contribute. Also Lossang Tsondu Kachar, Lossang Zadpa Khanpo Koncho Tonzin present their learned articles on Ladakhi, monastic dance *'chams'*.

POEMS

A. Dkon mchog dar rgyas:
'Bri gun skyabs mgon (LDSRZ 1991, nos. 2, pp. 8-10.
A. Geshe Bkra shis rab rgyas
Chos zla dang po (LDSRZ 1991, nos.1-2, pp. 89-32.
Bsod nams kyi nor bu (Jewel of virtue) LDSRZ 1983, no.2, pp. 57-57-63.
A. Ge she Ngag dbang rgya mtsho
Ka bshad (Verses in series beginning from Ka) (LDSRZ, 1991, nos .1-2, pp. 126-129.
A. Bka' chen Blo bzang szad pa, pa (LDSRZ 1981, pp. 15-26.
Chang la smad pa'i ka bshad (Ka shad of a drunkard) *Pan Chen ldum ra pa* (a garden of Great Pandit)LDSRZ 1980, pp. 1-14.
A. Ge she Dkon mchag rnag rgyal rtag ma cig.
Ka shad(Verses in series beginning from Ka) LDSRZ 1991, nos. 1-2, pp. 121-122.
Rten rnying srung skyob (LDSRZ 1990, 1.2, pp. 86-90).
Gzhan gyi lad mo (Other's service) LDSKI, 1984.
A. Skyabs rje Rgyal sras Ba Ku la.
Shal gdams (Verbal teachings) LDSRZ 1986, no. 4, pp. 88-90.
A special number of La dovags yi shes rab zom in 1990 no. 5-6 was published to deal with the aesthetic mannerisms of poetic composition, with reference to the *Snyan ngag me long* Kavyadarsha of Dandin.

ABBREVIATIONS

HCSP - Himalayan Culture, a Symbol of Peace, Key Monastery.
LDSRZ - Siraz, published from Ladakh Academy of Art and Culture, etc.
SRIT - Bulletin of Sikkim Institute of Tibetology, Gangtok.

4

Buddhist Themes in Pre-Modern Bengali Literature: A Study on the Nava Caryāpada

Dipak Kumar Barua

A few books have already been published on the *Caryāpadas* or *Caryā*-Songs[1] discovered in 1907 for the first time by Mm. Haraprasad Sastri (1853-1931) who caused to publish in 1916 these Buddhist mystic songs as an anthology titled *Hājar Bacharer Purāṇa Bāṅglā Bhāṣāy Bauddha Gān O Dohā,* 'Buddhist songs and couplets in the 100 years old Bengali Language.' It is still being considered as the first literary composition in the pre-modern Bengali literature.[2] Since that sensational discovery of Haraprasad Sastri,[3] about 56 years later, Professor Shashi Bhushan Dasgupta (1911-1964), Ramtanu Lahiri, former Professor of Bengali Language and Literature at the University of Calcutta, almost in the same accidental manner could find out some more new Buddhist mystic songs from Nepal.[4] About 100 new such songs which also represented the earliest specimens of the Bengali literature were discovered, as already mentioned, by Professor S.B. Dasgupta from Nepal in 1963, and after his untimely demise, 98 of those songs as selected by S.B. Dasgupta himself had been published by the University of Calcutta in 1989 under the title *Nava Caryāpada,* 'New *Caryāpada*'. This new set of the *Caryā* songs was so named in order to distinguish them from those found out by Mm. Haraprasad Sastri. These Buddhist mystic songs, both old and new, called the *Caryāpadas* or *Caryāgītis* were composed by the Buddhist Siddhas who practised Tantricism that fourished in Northern India from about the 9th century AD to the 15th century AD.[5]

Buddhist themes as revealed in these newly-discovered mystic songs from Nepal as the earlier *Caryāpadas* was tantric in form. Hence the religious tenets of these mystic songs might be characterized in a general way as belonging to Tantric Buddhism. In order to understand the fundamental concepts of this form of Buddhism it would be necessary to go through at least two Buddhist tantric works, namely, the *Hevajra-tantra* and the *Pancakrama.* The basic concept of Tantric Buddhism as revealed in these newly-discovered songs, is the Vajra. That was why this Buddhist movement was called Vajrayāna. But the tantric ideas and practices had never existed independently of Mahāyāna, as for example, Advayā-Vajra, a tantric teacher according to the Tibetan tradition, divided Mahāyāna into *Pāramitā-Naya (Sūtras)* and *Mantra-Naya* (*Tantras*). In fact, the basic ideas of Mahāyāna were always a subjacent to tantric rituals and the goals of Bodhisattva were never lost sight of. These new songs, which represented Vajrayāna form of the Buddhism, were unique in nature because of the following reasons:

(i) In these mystic songs the images of Vajrayana gods and goddesses as well as prayers and worship to them was more discernible as reflected in the minds of the meditators than the Sahaja-doctrines and Sahaja practices.

(ii) Almost all the songs represented the *Maṇḍala-caryā* of the Vajrayāna meditators, e.g. *Karṇa-pā maṇḍala-caryā gāvay bāhire pūjaa hoi* (Song 31).

(iii) These songs were actually the *carita-gīti* 'feature songs' or *Vajra*-songs to be sung worshipping the gods and goddesses of the relevant *Maṇḍala, Gīta-carita* (Song 71) or *Vajra-Gīta* (Songs 86, 89).[6]

The fundamental concept of Tantric Buddhism, as of Mahāyāna in general, was manifested in these mystic songs, in a term *Bodhicitta*, 'Thought-of-Enlightenment', of which unique treatment had been made therein. The original concept of *Bodhicitta* as described in the Mahāyāna texts, was the resolution to attain *Bodhi*, 'Enlightenment', of the 'would-be-Bodhisattva' and the attainment of the *Bodhicitta* through the *Daśabhūmi*, 'Ten Stages', would signify the purification of the mind in successive stages of meditation.[7]

The predominating deity in these songs of the *Nava Caryāpada* was Hevjra or Hevajja or Hetuvajra who was called therein, *Krodhādhipati* (Song 83), *Śrīyogāmvara* (Songs 55, 61), *Trailokyanātha* (Song 76), *Śrīmañjughosa* (Song 76), *Śrimañjuvara* (Song 60), *Śrīmañjukumāra* (Song 84). But in most of the *caryā* songs of this group Vācchali played an important role, e.g. *Jaya jaya Vācchali sayala subhāskarī* (Song 25). S.B. Dasgupta opined that the goddess Śuṇ or *Śūṇyatā* or

Vajravārāhi or Vārāhi later on became goddess Vācchali from whom might be obtained the link with goddess Vāśuli, Viśālākṣi, or Vajreśvari who held away over Nepal, Mithīlā, Kāmarūpa, Gauda, and Vaṅgā from the 12th to 16th centuries AD. If that presumption would be true, then the geneology of the goddesses in the *Sahajiyā-sadhanā* would be as follows: Prajñaña/Sahajasundarī/Advayarupini/Vajravārāhi/Vācchali/Vāsuli/Vāśulī.[8]

Further, in these songs were mentioned the goddesses named Yoginī, Ḍombinī, Śavarī, Caṇḍālī, Śrīvidyādevi, Śrīvajradevī, Vāṃchali, Vajradhātveśvarī, Vajrayoginī, Vajradevī, Śrīvāgiśvarī, Nairātmādevī, Jñāneśvarī, Kālī, Vajrasattva-parameśvarī, Vajravairocanī, Vajratāruṇī, Vajravāruṇī, Śrīcintadevī, Nirañjanadevī, Śrīugratāruṇī, Buddhaḍākinī, Śrīvidyādharī, Caṇḍikā, Mahāḍākinī, Tribhuvaneśvarī, Nairātmā. In the same songs, the following gods had been worshipped, namely, Śūnyanirañjana, Ádi-Buddha, Śrīsamvararāya, Śrīsamvaranateśvara, Śrīherukanātha, Śrīvajrapānī, Śrīdharmarāya, Śrī Dipaṅkara Buddha, Śrī Śākyamuni, Trailokyanātha, Śrīvakreśvara, Śrīmahākala, Śrīmanjukumāra, Kālabhairava and the like.[9]

In the following Song 73 (*Rāga*-Bhairavī; *Tāla*-Ektāla), the composer had expressed his sentiment that would reveal a blending of Theravāda and Mahāyāna ideals:

Praviśatu Bhagavan Mahāmokṣapure deśaī anuttara bodhipadaṃ

Jarāmaraṇabhayabandhana mocaye paramāmṛtamaya paramaguru.

Ehi vatsa Mahāyāna Nayottama dehi cintāmṛta pānarande

Deśai kṣara ham gocara guhya Tathatānuttara Bodhipadaṃ.

Sarvatathāgata pūjayāmi ghātayāmi me pāpatanu

Prajñopāya dikṣita parivastita kamala-kulisa paribhramare.

Kusuma udaka mukuṭāśani Kamala Jinakulasamayacaryā padaṃ

Mantrāñjan darpaṇ sarakṣepa Daśabalamatipadabhāsuraṃ.

Namāmi Śrīcakrasamvara guruvākya dṛḍa dhariyā

Satguru caraṇakamala prasāde anuttara siddhipada mokṣa phaladaṃ.

—'Let the Lord enter the Great City of Emancipation, (and reveal) (an) incomparable Seat of Enlightenment.

Oh the Great Master Who is full of nectar, liberate (me) from the fetters of old age, death and fear.

Oh Mahāyāna disciple, the best of human beings, offer me the nectar of the Bodhicitta at the end of the pleasure of drinking;

Show me the field of mystic incomparable Tathatā and the seat of Enlightenment.

I worship all the Tathāgatas and destroy my sinful body,

Having initiated, encircled me in knowledge Lotus-kuliśa emancipate.

Flower, water, with the head-dress of thunderbolt Lotus-like the feet of the preceptors of the lineage of the Conqueror,

The mirror with the collyrium of the mystic incantations and having thrown the arrow (I) salute at the feet of the One Who has concentrated His mind to the Person endowed with the 'Ten Powers'.

(I) offer obeisance to Śrīcakrasamvara having kept (in mind) the teachings of the preceptor strongly,

By the blessings of the Lotus-like feet of the true preceptor obtains my mind the best of success and the fruits of emancipation incomparable.'

The basic philosophy of the newly-discovered *caryā*-songs had primarily been stated in the very first song of the *Nava caryāpada* as follows:

—*Rāga* Karnāti, *Tāla* - Jhapa
Tiaḍḍā cāpi, joini de aṅkavālī,
Kamala-kuliśa ghāṇṭa karahuin viāli.
Joini tai vinu khanahu na jīvami,
To muha combi kamalarasa pīvami.
Khepahu joini lepa na jāya,
Maṇikūle bahiā Oḍiāne samāa,
Sāsu ghare ghāli kuñcia tāla,
Cānda Suja veṇi pekhā phāla,
Bhaṇai Guḍarī ahme kunduru vīrā,
Naraa nārī mājhe uehila cīrā.

—'Pressing the girdle of three strings (or placing the pot on the oven), O Female Ascetic, give embrace.

Prepare the afternoon meal cooking the hotchpotch of the Lotus and Thunderbolt.

O Female Ascetic, without you I cannot live for a moment kissing your mouth I drink the nectar of the Lotus.

The Female Ascetic becomes solied at (every) movement. She enters into Oḍiāna passing by Maṇikule (Maṇikula).

Putting lock and key in the house of the mother-in-law (breath), cut down the two sides, the Moon and the Sun.

Guṇḍari (Gudari) says: 'We are heroes in intercourse. The genital organ was raised between men and women.'

This song also appeared as the Song 4 in the *Caryācaryaviniścaya* edited by Haraprasad Sastri.[10]

In the earlier *caryā*-songs of this second series, i.e. *Nava Caryāpada*, epistemology had been explained with the help of symbolism so that the words in their ultimate sense got more importance than their apparent meanings.[11] But in most of the songs the union of *Prajñā* and *Upāya* had been metaphorically stated with the sexual appeal describing the intercourse between a man and a woman. Many of these verses vividly illustrated the union between Hevajra or Heruka and goddess Vajravārāhi or Śuṇ or Śūṇyatā.[12] According to S.B. Dasgupta such verses might be composed in respect of 'Heru and Devī' under the influence of 'Hara and Pārvatī'.[13] In fact, the change that occurred in the *caryāpada* with regard to poetic form and content might be due to the impact of Hara-Pārvatī Meditation, as for example,

Ūrddhva rakta piṅgala keśā
nācai Herua unmattaveśā
Heruo Heruo de moru kolā (Song 22)

In the conception of the *advaya* or the *yuganaddha* position of Śrī Herukanātha and Śrī Vajrayoginī had been realised through the *yogic* practices of the *Sādhaka* and his female counterpart.[14] Thus it might be unhesitantly remarked that the sudden discovery of the *Nava Caryāpada* by S.B. Dasgupta revealed not only the mystic thoughts of Vajrayāna Buddhism, but also would compel researches to explain the Bengali attitude, consciousness, and mental factors from the historical perspective. Although these songs had been discovered and collected from Nepal and adjoining areas, they very much represented the philosophical speculations and the specimens of early Bengali literature relating to Buddhist tantric rituals and practices. However, it should be noted that save the Songs Nos. 1, 2,

3, 4, 10 and 19, other songs of the *Nava Caryāpada* are remarkable additions to Indian literature. The title *Nava Caryāpada,* the collection of these newly-discovered *caryā*-songs, is quite appropriate, since S.B. Dasgupta, the compiler of these songs, had probably been inspired by the expression *gāvanti navagiti,* 'sing the new songs' (Song 84).

Before this discourse is concluded it would be better to translate and reproduce some of the remarks made in Bengali by Professor S.B. Dasgupta in his maiden lecture on the topic delivered at the Conference Room of the Bangiya Sahitya Parishat, Kolkata, on September 07, 1963 as follows:

'Acarya Haraprasad Sastri, Dr. Prabodhcandra Bagchi and Pandit Rahula Sankrityayana had discussed the *Caryāpada* and *Dohākosa.* I had obtained many evidences in favour of the information and theories advanced by them. Rahula Sānkrityayana mentioned the *Dohās* of Sarahapāda ... I saw those verses.'

The verses or Vajragītis compiled in the *Hevajra-Tantra* are now known as 'Kolāi Gān' in Nepal.

It appeared to me that the *Caryāpadas* of Haraprasad Sastri formed a collection of some select fifty verses. These verses were virtually faultless—in meters, in expressions, in statements. I thought that they were the jewels of the *Caryā*-songs ... I considered that the *Caryāpadas* were composed even after the twelfth century. There were, of course, also many other *caryā*-songs from those discovered and discussed by the above-mentioned three great scholars.

I had the evidence of my supposition. I obtained three new *padas* in my collection:

1. The *pada* with Sagata-bhaṇitā:
   Emahimaṇḍala meru samudrā
   Dhana jana jauvana uḍavindu candrā
   Pekhure anudin loane gaane
   Phulla parihāsai jinaguṇa raane
   Skandhe dhārī indiviṣaya savva ekā
   Samudra taraṅga jimu eku anekā
   Pavana dui bhediyā dṛḍha thire ciā
   Jvalai vajrānala dahadiha dahiā
   Sugata bheda bhāvaiā na hoi re śodhā
   Sugata bhaṇai acintālaya bodhā. (Song 5)

2. The *pada* with Macchīndra-bhaṇitā :

Pahu maitrī bhūvi vajra ahomā śuṇṇa sahāva
Tajhū via ehi niti sarvasattva hito va, etc. (Song 7)

3. Ḍombinī sarovara vilāsai kaise
Evaṃkāra kamale jagata nibbāsiye, etc. (Song 8)

These *Caryāpadas* of the second series would reveal some new indications in the language and meters. They would form a bridge between the old and medieval Bengali literature. ...

Till recently we knew that the first poet of the *Caryāpada* was Luipā (10th century), the last poet was Kāṇupā (12th century). But now we see that the first poet was Sarahapā (middle of the 9th century), the last poet was Kāṇupā (12th century). It would, therefore, not be wrong to remark that the *Caryā*-songs had been composed in a period covering 300 years.

Mithilā-Orissā-Magadha-Kāmarūpa-Rāḍha, Gauḍa, Vaṅga—in this vast tract of land due to the influence of the language of the *Caryāpada* (literary language) from the 12th to 14th-15th century, Vrajabuli (literary language) grew up.

The ninty-eight Buddhist mystic songs collected and published in the *Nava Caryāpada* would appear as very significant from the following Buddhist historical perspectives:

(i) The discovery of these mystic songs of the *Nava Caryāpada* was a sensational one, since it revealed that the followers of the Vajrayāna sect of Buddhism composed mystic songs also in Bengali and *not* exclusively in Sanskrit as thought before this discovery.

(ii) These mystic songs of the *Nava Caryāpada* were so far probably the last additions to the Buddhist tantric literature in the Bengali language.

(iii) The subject-matter of most of these songs was presented in an atmosphere of the *Sammohana-Tantras*[15] of the 14th century AD, although similarities between them and the Buddhist tantric Ḍākārṇava composed after the 12th century were also prominent in some instances.[16]

All these statements reveal that the *Nava Caryāpada* needs immediate attention for the sake of study and research in Buddhism, particularly Vajrayāna Buddhism.

NOTES

1. Kvaerne, per. *An Anthology of Buddhist Tantric Songs: A Study of Caryagīti*, (Oslo, The Norwegian Research Council For Science and the Humanities, 1975), pp. 7-8.
2. Sastri, Mm.Haraprasad (ed.), *Hājār Bacharer Purāṇa Bāṅglā Bhāṣāy Bauddha Gān O Dohā*, Calcutta, Bangiya Sahitya Parishat, B.S. 1388.
3. In both the snar-thaṅ (Narthang) (fol.215a) and sDe-dge (Derge) (fol.206a) editions of the Tibetan bs Tan-gyur (Tanjur 1) are recorded: pandita chen-po Kīrti-candra i Zal-sṅa-nasgdams-pa daṅ bcas-pa legs-par zus-śih/ chos-kyi rje dpal-Idan Sa-skya-pa khu-dbon-mams-kyi sku-drin-la brten-nas Bal-yu Yam-bu'i groṅ-khyer-du-Bod-kyi lo-cā-ba bande Grags-pa rgyal-mchan-gyis bsgyur-ro.
4. *The Statesman*, Calcutta, April 23, 1963, *Ānanda Bāzār Patrikā*, May 5, 1963; *Catuskon* (Nava Paryāy), Śrāvaṇa 1371/August 1964.
5. *Buddhist Literature: Its perspectives*, Proceedings of the XIXth International Buddhist Conference, 1994, Vol. XIX (Bodhgaya, International Buddhist Brotherhood Association, Tokyo, Japanese Temple, 1995), pp. 7-22 (Barua, Dipak Kumar, *Nava Caryapada: Perspectives of the Discovery of some New Buddhist Mystic Songs from Nepal*).
6. Dasgupta, Sashibhushan coll. & comp., *Nava Caryāpada*, edited by Asit Kumar Bandyopadhyay (Calcutta, University of Calcutta, 1989), pp. 99-102.
7. Shahidullah, Muhammad (tr.) *Buddhist Mystic Songs: Oldest Bengali and Other Eastern Vernaculars*, Dacca, Renaissance Printers, 1974.
8. Dasgupta, Shashi Bhushan, *op. cit.*, pp. 27-28.
9. Snellgrove, D. (ed.), *Hevajra-Tantra*, II, IV, 6 12.
10. Mojumdar, Atindra, *The Caryāpadas* (Calcutta, 1967, 1973), p. 2, n. I.
11. Dasgupta, Sashibhushan, *op. cit.*, p.102.
12. Sankrityayana, Rahula, *Dohā-Koṣa* (Patna, Bihar Rastrabhasa Parishad, 1957), (*Introduction*) p. 70.
13. Sen, Sukumar, *Caryagītipadāvalī* (2nd ed.), p.181.
14. Veaudeville, Charlotte, *Kabir*, Part I (London, 1974), p. 54.
15. Tucci, G, *Tibetan Painted Scrolls* (Rome, 1949), Vol. 1. pp. 209-249.
16. Bharati, A, *The Tantric Tradition*, London, 1965; Dasgupta, S.B, *An Introduction to Tantric Buddhism*, Calcutta, 1950.

5

The Influence of Buddhism on Bengali Literature

Sumita Chakrabarti

Buddhadeva was not only a great religious teacher or the founder of a new religion in India, he was a phenomenon. The history and culture in Indian sub-continent have never been the same since Buddhadeva's arrival. Now the Buddhist culture has been so incorporated in every sphere of the cultural heritage of India that it cannot be identified separately. Here we shall try to draw a preliminary outline of the influence of Buddhadeva's life, religion and philosophy that has found its way in the elite minds of Bengal and in Bengali literature.

There was a prince named Siddhartha born in 560 BC to a king of the Shakya clan in the northern part of Eastern India. He was very disturbed to see the human sufferings and was keen to search for a path to end the sorrow and pain of human life. He left home and took great trouble to fulfil his goal. Finally, after long meditation he found out a way to liberate the human soul, which is entrapped in this world of pain. It revealed in the Buddha's mind, a faith of attaining the supreme, peaceful and blissful existence for man. Siddhartha became the Buddha when he attained 'Bodhi' or supreme knowledge. This new religious path preached by Buddhadeva, his directive about the behaviour of everyday life and his moral teaching together with the religious philosophy have come to be known as Buddhism. The Buddha gradually became the manifestation of God to his followers and was called Buddhadeva or Lord Buddha. Originally, the Buddha stood against the scriptures, rituals and the orders of Brahminism in Hindu society. Later, Buddhadeva came to be known as one of the ten incarnations (*avatara*) of Lord Vishnu of Hindu *Puranas*.

We see that four aspects of Buddhadeva and Buddhism have influenced Bengali literature from four different angles.

Firstly, his personal life is an example by itself. He sacrificed his luxurious home, his throne, his young and beautiful wife and the infant son and went through great hardships and physical affliction. This kindled the imagination of the writers and artists. When the young and sensitive prince emerged as the Buddha, the enlightened one, he preached the message of not only individual *Nirvana* (liberation of soul) but of peace, friendship, non-violence, love and forgiveness towards the entire human society. And then came the great event of his passing away (*Mahaparinirvana*) in a quiet and completely blissful state of mind while accepting the food, probably, pork-meat (*Suaramajjapam*) which was unfit to be taken by a person of eighty years old but could not be refused as it was the sacred alms (*Bhiksha*) to a Buddhist. The story of the Buddha's life is simple, touching and immensely significant to Indian history and society which never failed to attract the writers and thinkers of Bengal.

Secondly, the Buddhist religion and philosophy had its own attraction. It stood somewhat against the traditional set up of the Hindu society, dominated by the hereditary and priestly elite class who called themselves Brahmins. The downtrodden and the oppressed people considered the Brahmins to be superior to them and the Brahmins themselves held the same idea very strongly. It was a feudal society and the kings also had strong belief in casteism. The so-called 'lower caste' people had to go through unending exploitation. The Buddha emerged with a religion with no caste-barrier. Immediately it was hailed by the common people. The religion got an acceptance in the merchant class too who had money but was considered of having lower status than the Brahmins.

The Buddhists laid very little or no stress upon God and Brahmins. The concept of heaven and hell was of no importance. The process of rebirth was accepted as it was thought that the long worldly bond cannot be broken in one single life. But human beings irrespective of their caste came first in Buddhist religion, not the deities or God.

The Buddha did not believe in complicated rituals and various established forms of worshipping. He was against icon-worship. For him religion meant living a simple, truthful and honest life, to help the distressed, to love and forgive others; to follow the path of extreme non-violence. In Buddhism liberation of soul comes when supreme knowledge (*prajna*) is attained. This comes through learning and meditation. Meditation in Buddhism goes with the rationality of mind. It is not a blind faith.

In due course, around one hundred and ten to twenty years after the death of Buddhadeva, Buddhism was divided into two groups called Hinayana and Mahayana. The Hinayanis maintained the traditional philosophical thought where *Nirvana* can be attained for one's own self only. Mahayanis went for a reformatory change and saught *Nirvana* for all.

Around 9th century AD when Mahayana faith was popular in Eastern India, it was divided again in three groups—Vajrayana, Kalachakrayana and Sahajayana. However, the basic idea remained the same—the attainment of *Nirvana* which means to stop the cycle of rebirth by a long process of learning which comes through the experience from many past lives and also by deep meditation. When it is attained, the soul dwells in an eternal bliss of spiritual existence (*Mahasukha*).

The intelligentsia and the reformers of the 19th century Bengal, mostly Brahmins, were particularly attracted by this philosophical aspect of Buddhism which seemed to cast a deep social and religious impact upon their thinking. They wrote many articles and essays on Buddhism; some of them were engaged in thorough research on the subject and produced some good academic work.

Thirdly, Buddhism appeared at a very crucial period of Indian history. During sixth century BC India was a land of religious and political turmoil. The social scene was also very disturbed. The north-western part of India was dominated by the Indo-Aryans. The north-eastern and eastern part was a peculiar amalgamation of Indo-Aryans, non-Aryan tribes and the tribals of the hill areas. Many small kingdoms were fighting with each other continuously. Brahminism was the dominant social force, which was harsh on the so-called lower caste people. Under the circumstances, people suffered and naturally began to question the values of life and worth of living. Buddhadeva appeared with an answer. Since no caste-bar was attached to this new religion, common people came to Buddhadeva for advice. His doctrine was of love and mercy. Buddhist monks also rendered consolation to the distressed as they never considered anybody as a sinner who could not be forgiven. They never gave punishment as such but provided refuges instead.

Buddhism attracted the attention of some rulers of north-eastern states. King Ashoka was converted to Buddhism. The Pala dynasty was of Buddhist faith. Though the Buddhist kings were not unkind to Hindu religion, Hindu upper castes were unfriendly to Buddhism. The situation did not alter after Buddhadeva's death but only increased after the second Buddha Sangeeti (The great conference to straighten up the differences among various Buddhist sects). The differences among the Buddhists of various groups were never reconciled.

The conflict between Buddhism continued till the 9th century AD. Gradually by the 10th and the 11th century, Buddhism changed considerably. Earlier Buddhism denied the existence of God. In this period, however, the concept of many deities was introduced. Complicated patterns of rituals and forms of worship also crept in. *Charya-geeti* or *Charyapadas* are the oldest form of Bengali poetry known till date. These were written between the 10th and the 12th century AD. The context of these musical poems is derived from contemporary Buddhist religious practice. The poems are the symbolical expressions of a concealed religious meaning in a religion where the ultimate blissful state can be attained through following the 'guru' (religious teacher) only.

When the invaders from Western Asia—the Turks and the Pathans—began arriving to conquer India, Buddhism slowly moved towards the Eastern Asian countries. The period, from the 5th century BC to the 12th century AD has been marked as Hindu-Bauddha Yug (the period of Hinduism and Buddhism) by some academicians. This particular span of time with all its collisions and rivalries has largely attracted the novelists and short story writers in Bengali literature. We shall state the examples later.

Lastly, Buddhist scriptures have a large number of beautiful anecdotes of their own. They were written mostly in Pali, a language developed by the Buddhists simplifying the elite Sanskrit language for common, little-educated masses. The *Jatakas* and the *Avadanas* are practically great collections of various stories. On one hand, these stories explained Buddhist religion and philosophy, on the other, are unparallel documents of Indian social and cultural history of the ancient period. Some modern writers have re-written these stories in Bengali. Sometimes they have used the stories in such a manner that contemporary social questions have arisen from that remodelling. But the general themes of the stories have remained the same—entirely human. Rabindranath Thakur himself has made use of quite a number of these stories to write some beautiful poems, plays and dance-dramas.

Presently, we shall come to the literary examples of these four aspects depicted in language-art-form. Leaving the examples of manifestation of Buddadeva's life, to be discussed later on, we shall bring forth the second aspect, i.e., the academic and institutional studies on Buddhism in Bengal.

The Christian missionary of Srirampur initiated the earliest researches on Pali language and literature. In 1908, Felix Carey, son of William Carey, went to Rangoon for spreading Christianity and came in contact with Pali language and literature. He studied Pali, authored a grammar book on the language and translated some of the *Suttas* (religious hymns or ethical instructions composed in meter) into English.

Devendranath Thakur, father of Rabindranath, the first Indian to take interest in Pali literature and Buddhism, went to Ceylon (now Sri Lanka) in September 1859 and joined in prayers and worships of the Buddhist monks. The peaceful meditation of the Buddhists, their negation of casteism and idol worshipping and almost no ritual practice attracted his attention. He came back in the same year to found a religious institution called Brahma-Vidyalaya. Brahma faith and Brahma schools were based on some of the Buddhist ideas and practices.

Keshavachandra Sen who had accompanied Devendranath Thakur was a zealous Brahma youth. On returning from Ceylon, he started celebrating the birthday of Lord Buddha on *Baishakhi Purnima* (full moon day of the month of *Baishakh*). He went to visit Bodhgaya and initiated an annual programme for religious discussions called 'Shakya-Samagam' in 1880. Dwijendranath Thakur and Satyendranath Thakur, both Devendranath's sons, wrote books on Buddhist history and philosophy. Rabindranath acquired his long-term attachment with Buddhism out of this atmosphere.

There were other Bengali scholars too who, in the last three decades of the 19th century, shouldered the responsibility of bringing the glorious ideas of Buddhism to the Indian people and to the Bengalis. A select bibliography follows:

	Book		Author
1.	*Shakyamunicharit o Nirvanatattva*	1881 (?)	Aghornath Gupta
2.	*The Sanskrit Buddhist Literature of Nepal*	1882	Rajendralal Mitra
3.	*Buddhacharit*	1892	Krishnabihari Sen
4.	*Ashokacharit*	1892	Krishnabihari Sen
5.	*Aryadharma o Bouddhadharmer*		

	Paraspar Ghat Pratighat o Sanghat	1899	Dwijendranath Thakur
6.	*Bouddhadharma*	1901	Satyendranath Thakur
7.	*Dhammapada (Tr.)*	1904	Charuchandra Basu
8.	*Paliprakash*	1911	Bidhushekhar Shastri

We may conclude from this very short survey of the contemporary scene by quoting a few lines from the preface of the book *Bouddhadharma* (2nd ed., 1923) written by Satyendranath Thakur. These lines sum up the general theory of the Bengali intelligentsia about Buddhism in Indian history and culture.

> "আজ আমরা প্রাচীন ভারতবর্ষের ইতিহাস বলতে প্রধানত বৌদ্ধযুগের ইতিহাসই বুঝি। আমরা হঠাৎ আবিষ্কার করেছি যে, ভারতবর্ষের বৌদ্ধযুগক্ক হচ্ছে এ দেশের সভ্যতার সর্বাপেক্ষা গৌরবমণ্ডিত যুগ।"

"Today, we particularly mean the history of Buddhist period as the history of ancient India. We have suddenly discovered that the Buddhist period in India is the most glorious age of the civilization of this country."

Next, we come to the historical side of Buddhism, which has influenced the sphere of Bengali literature considerably. The Buddha and his followers made their presence felt very deeply in the political surrounding of ancient India and constantly clashed with the social and political forces of the Hindu society.

When the Buddha appeared in the 6th century BC, no single ruler ruled the vast north-eastern part of the country. There were many small groups and clans constantly fighting for power and territory. The common people were endlessly exploited economically by the king's court, the feudal lords and by the Brahmin priests. Buddhadeva and his disciples brought at least some discipline in the religious order for a section of common people in the country.

The first great conference of the Buddhists or Bauddhasangeeti was held just after the death (*Mahaparinirvana*) of Buddhadeva in 480 BC at Rajagriha (Now Rajgir in Bihar near Patna) convened by Sthabira Mahakashyapa. The messages of the Buddha were collected there for the first time in three different sets called *Pitakas.* The second Mahasangeeti was held in Vaishali after 110 years of *Mahaparinirvana.* In this very gathering the difference within the Buddhists (Bauddha Sangha) became evident. They were divided into two groups, Hinayanis and Mahayanis. The former were traditional practitioners of Buddhism who aimed at the liberation of one's self. Only the latter developed a philosophy where all could attain liberation.

The political scene of the country was devoid of any united force till the 4th century BC. There were no prominent rulers. Alexander came to conquer India around 325 BC. Out of the unprecedented turmoil a great king appeared and rose to the occasion. He was Chandragupta Maurya, a king who descended not from the caste of Brahmins or upper class Kshatriyas. He was probably a lower grade Kshatriya, might be a Shudra, at least born of Shudra mother. He was the first powerful king in Eastern India to establish a well-founded kingdom and a dynasty. Buddhism was well established then but could not dethrone Brahminism at that time.

Chandragupta's grandson Ashoka, son of Bindusar, became the king in 232 BC. After winning Kalinga war he was converted to Buddhism and embraced this doctrine of peace whole-heartedly. This was the time of glory for Buddhism. The third Bauddha-sangeeti was held in King Ashoka's period. He sent messengers of peace to Singhal (now Sri Lanka) and the path of Buddhism was spread towards Eastern Asian countries. Numerous *Viharas* (lodges for Buddhist monks) were established. Buddha *Viharas* became the centres for learning. Some of them like Vikramashila, Nalanda, Sompur, Takshashila were not meant for studying Buddhism only but were regarded as full-fledged universities where many subjects were taught and students used to come from all over Asia.

Though after the Maurya dynasty, Hindu kings like Pushyamitra and Satavahana came into power for a short period, the next great king Kanishka in the 1st century AD was also a Buddhist.

From the rise of the Gupta period in the 3rd century AD to the decline of the Pala dynasty in the 11th century AD north-eastern India was a union of quite a few prosperous states. The citizens practised Buddhism and Hinduism both.

It can be easily understood that the historical perspective of this period was very significant and colourful. The time was changing very fast. There was a constant interaction among the king, the merchant class and the guardians of the religious order; conflicts grew naturally between the exploited mass and the feudal landlords. The reality of life in this fast-moving time seemed attractive to the fiction writers because fiction is a form of literature where the reality of life and the heartbeat of the people from every section of the

castes like Dom, Chandal, and Kaibarta were treated with contempt. On the other hand, Buddhist institutions that earlier provided some refuge to these so-called 'lower-class' people were themselves involved in ugly tantrik practices. They used bodies of these lower-caste people for their worship and did not hesitate to murder them for the said purpose. They also kidnapped women from the similar castes to use them as *Sadhan Sanginis,* forcefully carrying out sexual malpractices. Dineshcandra Sen, a scholar of historical sender and outlook sadly opened up the scroll showing the pattern of social changes. Consequently, these lower-castes gradually started adopting Islamic faith to escape the various exploitations of the upper class Hindus and tantrik Buddhists.

Sharadindu Bandyopadhyay was a very popular Bengali writer who wrote historical novels as well as detective fiction during the fifties and the sixties. Many of his historical novels are set in ancient Indian background. *Kaler Mandira* (The bell of the time, 1951) is about a Hun king who was a convert Buddhist at the time of Skandagupta around 5th century AD. The novel is nothing but a romantic story but the author is deeply respectful to Buddhadeva's teachings and Buddhist monks. *Gourhmallar* (The Mallar, an Indian classical musical note of Gourh, 1954) is also a historical romance. The period is the span of one hundred years in Bengal after the death of King Shashanka. Buddhism was somewhat decaying in this period. From the 8th century AD it started mixing with Hinduism.

It is the story of Bajradeva, the grandson of Shashanka who after his father's death in exile comes to Gourh and incidentally occupies the throne of Gourh for one day only. Then he leaves the kingdom to return to his mother and childhood sweetheart for the rest of his life. There are beautiful descriptions of Bauddha-*Viharas* of Karnasuvarna and Nalanda. Bajradeva was summoned by Aacharya Sheelabhadra and was requested to try to regain the kingdom. Bajradeva became intimate with the young Buddhist monks. The whole narration gives us a fine picture of the Buddhist institutions of the 8th century AD in eastern India.

The third novel of this kind by Sharadindu Bandyopadhyay is *Tumi Sandhyar Megh* (You are the evening cloud, 1958). The novel is a historical one. The episode and descriptions of falling in love of Vigrahapala, a crown prince of Pala dynasty and Yaubanashree, the daughter of Karnadeva, the king of Chedi with each other is imaginary to a large extent but the marriage is a historical fact. The main theme of the novel is the insecurity of the Buddhist institutions when Turkish invaders used to attack the *Viharas* repeatedly and the monks tried to preserve the scriptures in safety by carrying the old manuscripts to Nepal and Tibet from India. The protagonist of this part of the novel is the famous and great Buddhist monk and teacher Dipankar Shreejnana who is a historical figure. The atmosphere of the *Vihara* is vividly described in this novel.

Sharadindu Bandyopadhyay wrote a few short stories too on Buddhist themes but before him, Bibhutibhushan Bandyopadhyay wrote a couple of such stories using some supernatural elements. In the story *Meghmallar* a power-loving Tantrik Buddhist monk captured the goddess of art and learning (Saraswati). At last the young man who unknowingly gives a hand to the Tantrik earlier sets her free. The young man turned into a stone-figure. This story holds nothing of Buddhist thought or Buddhist history but another story called *Pratnatattwa* (Archaeology) spins around the character of Dipankar Shreejnana again. A beautiful stone image of Saraswati is found in an archaeological excavation. The narrator of the story or the author himself is enchanted by the statue and cannot resist from meditating upon it all the time. Finally, one night, Dipankar Shreejnana appears in his dreams. He showed him the glorious moments and events of his life connected with Buddhist period. The statue was carved out of stone by himself. He was a fine sculptor too, a fact few people knew. The narrator wakes up from his dream knowing everything about the image and acquires his normal self again.

Sharadindu wrote a few short stories on Buddhist events and ideas such as *Amitava*, *Mrit-pradip* (The earthen lamp), *Chandan Murti* (The statue of sandalwood), *Maru O Sangha* (The desert and the monastery), etc. All the stories are attractive with historical reference on Buddhism and touches of Buddhist culture.

We may refer to two Bengali novels written by two well-known writers from Bangladeshi Selina Hossain's *Neel Mayurer Yauvan* (The youth of the blue peacock) which depicts the period between the 10th and the 12th century AD when Buddhism was spread widely to the backward communities. The poets wrote Buddhist religious songs and occasionally referred to the backward classes like Doms, Chandals, and Shabaras. The songs express their livelihood, their poverty, untouchable social status and their love. Selina Hossain has written about the story of their struggle and faith of these common people.

The other novel is written by Shaukat Ali named *Prodoshe Prakrita*

Jan (The common people at the end of the day, 1984). The state of Buddhism during the Sena period and the arrival of the Muslim invaders are narrated in the novel. The author tries to establish the historical point that the downtrodden people of the so-called lower castes were inclined to be converted to Buddhism before the Muslims came. But, gradually, the Islam held that position. We note that Dinesh Chandra Sen's observation in *Shyamal O Kajjal*, was the same. It is a very well written, thought-provoking novel.

Last but not the least, we name a very significant novel titled *Maitreya Jataka* (The Maitreya born) published in 1994 by Bani Basu. It is a novel inspired by the life and teachings of the Buddhadeva. It is a great historical novel too. The political scene of Eastern India was disturbed by the conflict of power. In society the merchant class were dominant and they took to Buddhism more and more. It is a multi-dimensional novel with contemporary social, political, cultural and ethical aspects of the Buddhadeva, the merciful lord whose personal influence carries a man's wounded and inflicted heart towards eternal peace and bliss.

We have stated earlier that Bengali writers in various forms have adopted stories from Buddhist scriptures. While some of them are only translations (we are not considering the translations here), most significant literary creations are found in Rabindranath Thakur's writings.

Rabindranath Thakur was himself an institution regarding Buddhist studies and Buddhist literature in Bengal. He, like his elder brothers, inherited this interest from his father. Rajendralal Mitra's *The Sanskrit Buddhist Literature of Nepal* was an all-time companion to him.

He has referred about Nepali Buddhist literature in *Chhinnapatravali*, his collection of letters written to Indira Devi Chaudhurani (letter No. 16, dt. March 3, 1893). Interest in Buddhism, was evident in contemporary Western countries also. *The Light of Asia*, the well-known epic poem showing the greatness and glory of Buddhadeva's life was written by Edwin Arnold (published in 1879). The translations and appreciation of Buddhist literature by Rhys Davids also appeared during this period.

Rabindranath initiated the studies of Pali, the language of the Buddhist scriptures in Santiniketan. Bidhushekhar Shastri, a great scholar on the subject came from Varanasi in 1909 and wrote *Pali Prakash*, the first Pali grammar in Bengali (Published in 1911).

Rabindranath sent Nityananda Vinod Goswami, a teacher in Santiniketan, to Singhal (now Sri Lanka) and Burma (now Mynamar) to collect old Buddhist manuscripts, which he did. Rabindranath loved *Dhammapadas* included in *Sutta-Pitaka* and he wrote the introduction of the translation of *Dhammapadas* by Charuchandra Basu. According to Thakur *Dhammapadas* is one of the best religious texts in the world and it is the voice of India's soul. In 1919, Thakur invited the well-known Buddhist monk Dharmadhar Mahasthavira at Santiniketan to deliver speeches and explain Buddhism. Sylvain Levi, the French scholar on Buddhist scriptures who knew Chinese, Japanese and Tibetan, came to Santiniketan in 1921. An executive body called Visvabharati Parishad was formed in Santiniketan in 1921 when Rabindranath was re-modelling the establishment as a full-fledged educational institution. In its inaugural function Rabindranath said, "This institution has been planned after the Sanghas and Viharas of ancient India when they fulfilled the needs of the country. The changes only have been made to suit the modern age."

Scholars, teachers and students from China, Japan and Tibet used to come to Santiniketan regularly. Rabindranath Thakur was the first educationist in India who started regular Chinese, Japanese and Tibetan departments in his institution. He himself visited China and Japan (1924) and the Eastern Asian island states—Malay, Java, Bali, and Siam in 1927. Suniti Kumar Chattopadhyay has narrated the description about this tour and Rabindranath's interest and respect towards Buddhist culture in his travelogue *Rabindra Sangame Dweepamay Bharat O Shyamdesh.* Suniti Kumar Chattopadhyay accompanied Thakur on this tour. The paintings, murals and sculptures in Santiniketan on Buddhist subjects by painters and sculptors like Nandalal Bose and Ramkinkar Bej are the treasures of the world of art.

Rabindranath Thakur wrote quite a number of poems on Buddhist themes and stories. Here we present a very short account of them showing the changes he made while using the stories. All these poems have been collected in *Katha O Kahini* (1900).

1. *Shrestha Bhiksha* (The great alms)
   Story from *Bastravadana* of *Avadana-shataka*:

The original story:

Anathapindatha, a principal disciple of Buddhadeva, went to the city to beg for Lord Buddha. He was not satisfied by the various offerings of rich people. A poor woman offered her only worn-out piece of cloth to him and hid herself in the forest. After that she was given valuable garments and went to the abode of the gods.

The changes: Almost no change. But the last part of the story of the woman's receiving valuable garments and leaving the world has been omitted.

2. *Mastak Bikray* (The sale of the head):
   Story from *Ajnatakaundilya Jataka* as narrated in *Mahavastu Avadana.*

The original story:

The virtuous king of Kosala was known for his kindness. He sacrifices his throne and kingdom to avoid bloodshed in conflict with the king of Kashi and goes into exile. He meets a poor merchant who is in need of help. The king of Kosala takes him to the king of Kashi to request him to give the poor man the sum of money that has been set as the price of his own head. Such self-sacrifice moved the king of Kashi deeply and he reinstated the king of Kosala on his throne.

There has been no change in the poem of Rabindranath Thakur.

3. *Pujarini* (The woman worshiper) and *Natir Puja* (The worship of the dance, 1926).
   Story from the anecdote 'Shreemati' from *Avandana Shataka.*

The original story:

King Bimbisara, a disciple of Buddhadeva, begs for a piece of nail and some hair of Lord Buddha. On receiving those, he builds a Stupa and orders the ladies of his household to clean the place everyday. His son Ajatashatru is against Buddhism and prohibits the practice. But Shreemati, a maidservant, washes the place in the evening as usual and lights the lamps. The king is enraged and orders her execution. After death she is made a goddess.

Here also the story has remained unchanged in the poem but for the last miraculous portion which has been dropped. Rabindranath Thakur wrote a full-fledged drama also titled *Natir Puja* (1926) based on this story. Many characters and episodes have been invented there. Shreemati is a dancer here, not a servant. But the spirit of the story is the same.

4. *Abhisar* (Going secretly to meet one's lover), story named 'Upaguptanam' from *Boddhisattvabadanakalpalata.*

The original story:

Upagupta, a handsome young man, is a disciple of a monk. Vasavadatta, a prostitute is attracted to him and invites him to her place. Upagupta refuses and says that he would call on her at proper time. After some time Vasavadatta poisons one of her paramours at the instigation of another. She is severely punished. The executioners cut her nose, ears and hair. They take away her clothes and leave her in isolation. Upagupta comes to her and consoles her. Then Upagupta became a Buddhist monk of reknown.

The changes: Rabindranath has transformaed the character of Vasavadatta for better. Neither does she murder anyone, nor she gets punished. She is suffering from small pox and is left helplessly alone when Upagupta comes and nurses her with great care.

5. *Samanya Kshati* (A little loss).
Story from the episode of 'Shyamavati' included in *Divyavadanamala.*

The original story:

The story is a complicated one with too many sub-plots and episodes. The story of Shyamavati is a tale within a tale narrated by Lord Goutama to King Udayana. Brahmadatta is the king of Varanasi who has five hundred wives. One day after bathing in the river, they feel cold and in order to make themselves warm, they set fire to a hut nearby. The hut belongs to a hermit who escapes and by supernatural power he rises to the sky to bless the ladies. The women, Shyamavati being in the leading role, is astonished and begs punishment for their sins. They pray for supreme knowledge also.

The changes: Rabindranath did not use the supernatural part of the story. In his poem, the queen sets fire to a hut causing the whole village to be burnt. The homeless villagers come to the king and state the events. The king makes his queen to beg from door to door for money in order to rebuild the village huts. Thus the king appears as a man of justice in the poem.

6. *Mulyaprapti* (Getting the price)
Story from 'Padmabadana' collected in *Avadana Shataka.*

The original story:

A gardener of Sravasti brings a big lotus for King Prasenjit. At the moment Anathapindada, a disciple of Buddhadeva, comes and doubles its price. He wants to give the flower to Lord Buddha. The king and the monk keep bidding against each other till the price rise to a hundred-fold. The gardener then refuses to sell it and presents the flower to the Lord himself. Instantly the lotus swells out to the size of a wheel standing over Buddhadeva's head.

The changes: The poet drops the name of Anathapindada and the king. In the poem the traveller is the bidder against the king. The supernatural portion has been omitted.

7. *Nagaralakshmi* (The goddess in-charge of the city).
Story of Supriya from 'Kalpadrumavadana' included in *Avadanashataka.*

The original story:

Anathapindada's daughter Supriya is deeply religious since her birth. She eventually becomes a nun. A famine breaks out in the city and Supriya begs alms from the common households to relieve the poor people.

The changes: The story of Supriya in *Avadanashataka* includes many other episodes. Rabindranath selects only one of them. In the poem there are some slight changes only, that is, when the famine breaks out, Lord Buddha asks his rich disciples to undertake the task of feeding the citizens. None accept other than Supriya who declares that she would beg to feed the famine-hit people of the city.

8. *Parishodh* (Paying off the debt) and *Shyama* (1939).

Story from *Kanabera Jataka* and also from *Shyama Jataka* included in *Mahavastu-Avadana.* There is a slight difference in these narrations.

The original story from *Jataka*:

Once Bodhisattva was born as a thief and was arrested by the king's men. The famous prostitute of Varanasi was Shyama who fell in love with the handsome young man. She sent one of her lovers to the police and Bodhisattva was set free. Shyama and Bodhisattva lived happily for some time. But Bodhisattva one day killed Shyama and left taking away all her valuables. Shyama revived and searched for him but Bodhisattva did not return.

In the story of the *Avadana* the name of the protagonist is Vajrasena who is a horse-dealer and is caught by the police as a thief. Shyama rescues him in the same way as narrated in *Jataka*. Vajrasena, after spending some time with Shyama gradually feels distressed over her cruelty towards the other man who is executed. He makes her senseless with wine and drowns her. Vajrasena goes away. Her maids revive Shyama. She sends for Vajrasena and invites him again. Vajrasena accepts her message and love. But whether he comes back to Shyama or not, is not stated clearly in the story.

The changes: Rabindranath Thakur uses the version of *Avadana*. In his poem *Parishodha* and the beautiful dance-drama *Shyama* written many years later, the name of the protagonist is Vajrasena. He is a merchant, not a thief. Though he rejects Shyama for her cruel deed, he never tries to kill or punish her. He is sorry for Shyama but feels helpless because he cannot make himself to accept the woman who arranged to kill an innocent man. Thus, Vajrasena stays apart though he loves Shyama.

There are some dramas by Rabindranath Thakur which are adaptations from the stories of Buddhist scriptures. We may take account of these now.

9. *Raja* (The king, 1910), *Arupratan* (The treasure invisible, 1920), *Shapamochan* (Release from a curse, 1931).
   Story from *Kusha Jataka* collected in *Mahavastu-Avadana.*

The original story:

Kushakumar is a prince of great knowledge, sweet personality and fearless bravery. But he is ugly. He marries a beautiful princess but his mother does not allow the couple to meet in day-light. When Pravabati, the princess see her husband at last, she is so shocked by his ugly appearance that she goes back to her father's residence. Kushakumar is deeply in love with Pravabati and follows her in disguise. When seven kings attack Pravabati's father at a time, Kushakumar fights bravely to save him. Pravabati then overcomes her initial feelings of dislike. She gratefully and lovingly accepts her husband.

The changes: Certain changes have been made in Rabindranath's adaptation of the story. In the dramas—'Raja' and 'Arupratan'—the character of Surangama has been introduced. Surangama is a companion to the queen Sadarshara, and is unconditionally devoted to the king. The appearance of the king makes no difference to her. A symbolic character of a grandfather-like old man 'thakurda' has become the mouthpiece of the author's thought in both the dramas. In the dance-drama 'Shapamochan' the queen leaves the king but does not go back to her parents. She goes to a secluded place. In course of time, she realizes her own shortcomings herself. There is no external force like the attack of enemies. The names of king and queen have been changed also to Aruneswar and Kamalika.

10. *Chandalika* (The Chandal girl, 1933), Chandalika, the dance drama (1937).
    Story from *Shardulakarnavadana* collected in '*Avadana-shataka*'.

The original story:

Ananda, the favourite disciple of Buddhadeva was returning to the *Vihara* when he feels thirsty and asks for water from a young woman of Chandal caste. Prakriti, the woman says that she is untouchable to the upper-caste people. But Ananda accepts the water from her because Buddhists have no caste-restrictions. Prakriti is attracted to Ananda and requests her mother to bring her beloved to her by force of her magic. Prakriti's mother does the same. Ananda comes to Prakriti at night but when Prakriti is busy making the bed, suddenly Ananda comes back to his senses and prays to the lord to rescues him. The lord utters a 'mantra' so that Prakriti's mother cannot hold the spell of magic. Ananda returns to the *Vihara* safely.

The changes: The first half of the story is the same in Rabindranath's version. He makes one major change. When Ananda comes to Prakriti's house, Prakriti herself becomes repentant realizing that she is bringing disgrace to a pure soul. After begging pardon Prakriti lets Ananda go his own way. Both the characters of Ananda and Prakriti have been uplifted in Rabindranath's creation.

11. *Malini* (1896)—a drama
    Story from *Mahavastu-Avadana.*

The original story:

Malini is the daughter of the king of Varanasi. She is attracted to the new religion and invites Lord Kashyapa to entertain him with a meal. The Brahmins of the king's court are angry. They induce the king to banish her. Malini begs for a week's respite and during those seven days many of her kinsmen and the ministers of the court are converted to the new religion. Armed men are sent to kill Kashyapa but they are also converted. Then the Brahmins themselves go to confront Kashyapa but are crushed to death by his power.

The changes: The original story is of the confrontation of the Brahmins and Lord Kashyapa. Rabindranath has written the play around Malini as the protagonist. The daughter of the king takes to the new religion. She influences Supriya, her lover to embrace the new religion too. Kshemenkara is Supriya's friend. A staunch believer of Brahminism, he rebels against Buddhism and is put to jail. When Kshemenkara is brought to the king's court he calls Supriya near and kills him with one strike of the heavy iron-chain of his hands. Malini is shocked but according to her religion of mercy she requests the king to forgive Kshemenkara.

The change: We see that Rabindranath has invented the whole plot of the play with the dramatic characters. Kashyapa has almost no importance in Thakur's version. It is new creation of the author and the spirit of Buddhism is more explicit here than the original story.

12. *Achalayatan* (1912), Guru (1918)
Story of *Panchaka* from *Divyavadanamala*

The original story:

Once an educational institution is set up by Aryaguru (the teacher of the Aryans). In course of time, lifeless rules and meaningless regulations become dominant there. Mantras and tantrik rituals are practised instead of normal teaching and simple meditation. Panchaka, a student of the school is unhappy over the whole business. He is anxious to break these chains and to come out in the open world near common people.

The changes: Rabindranath has retained the character of Panchaka and has invented the other characters—chiefly Mahapanchaka, a hard-core protector of the traditional system and the Guru who supported the notion of Panchaka—a simple, joyful, humane way of education and worship.

13. Next we come to *Rajarshi* (a sage-like king, 1887) and *Bisarjan* (immersion, 1890), the former, a novel and the latter a verse-drama

on the same theme. Rabindranath expresses his views against animal sacrifice as a form of worship. The theme has been expanded in the novel and in the play. The story has remained the same. The king wants the animal sacrifice to be stopped in the temple. The priest supports the tradition and confronts the king. The new religion is accepted after tragic consequences. The idea comes from Buddhism but there is no particular story behind the plot.

Rabindranath has written many poems and songs on Buddhadeva's life and Buddhist thoughts. He has written a few articles on Buddhism also like 'Bauddhadharme Bhaktibad' (The Bhakti-cult in Buddhism) and others. In the year 1931, a Buddhist *Vihara* was inaugurated on October 24th at Sarnath. Rabindranath wrote a poem on that occasion:

বোধিদ্রুমতলে তব সেদিনের মহাজাগরণ-
আবার সার্থক হোক, মোহ, আবরণ-।
"Your great awakening under the tree of knowledge-
Let that the victorious, let the false ideas fall apart."

We may quote one only
Among his many songs on Buddhadeva:

নূতন তব জন্ম লাগি কাতর যত প্রাণী
কর ত্রাণ মহাপ্রাণ আন অমৃতবাণী।
"The mankind awaits earnestly the new advent of yours-
Deliver us, oh great soul; bring us the message of immortal peace."

But, in spite of all the respect Rabindranath had for Lord Buddha and Buddhism, it may be pointed out that he did not accept the essential philosophy of Buddhism. Buddhism seeks to break the ties with the world while Rabindranath wants to maintain that loving bond with the human world forever.

We know very well that the specimens of oldest Bengali language and literature found so far does Haraprasad Shastri discover the manuscript of *Charyacharyabinishchaya* in 1907 from Nepal. Scholars are more or less of same opinion that these verses (forty-six and one incomplete) were written not later than the 12th century A.D. The earlier ones might go back to the late 10th century AD.

The poems were meant for singing and they reveal the Buddhist religious philosophy of the contemporary period. The variation of the Mahayana philosophy evolved as Mantrayana. It was divided into three branches called Vajrayana, Sahajayana and Kalachakrayana.

Their religious practice amalgamated with Tantras and they were staunch followers of the Guru. To be liberated from the worldly chain and to attain *Nirvana* with the help of Guru's teachings are the content of these songs. But they have literary flavour also. Contemporary social life has been depicted. The content has been displayed through many images—some of them quite beautiful like deer running in the forest, women wearing flowers, a girl dancing on the petals of lotus, a boat full of golden treasure, etc.

In the medieval period, Buddhism on the whole was devoured by Hinduism in Eastern India. The reason behind might be the great movement of Bhakti-cult promoted by Chaitanyadeva in the 16th century. Some traces of Buddhism might be noticed in the practices of the Natha Yogis and in the worship of Dharmathakur around the 18th century in some areas of Bengal like Bankura, Birbhum, etc.

In the second-half of the 19th century the enlightened Bengali middle class was respectfully conscious about Buddhadeva and Buddhist culture again on chiefly due to the Brahma society. In Bengali literature it is to be noted that Girischandra Ghosh, the famous playwright of the day, wrote a five-act play named *Buddhadeva Charit* (The life of Buddhadeva). It was written and staged in Star theatre in 1887. In the introduction, Ghosh has acknowledged his indebtedness to *The Light of Asia* written by Edwin Arnold.

Another long poem on a similar theme depicting the life, character and teaching of Buddhadeva was written by Navin Chandra Sen titled *Amitava* (published in 1895). It is written in metrical verse form, divided into nineteen cantos and the focus is on the life of Buddhadeva from his birth to his passing away.

In these writings we feel that Buddhadeva, the person with his charm, nobility and greatness of character is the centre of attraction of the authors. They do not care much about the religion or even the philosophy. They express their deep respect to a person who preached non-violence and stood by the distressed people offering them love, mercy and solace.

Manmatha Roy, another renowned Bengali playwright, also wrote a few plays where Buddhist influence in Bengal has been treated in its proper perspective. In 1923 he wrote *Muktir Dak*, one of the earliest one-act plays in Bengali. Buddha's disciple and Buddhism here have saved the afflicted soul of a woman. In 1933, he wrote *Ashoka*, a five-act play about the king who was converted to Buddhism and became an ambassador of peace. Again in 1945, Manmatha Roy composed a one-act play called *Rajpuri* where the greatness of Buddhism has been established as the path of truth.

Abanindranath Thakur wrote a beautiful novelette on Buddhadeva's life. Though originally meant for teenage readers, it is an all-time masterpiece of literary craftsmanship. The book *Nalak* was published in 1916. Nalak is the name of a boy of about twelve. He lives in the *Ashrama* (abode) of Rishi (sage) Devala as a student. One day, Devala goes to see Lord Buddha at Kapilavastu. Nalak is also very keen to see Buddha but as he is unable to go, the entire life of Buddhadeva flashes in his mind's eye. He sees every scene from newborn Siddhartha in the king's palace to the meditation that transformed Siddhartha's life under the Bodhi *Vriksha* (the tree of enlightenment). Nalak waited long to meet Buddhadeva. But the boy had left his mother for a long time too. The day he starts for his home crossing the river, Buddhadeva arrives on the bank of the same river that very day. Nalak could not meet the Buddha in person; he carried Lord Buddha's image in his heart forever. Abanindranath, a great painter, has sketched beautiful, subtle pen-picture of the forest, the *Ashrama* and every stage of Buddhadeva's life, seen through the eyes of the devoted boy Nalak.

Bengali poets during the twenties and thirties of the 20th century wrote some poems on Buddhadeva. They also laid emphasis not on the religion or philosophy but on the divine personality of the great man. Here are some examples:

1. মহামানব

মোহিতলাল মজুমদার

চিনেছি তোমারে যুগে যুগে অবতীর্ণ তুমি
হে বোধিসত্ত্ব। বুদ্ধ। তোমার চরণ তুমি।

মৈত্রেয় তথাগত
মহাদেব নয় মহামানবের চরণ চুমি।

The Great Man by Mohitlal Majumdar—"I know you—you come often in various ages. Oh, Boddhisattva! O, Buddha! I kiss your feet! Oh, Maitreya O, Tathagata

I kiss not the feet of the great god—but the feet of the great man."

2. বুদ্ধ পূর্ণিমা

সত্যেন্দ্রনাথ দত্ত

মৈত্রী করুনার মন্ত্র দিতে দান
জাগ হে মহীয়ান মরতে মহিমায়

নিরীহ মরালের শোণিতে অহরহ
ভাসিছে সংসার হৃদয় মোহ পায়-

হে বোধিসত্ত্ব হে, মাগিছে মর্ত্য যে
ও পদপঙ্কজে শরণ পনরায়।

Budhapurnima
(The sight of the full moon on Buddhadeva's birthday)
by Satyendranath Datta

"Oh Lord!

Arise again to preach the message of mercy in this world

Lots of blood of innocent swans
Have been shed in this earth,
Oh, Lord Boddhisattva
People are praying at your feet for solace."

3. সুচেতনা

জীবনানন্দ দাশ

সেই শস্য অনগণ মানুষের শব,
শব থেকে উৎসারিত স্বর্ণের বিস্ময়
আমাদের পিতা বুদ্ধ কনফুশিয়সের মতো আমাদেরও প্রাণ
মূক করে রাখে; তবু চারিদিকে রক্তক্লান্ত কাজের আহ্বান।

Suchetana (The good sense)
by Jibananda Das

"The harvest is nothing but the corpses of men.
The corpses bring wonderful wealth to some people.
We remain speechless and dumb
Like our forefather—Buddha Confucius
The grave and tiring duties are to be done."

4. পরাবত

সুধীন্দ্রনাথ দত্ত

ছুটিছে গৈরিক পথ নির্বিকার সন্ন্যাসীর মতো
নির্পূণ নির্বাণ ভরা, নিরাকার শূন্যের অন্বেষে,

Parabarta (The cycle of time)
by Sudhindranath Datta

"The saffron road is running like an indifferent sage
Devoid of any quality, full of Nirvana,
In search of the emptiness that has no form."

5. মহাদেবের দুয়ার

বীরেন্দ্র চট্টোপাধ্যায়

(চার সংখ্যক)

গাছ তলায় ঐ যে মানুষ
উপোস জানে না,

....

যদি সে উপোস জানত
তার জন্য প্রতিদিন সোনার থালায়
পরমান্ন আনত সুজাতা
কিন্তু সে সন্ন্যাসী নয়, সাধারণ নির্বোধ মানুষ।
কিন্তু সে সন্ন্যাসী নয়, সাধারণ নির্বোধ মানুষ।

Mahadever Duar (The door of God)
by Birendra Chattopadhyay
(No. IV)

"The man under the tree
Does not know fast;

Had he known fast
Sujata would have brought him porridge
In golden plate.
But the man is not a hermit—
Only an ordinary simple man."

6. বামিয়ান

অমিয় চক্রবর্তী

গিয়েছিনু বামিয়ান

....

শিলাকাটা গুহা।

গ্রানিট পাথর খোদাই মূর্তি আকাশী বুদ্ধ।

হিন্দুকুশের হিমশাখা, নীচে গম্ভীর নীল।

....

হিন্দুস্তানের গিরিসংকটে ঊর্ধ্ব আকাশে স্থির

যাত্রীরা দেখে মানবোত্তম

অভয়মুদ্রা।

Bamiyan
By Amiya Chakravarty

"I had been to Bamiyan

....

The stone-carved caves
Carved out of granite, stands the statue of Lord Buddha
Reaching the sky.
The cold flames of Hindukush,

The profound blue at the feet.

....

The mountain pass of Hindustan
Unmoved towards the sky above

The travellers behold
The sign of the fearless fingers
Of the great divine man."

The enemies of civilization have destroyed this statue. But the statue of the great and divinely merciful still reaches the sky. The state has been made immortal in this poem, and it spreads the sign of fearless fingers to the mankind forever.

6

Aspects of the Buddhist Influence: Bengali and other Indian Literature

Biplab Chakrabarty

I

The familiar Buddha image of a meditating sage has been imprinted in the Indian minds for more than two thousand years. Many of the Buddha's doctrines and teachings flourished in India and abroad for over one thousand five hundred years or so. At the end of the nineteenth century there was some sort of revival of the Buddhist teachings and religion in modern India. The Buddhist symbol of the wheel of righteousness (*dharma-chakra*) adorns the national flag of India. Emperor Ashoka inscribed the Buddha's sermons on stones and the four roaring lions of the Ashoka pillar symbolize the first sermon of the Buddha. Thus *Simha-nada* (or the lion's roar) is compared to the discourse of the Buddha and *Sakya Simha* is one of the popular epithets used for him. The *Simha-nada* sculpture are the national emblem of India. The life and teachings of the Buddha may be called an indistinguishable part of Indian culture and literature.

II

The life of the Buddha is full of marvellous episodes. There are various legends that tell us how he felt when he met an old man, a sick man, a corpse and an ascetic and finally, he resolved to gain freedom from old age, sickness and death. Human life is subject to frailties of age, sickness and death and the Buddha showed the world the way to salvation. He left home, his wife and child in order to meditate on causes of human suffering and on the possible means by which one can overcome it. The popular legend of Sujata tells us how he accepted milk and rice sitting under a sacred tree from Sujata who mistook him for a tree-spirit. This time he was very weak because he suffered the severest austerities but he realized that the attainment of the truth would not be possible by mere mortification of the flesh. So he abandoned his strict adherence to the path of austerities. Having refreshed himself in the water of River Niranjana, he sat under the Bodhi tree, accepted milk-rice from Sujata and finally absorbed in the most profound meditation till he ascended the fourth stage *dhyana* or pure consciousness and equanimity. He had spent seven weeks there sitting under the tree till he attained enlightenment.

The Buddha is one who gains an insight into the nature of things through intuition, thus attains the *Bodhi* or the extinction of passion and craving. Thus *Nirvana* is a kind of freedom from rebirth and transmigration. But the Buddha wanted the end of sorrow for all mankind and not for himself alone. So he taught for forty-five years until his death at Kusinagara at the age of eighty. There are numerous stories associated with the gospel of the Buddha. There are also many supernatural episodes that are fascinating. The image of the Buddha as a saviour and teacher has also fascinated millions of people through the ages. The idea of salvation for all mankind has also become solace for many more.

Modern Indian writers have been influenced by the image of the Buddha and Buddhist philosophy as well. The Buddha never announced a new religion but his insistence on deliverance from human sufferings with all spiritual freedom attracted many people, whether a writer or a common man. Buddhism offers neither rigid customs nor any ceremonials. The Buddha taught a new humanism that is free from prejudices and narrow social barriers. All these must have influenced Indian writers to take up the life of the Buddha as a major theme. Legends and episodes concerning the great Buddha have been reflected in Indian literature in many ways and on many occasions. Even the history of Buddhism with its rises and fall and subsequent regeneration has also been a matter of great importance to Indian writers.

In classical Indian literature, *kavyas* and epics have been composed on the Buddha and Buddhism. Asvaghosa's *Buddhacharita* deals with the life of the Buddha from his birth to death in 28 cantos that has been described as a matter-of-fact narration in epic style. Again *Manimekalai,* a Tamil epic composed by Chattan in about AD 600 is said to be the mouthpiece of the Buddhist propaganda. Manimekalai, the heroine, turns to vows of austerity and in her firm pursuit of truth fights herself in order to free herself from all human temptations. Manimekalai is a spirit that performs many miraculous deeds. Finally, she learns the Buddhist philosophy from an enlightened Buddhist seer and saint, then performed *Tapas* (penance) in order to put an end to all her future births. Thus *Manimekalai* is a storehouse of information on Buddhism and Buddhist philosophy in poetic form.

Both the Sanskrit and the Tamil epic stand as models for the later poets and writers who composed poetry on the life and teachings of the Buddha. Modern Indian writers have also used these sources. But modern Indian writers have their own ways of projecting the Buddha and his thought. The bulk of modern Indian literature on the Buddha and Buddhism may primarily be divided into three categories as under:

1. Literature that is directly related to the Buddha and Buddhism
2. Literature that is indirectly related to the Buddha and Buddhism
3. Literature that is distantly related to Buddhism

The first category of writings may be further subdivided into two groups, namely, literature directly related to the Buddha and literature directly related to the Buddhist philosophy and religion. Since the second categories of writings are all indirectly related to Buddhism, they refer to the Buddha and Buddhism both. Over and above, there is a mark of difference between the first two categories that cannot be diffused. While all the writings belonging to the first category are composed with high mark of respect and regards to the Buddha, some of the writings in the second category happen to be a critique of the Buddhist philosophy and religion. The third category of writings are more or less distant echoes of Buddhist teachings and philosophy in the background of contemporary reality.

Asvaghosa's *Buddhacharita* and Chattan's *Manimekalai* may be regarded as typical example of two types of writings under the first category. While *Buddhacharita* is the most noteworthy poetic composition on the life of the Buddha, *Manimekalai* is composed on the basis of Buddhist teachings and the storyline follows the essence of such teachings ardently. *Buddhacharita* inspired many Indian writers in the later period. Modern Indian writers have composed poetry, drama, fiction and essays focussing on the salient aspects of the life and teachings of the Buddha.

Among a host of modern Indian writings on the life of the Buddha, here are some typical and prominent examples:

	TITLE	AUTHOR	TYPE	LANGUAGE
1.	*Buddha Charita*	GirishChandra Ghosh	Drama	Bengali
2.	*Amitava*	Nabin Chandra Sen	Poetry	Bengali
3.	*Sri Buddhacharitam*	Kumaran Asan	Poetry	Malayalam
4.	*Nagar Lakshmi*	Rabindranath Tagore	Poetry	Bengali
5.	*Mulyaprapti*	Rabindranath Tagore	Poetry	Bengali
6.	*Nalak*	Abanindranath Tagore	Story	Bengali
7.	*Simha Senapati*	Rahul Sankrityana	Fiction	Hindi
8.	*Amitava*	Saradindu Bandhyopadhyay	Story	Bengali
9.	*Seshlekha*	Bibhuti Bhusan Bandhyopadhyay	Story	Bengali
10.	*Nirranjana Nadir Dheu*	Jahanabi Kumar Chakraborty	Story	Bengali
11.	*Jatak*	Binda Karandikar	Story	Marathi
12.	*Ambapalira Buddha Bandana*	Baikuntha Nath Pattanayak	Poetry	Oriya
13.	*Buddhadev*	Rabindranath Tagore	Essay	Bengali
14.	*Buddha Dever Jibane Nari*	Banaphul	Essay	Bengali
15.	*Buddha bani Gana*	Subodh Ghosh	Essay	Bengali
16.	*Sundara Nandam*	Pingali Lakshmi Kantam and Katuri Venkateswar Rao	Poetry	Telugu
17.	*Premviksha*	Siddhakobi	Poetry	Telugu
18.	*Santi Patham*	Narayan Rao	Story	Telugu
19.	*Goutam Buddha Natak*	Acharya Atre	Drama	Telugu
20.	*Satya Deepam*	Narayan Menon	Story	Telugu
21.	*Yasodhara*	Shankara Kurup	Poetry	Malayalam
22.	*Bodhi Vriksamu*	M. Satyanarayan	Story	Telugu
23.	*Buddhadeva*	Bipin Chandra Barua	Drama	Assamese

The list is incomplete, as many more titles from different Indian languages could have been added to it. All the titles cited alone, however, are directly related to the life or numerous episodes of

Gautama Buddha. Certainly, some of the compositions are devoted to what may be called an overview of Buddha's life. *Buddha Charita* by Girish Chandra or *Amitav* by Nabin Chandra Sen may be regarded as life-sketch of Gautama Buddha in the form of drama and epic poetry respectively. The Assamese drama *Buddhadeva* by Bipin Chandra Barua is also a life-sketch of the Buddha. While Sri *Buddhacharitan* by Kumar Asan is a commentary of a poet on the life of the Buddha in poetic form, *Buddhadev* by Rabindranath Tagore is again a unique piece of commentary on the life and teachings of the Buddha in prose.

III

Rabindranath expressed his high regard for the Buddha on many occasions. In *Buddhadev*, a penetrating piece of revelation in prose, he explains how and why Gautama Buddha remains ever a *Mahamanav* in the long-drawn history of mankind. Moreover, he has pointed out how the Buddha revealed the sparkling truth of India spreading throughout the world crossing the stone-walls of racial discrimination. Again Rabindranath, like many other Indian writers, felt the need and relevance of the teachings of the *Mahamanav*. Similarly, Rabindranath composed a number of beautiful poems dealing with fragmentary incidents in the Buddha's life.

Poems like *Buddha janmotsava* or *Buddhadever Prati* by Rabindranath are well known. *Buddhadever Prati* (to Buddha Deva) for instance, was composed on the occasion of the foundation of Mul Gandhakuti at Sarnath and all such poems as this are what may be called adoration of the Buddha in poetic form. There are yet other types of poems composed mainly on some incidents in the life of the Buddha. *Nagar Lakshmi*, for instance, relates a story taken from Kalpadrumavadan. The story line of the poem *Mulyaprapti* is found in *Avadan satak*. There are many more examples. The leitmotif of such sort of poems lies not in the delineation of the story alone, but in describing the same in the light of the Buddhist sociology and philosophy as well. *Nagar Laksmi* is a poem that relates the principle of wealth distribution and related sociology.

Modern Indian poets more or less follow a similar method in composing poems dedicated to the Buddha in their own style. *Ambapalir Buddha Vandana* by Baikunthanth Pattanayak in Oriya, *Yasodhara* by Shankara Kurup in Malayalam, *Premviksha* by Siddhakobi in Telugu, *Buddher Smritite* by Sunil Gangopadhyay in Bengali, *Sundara Nandam* by Pinguli Lakshmi Kantam and Katjuri Venkateswara Rao in Telugu are but a few examples. In such cases, the accepted method is to take up a Buddhist legend and remodel or recreate it in the style of the poet concerned. All such poems are directly related to the Buddha, as he is seen present amongst his followers and disciples. Thus, Baikuntha Nath Pattanayak takes up the Ambapali episode; Shankara Kurup selects *Yasodhara* as the focal point of his poem. In each case, the characters or the story may be different but the Buddha is the central figure, thereby opening their eyes to the truth and sufferings of life.

Nagar Lakshmi by Rabindranath Tagore, for instance, begins with a question posed by the Buddha himself to the citizens of Shravastipur amidst heart-rending cries of the famine-stricken people in the following lines:

Buddha nija vaktagane
Sudhalen jane jone
'Kshudhitere Anna-dan-Seva
Tomara loile balo keba'[1]

(The Buddha asked his own disciples one by one, who amongst you would like to take up the responsibility of serving the famine-stricken people with food?)

Now the whole poem describes how everyone refused excepting Supriya, daughter of Anath Pindad. But the question that troubled every follower of the Buddha was how a destitute like Supriya could shoulder such a heavy responsibility as this. Supriya answered herself thereby exposing a major principle of Buddhist sociology:

'Amar bhandar ache bhare
Tomaa saba kar ghare ghare'
Tomar chahile sabee patra akshay hobe
Viksha anne bachaba basudha
Mitaiba durbhiker khudha.[2]

(My treasure-pot is full in your house. If you all want, this pot will remain ever full. I'll save the world and the people from want of food by alms received from you.)

Supriya, the central character in the poem *Nagar Lakshmi* is one who according to the teachings of the *Dhammapada* has the ability and courage to cross the sea of suffering while others rest on the shore.

Appaka te Manussesu je jana parogamino
Athayam itara paja teermeba anudhabati.[3]

It is because Supriya wanted to follow the teachings of the Buddha that wealth is not for the purpose of public exhibition or ostentation. One has to make use of the wealth for one's own comfort and also for that of others. Thus the Vikhuni wanted to say, as per the teaching of the Buddha, the wealth becomes cause of happiness of oneself as well as others.

The Buddha showed how the righteous life in the world eventually leads to a happy life: '*dhammacari Sukham seti asmin loke Paramhica*'. He always laid emphasis on the good and virtuous life in this world and not on that of the other world. Even *nirvana* could be attained in this very world itself. The Buddha taught his step-brother Nanda how to control one's own mind in order to win success in the attainment of the truth. He said:

Yatha agarang Suchhannag, butthi na Samatibijhati
Evang Subhabitang Chittang rago na Samatibijhati.[4]

Some modern Indian poets and writers have been inspired by this episode of *Nanda-Sundaram* to write poems. Pingali Lakshmi Kantam and Katuri Venkateswara Rao composed a poem *Nanda-Sundaram* (1932) based on this episode. It is a long narrative poem. Nanda, brother of the Buddha, was enslaved by the alluring charm of his wife Sundari and as such could not respond to the call of the Lord Buddha for alms. Later the Master taught his brother the right way of overcoming problems of allurements and suffering of life.

Nanda-Sundaram, the poem, begins with a description of the Buddha addressing his brother, Nanda like this:

The sage seated himself
and urged his brother to sit, too,
lovingly caressing him with his tender hand,

He addressed Nanda in the gentlest manner. Finally, the Buddha made his brother rise up and gird his loins against the heartless onslaughts of tyranny of carnage and lust. *Nanda-Sundaram* is thus a beautiful piece of poetry with the teachings of the Buddha on the suffering and follies of human life.

It may be referred to in this context that Bibhuti Bhusan Bandyopadhyay was also inspired to write a story on the same episode. This story has been posthumously published under the title

Sesh Lekha. The story describes how the Buddha helped Nanda to get himself free from infatuation of women. The Buddha showed the way only and Nanda followed it. All illusionary world of Apsaras, as Bibhuti Bhusan recreates the story, was created by the Master set against the object of infatuation and finally it was Nanda himself who rescued himself from his sufferings. The core context of the Telugu poem and the Bengali story is the same but each of the works is a distinctive literary creation. In both the writings man happens to be the master of his own fate as the *Dhammapada* says:

Atta hi attano natho kohi natho parosia
Attanaib sudantena nathang lavati dullavang.[5]

A modern poet like Sunil Gangopadhyay builds up the ever-known image of the Buddha in his poem *Buddher Smritite* (In the memory of the Buddha). It is a narrative poem which describes Angulimala, a notorious character who committed numerous murders and later became a disciple of the Buddha. Angulimala is personified in this poem with a modern man drawn by greed and lust. So the poet builds up popular image of the Buddha as the Saviour who welcomes all Angulimalas of the world. The poet writes:

Many a Angulimala with ferocious greed lie in ambush at corners of different roads.
Sparkle brilliantly before eyes
He walks alone with gentle and measured steps.
Calling all the Angulimalas of the world he says
'Come close to me'.[6]

The Buddha calls everyone, irrespective of cast and creed, race or religion pronouncing the truth:

Sabbang rating dhammarating Jinati
Tanha Khayo Sabbo dukkhang Jinati[7]

Moreover, he warned us like this:

Natthi rago samo aggi natthi desho samo gaho
Natthi maha samo jalang natthi tanha samo nadi.[8]

But the modern poets and writers depict pictures of human follies of the Angulimalas, Nandas and, occasionally, the Supriyas.

Many a fiction writers in modern Indian literature have portrayed the Buddha as the Yogin performing the severest form of *Tapasya* in his encounter with the formidable 'Mara', the demon of lust and greed. This description is available in modern literature in two basic forms:

1. Encounter of the Buddha with 'Mara'
2. Encounter with a number of people who are enraptured and captivated by 'Mara'

In the first case, the writers, either in prose fiction or in simple discourse, prefer to describe life story of the Buddha. *Buddha charitam* by K.M. Panikkar, *Simha Senapati* by Rahul Sankrityayana, *Nalak* by Abanindranath Tagore, *Amitava* by Saradindu Bandyopadhyaya or *Sipra NadirDheu* by Janhabi Kumar Chakroborty or *Satya Deepam* by Narayan Menon may be worth mentioning. While the writers describe the Buddha-Mara-episode, they use either Asvaghosa's *Buddha Charita* or Edwin Arnold's *The Light of Asia* as their source material. *Sri Buddha Charitam* by Kumaran Asan or by K.M. Panikkar and *Satya Deepam* by Narayan Menon are primarily based on the *Light of Asia.* Abanindranath's description of the Buddha in *Nalak* is primarily based on Asvaghosha with Sanskrit quotations. In Asvaghosa's *Buddha Charita,* 'Mara' attacked the Buddha with his three sons namely, Vibhrama, Harsh and Darpa and three daughters namely, Rati, Priti and Trishna. Abanindranath, on the other hand, mentioned only three daughters of 'Mara' namely, Kamana, Chhala and Kala, and recreates the story as series of visionary pictures painted on the screen of Nalak's mind.[9]

In the second case, there are many descriptions of numerous people, who are weak and enraptured by follies, take refuge in the great teacher and revealer of truth, showing his followers the path of ultimate release, or *Nirvana.* Rahul Sankrityayana records an imaginary conversation between the Buddha and Sinha, the great warrior and the General of the republic of Vaishali. The narrator and the hero being Simha Senapati becomes the follower of the Buddha after he met the Lord. The conversation may be regarded as a discourse of the Buddha on various Buddhic principles and outlook. The novel further records contemporary social reality during the time of the Buddha.

In *Amitava,* a story, Saradindu Bandyopadhyay again records an imaginary conversation between Amitav, the Buddha, and Pundarik, the architect, and narrator of the story. The story describes how the hero was totally enthralled at the first sight of the Buddha. The story is a unique portrayal of the kingdom and polity of Magadha during the life-time of the Buddha. The architect hero was sent to the village of Patali in order to build up the fort and city of Patna. Being so engaged by the highest political authority, he was also warned of the enemy of Magadha during the region of King Ajatashatru. There are many stories under the title *Nirajanja Nadir Dheu* by Jahanabi Kumar Chakraborty based on some fragmentary history and legends of the Buddha.

There are many dramatized versions of the stories and legends of the Buddha. *Buddhadev Charita*, a play in Bengali by Girish Ghosh and *Buddhadev*, an Assamese play by Bipin Chandra Barua, may be mentioned here. *Buddhadev Charita* was enacted in 1885 in Calcutta and it was dedicated to Edrwin Arnold whose *The Light of Asia* was used as the primary source material. Girish Chandra dramatized the life of the Buddha from his birth to his attainment of *Nirvana*. The principal incidents narrated in this play are Nalak-Debal episode, the dream of Mohamaya, Chhandak, Kumar Gautama and the Mahaniskramana episode, the Buddha-Mara episode, etc. Bipin Chandra Barua's Assamese play *Buddhadev* was published in 1941 and was enacted many times by Bharammoman theatres in Assam.

There are many prose writings, which are essentially commentary of the life and teachings of the Buddha. Subodh Ghosh, for instance, explained the life and teachings of the Buddha as the first message of peoples' emancipation. Banaphul, on the other hand, explained the importance of the role of women in the Buddha's life. Mohitlal Majumdar, a major Bengali poet, could not, however, see eye to eye with the Buddhist outlook. Barring such typical examples, the poets, the playwrights and the story-tellers in the contemporary Indian literature portray an image of the Buddha that is very much held in high esteem, considering the importance of the teachings and outlook of the Buddha against the background of the contemporary world.

IV

Compared to the literature directly related to the Buddha and the literature indirectly related to the same portray neither any life story of the Buddha nor any legends, myths or history of the Buddha. This corpus of literature is not directly related to the Buddha because it chiefly deals with later period of the history of Buddhist religion.

Here the Buddha is present not in person, but as an image or as a statue being the source of inspiration to many. Both the rise and decline of the Buddhist religion as a movement are also depicted here. Here are some examples that are indirectly related to the Buddha:

	TITLE	AUTHOR	TYPE	LANGUAGE
1.	*Abhisar*	Rabindranath Tagore	Poem	Bengali
2.	*Pujarini*	Rabindranath Tagore	Poem	Bengali
3.	*Chandalika*	Rabindranath Tagore	Drama	Bengali
4.	*Shyama*	Rabindranath Tagore	Drama	Bengali
5.	*Sasanka*	Rakhaldas Bandyopadhyay	Novel	Bengali
6.	*Bener Meye*	Haraprasad Shastri	Novel	Bengali
7.	*Kanchanmala*	Haraprasad Shastri	Novel	Bengali
8.	*Amita*	Yashpal	Novel	Hindi
9.	*Niranjana*	Banaphul	Novel	Hindi
10.	*Chandanmurti*	Saradindu Bandhopadhyay	Story	Hindi
11.	*Sangha-O-Moru*	Saradindu Bandhopadhyay	Story	Hindi
12.	*Ashoka*	Girish Chandra Ghosh	Drama	Bengali
13.	*Ashoka*	Khirod Prasad	Drama	Bengali
14.	*Uttar Priyadarshini*	Agyeya	Drama	Hindi
15.	*Ashoka*	Golok Sharma	Drama	Assamese
16.	*Kalinga Vijoy*	Medini Thakuria	Drama	Assamese
17.	*Kunal Kanchan*	Satya Prasad Barua	Drama	Assamese
18.	*Asvaghosh*	Purushottam Das	Drama	Assamese
19.	*Uttar Priyadarshini*	Ratan Thiyam	Drama	Manipuri
20.	*Sei Sanghatik Lokta*	Subodh Sarkar	Poem	Bengali

Some of the poems and dramas of Rabindranath Tagore are indirectly related to the Buddha, although profound influence of the Buddha is there on the central character of the episode concerned. *Abhisar*, *Pujarini*, *Buddha Janmotsav* and such other poems may be referred to here. It is indeed a fact that Rabindranath paid his utmost respect to the Buddha as a 'Mahamanab', but whenever he took a skeleton story from any Buddhist source material, he moulded the characters in his own way featuring spring and alluring effects of life. So Prakriti in *Chandalika*, the famous dance drama by Tagore, is transformed psychologically. When Ananda is drawn to her by her mother's occult power, she felt pity and remorse. According to Sardula Karna-Avadana, Prakriti was converted into a Bhikshuni (a nun) by a mantra, called the destroyer of all evil. But Tagore remodelled the story available in Mahavastuabadan for writing the dance-drama, *Shyama.* Tagore ennobled *Shyama* going far ahead of the Mahavastu episode glorifying love and pity as well. *Malini* by Tagore is yet another example of how Tagore used Buddhist legends. *Malini* was recreated as a new woman reawakened.

It is interesting to note that a good many number of Indian writers have taken up one and the same episode distantly related to the Buddha. Episodes like Emperor Ashoka and Kalinga war or the episode of Kunal Kanchen during the period of Ashoka are but a few examples. Girish Chandra and Khirodprasad in Bengali, Golok Sharma in Assamese for instance, have chosen the story of Ashoka and his subsequent conversion to Buddism.

Again Medeni in Assamese, Agyeya in Hindi have focussed on the Kalinga episode in their respective works. Rantan Thiyam translated *Uttar Priyadarshini* in Manipuri as a mode of new theatre in Manipur... Agyeya's work is an experimental poetic drama in Hindi. Ratan Thiyam based it on the Hindi play but he transcribed the story of Ashoka's conversion after the Kalinga war with greater emphasis on collective movements and Buddhist chants as theatrical device. Thus a new search for Indian theatre has been motivated with such elements as are indirectly related to Buddhism.

A number of Indian authors have dramatized the history of Ashoka, with special focus on Kalinga war. In each case, dramatists have employed their own method and style. Girish Chandra's Ashoka, for instance, may be regarded as an episode of Mara-Vijay with a difference. In this play *Mara* along with *Trishna,* endeavours to influence Ashoka, but fails and finally bends to the Buddha in obeisance. Khirodprasad, on the other hand, depicts Ashoka as one who frees himself for inner agony and torments. Both the dramatists have used Kunal-Tishyarakhita and other episodes as sub-plots. Golok Sharma has also followed similar method in his Assamese play, *Ashoka.* Satya Prasad Barua and Medini Thakuria in their Assamese plays have focussed on Kalinga war and Kanchan-Tishyarakshita episode respectively. Of course, Purushottam Das' *Asvaghosh* is solely devoted to the author of *Buddha Charita.* All such dramas are based on some common elements of Indian history indirectly related to the rise and spread of Buddhism.

A number of Indian story-tellers have also taken up the common theme of Ashoka's Kalinga war and other related stories. *Kanchan*

Mala by Haraprasad Shastri in Bengali and *Divya* by Yashpal in Hindi are but a few examples. Haraprasad Shastri was an erudite scholar especially on the Buddhist period. While describing Kunal-Trishya rakshita episode, he portrayed contemportary social reality, especially the conflict of Brahamanism and the Buddhism. Of course, there are some debatable points as to whether the Brahmins were heaped with indignities by the principles of Ashoka in favour of Buddhism. Haraprasad never put his novels under the rubric of historical novel. He rather preferred to take up the background of Brahmin-Buddhist conflict. *Bener Meye*, another novel by Shastri, is what maybe called a fictional study of the social history during the decline of Buddhist influence in Bengal. The corruption of the later Buddhist monks and subsequent result have been highlighted in this novel. It would not be out of place to refer to Banaphul's novel *Niranjana.*

Niranjana is an inspired novel by Banaphul following Anatole France's famous novel *Thais.* Banaphul transformed the story of *Thais* into a story of a religious ascetic and anchorite monk against the background of corruption and downfall of a section of Buddhist followers in Bengal. The hero of the novel realizes at the end that all his endeavours to free *Niranjana* from the shackles of spendthrift pleasures have failed causing his own downfall. It is interesting to note that some other Indian writers like Premchand and Yashpal also attempted to remodel the story of *Thais.* Yashpal's *Divya* is a glorious example. Like Banaphul, Yashpal also used the Buddhist period as the backdrop of his novel. Yashpal's *Amita,* a histrorical novel on Kalinga Vijoy, may also be referred here. Yashpal, of course, raises the question of morality in historical perspective, and the contemporary socio-political reality looms large here.

The novels like *Sashanka* by Rakhaldas Bandyopadhyay and *Bodhibrikshamu* by Misatyanarayana Sastry may be referred to as novels indirectly related to the Buddha. Rakhaldas refers to the late history of the Bodhi Vriksha that was uprooted at the time of war fought by Sashanka. *Bodhibrikshamu,* on the other hand, concentrates on the tree as its central theme. *Charumarti* and *Sangha-O-Maru,* two stories by Saradindu Bandyopadhyay are set in two different backgrounds. *Charumarti* is a tale of a Buddhist monk who was perished in an earthquake while he was in search of a rare Buddha statue made of wood. In the second story, Saradindu portrays picture of human passion set against the path of austerities of a Buddhist monk. Both the stories like many other counterparts in modern

Indian literature echo victory of life over death and infallible spirit.

Subodh Sarkar, a modern Bengali poet, had published a poem 'Sei Sanghatik Lokta' (That Dangerous Man) which is indirectly related to the Buddha in the following manner:

> I know That man
> Who standing on the road of Egypt ordered three other men wrapped in blanket 'Burn down'
> and the library of Alexandria was burnt to ashes.
> I know that man.
> Sipping the best cup of tea in the morning
> that man said, 'do not allow the Jews enter Israel.'
> I know that man.
> Who said standing in between the Ganges and the Spear
> 'Babri Mosque must be destroyed within 48 hours'
> I know that man
> One of his eyes is covered with a dark glass.
> The man has been condemned
> for the last three thousand years
> by three hundred types of UNESCO.
> Hardly they could do any harm.
> The man walked down from Alexandria
> to Afghanistan via Ayodhya.
> He is charging the denominate
> standing in front of the Buddha
> one hundred seventy five feet high . . .
> The Buddha statue of one hundred seventy-five feet
> as high as Tata Center.
> 'O Buddha, calm and quiet',
> Someone asked, 'Who are you ?'
> God? an incarnation? a saviour?
> You said, 'I hear, I am nobody',
> 'I am the Awakened one'.
> How is that?
> Are you awakened? If so,
> why aren't two hands of your sky high statue coming down
> to make the eyes of that
> dangerous man white? [10]

V

There are numerous other examples of modern Indian literature distantly related to the Buddha and Buddhism. These are related to echoes of Buddhist teachings and philosophy expressed in artistic language. Some of the modern Indian poetry may be cited in this context. There are poems written in Oriya, Assamese, Bengali and in other languages that are very personal in tone with a mark of anguished sense of suffering and subsequent result. Sometimes the poems dramatized man's endeavours to win over greed and lust. The names of Guru Prasad Mohanty, Baikunta Nath Pattanaik, Lakshmi Kanta Mahapatra in Oriya, Nalini Bala Devi, Bhaben Barua in Assamese and many other poets in other Indian languages may be referred to. Guru Prasad Mohanty draws a picture of modern man who being wrought with fear and sin feels helpless:

> Harekrushna Das roams in
> the friendless and foreign city
> of namaskars, jaihinds, salaams.
> Harekrushna Das brakes suddenly.
> What is this fear,
> unexpected, suddenly
> of what calamitous times?
> of what terrible crime and sin?
> The time present is pregnant with fear and sin.[11]

Though the poets often record a feeling of loss and deprivation, they never abandon hope as poets like Lakshmikanta Mahapatra writes:

> My heart cries, I wait in vain.
> My pain and suffering are endless.
> But in that pain is present
> joy and solace in abundance.
> That misery fills my being
> with hope in this lonely state.[12]

Existentialists grappled with the problem of existence and modern writers are sometimes obsessed by existentialist thoughts. While projecting man as solely responsible for his own acts, they somehow relate that matter to Buddhist thoughts. They also draw pictures of human cravings, i.e., *Tanha* and subsequent frustration. There is a bulk of existentialist literature in Bengali and other Indian languages. This literature is what may be called literature distantly related to Buddhism.

Some other poets like Nalini Bala Devi portrays the supreme thirst of her anguished soul for the healing balm of infinite bliss. In the poem *Param Trisha,* she affirms that the unlimited thirst for beauty in man is not the desire for happiness of transitory earthly life, but for the eternally beautiful. Bhaben Barua, another important figure in contemporary Assamese poetry, records in his poem *Subhratar Swar,* how human heart glides down the deep pool of unfathomable aching and yet listens to the transparent voice or the voice of whiteness.

Thus modern Indian poetry records distant echoes of Buddhist thoughts on human life and suffering and on man's endeavour to find an everlasting solace. The poems are distantly related to the Buddha and Buddhism in various ways. Sunil Gangopadhyay co-related one of the poems on Neera to the Buddha in the following manner:

> 'Neera, just now you gave alms to one who has nothing to eat.
> Won't you give me?
> I sleep at the cremation ground,
> I eat ashes and my body is filled with ashes,
> I pass my days by the side of a river,
> That witnessed Gautama Buddha
> And was also covered by subsequent bursts
> You are that river.[13]

Here lies the picture of human thirst and subsequent longing for a lasting release from the same in a beautiful imagery. Sometimes, modern poems record human endeavour to win over greed and fear, dreading accompanists of 'Mara'. The following poem by Nirendranath Chakraborty, an epoch-making Bengali poet, may be regarded as a modern version of the 'Mara-Vijay'.[14]

> Greed first drew me to the forest.
> Then
> Within that unknown forest
> Fear drove me rushing in all directions.
> I had made up my mind
> I'd finish of these twin foes. First I'd see
> The dead face of Greed,
> Then of Fear.
>
> But then, how strange:
> No sooner had I plunged

My long sharp knife to the hilt in old Greed's throat
And shouted, 'I want nothing', on the instant
Fear too, like a deflated sack,
Sank at my feet.

I don't know when the day broke.
I can hear
The song of sunrise float from far away.
Like a heady wine
I feel its music range along my blood.
My frame feels lighter,
As though I am freed from some deep disease.

Greed had stood before me,
Fear behind. I had thought
I'd dispatch them one by one. There was no need:
As soon as I'd attacked one,
The other collapsed.

Carrying its morning tray of festal colours,
The sky comes to view my face. The birds sing hymns to me
Trees and creepers bend to me in obeisance.
—The double murder done, with my left foot
I kicked my two life-long foes into a ditch,
And whistling myself
I come out of the forest.

In fact, the influence of Buddhism is widely felt in modern Indian literature in various manner. Sometimes it is poignant and direct and sometimes it is felt indirectly and finally there are distant echoes too. It is an undeniable fact that the image of the Buddha with all legends, tales and thoughts has left a distinctive trail in modern Indian literature.

NOTES

1. *Nagar Lakshmi*, Rabindranath Tagore, Katha O Kahini.
2. *Ibid.*
3. *The Dhammapada*, III, 85.
4. *Ibid.*, I-14.
5. *Ibid.*, XII-16.

6. *Buddher Smritite*, Sunil Gangopadhyay, translated by Biplab Chakraborty.
7. *The Dhammapada* XIV, 35.
8. *Ibid.*, XVIII, 245.
9. *Buddha Charita*, Asvaghosa, Canto XIII, no. 1-2.
10. *Sei Sanghatik Lokta*, Desh, Sept, 2001, page 43, translated by Biplab Chakraborty.
11. Harekrushna Das, Guru Prasad Mohanty, Tr. Souvagya Kumar Mishra.
12. *Jivan Sangita*, Lakshmikanta Mahapatra, Tr. Souvagya Kumar Mishra.
13. *Neera, Tumi*, Sunil Gangopadhyay, Tr. Biplab Chakraborty.
14. *Joḍa Khun*, Nirendranath Chakraborty, Tr. Sukanta Choudhury.

7

Influence of Buddhism in Tagore's Literature

Sabuj Kali Sen (Mitra)

Rabindranath Tagore was born at a time when at least three movements had started giving to the culture of Bengal a new direction. One of these was religious, which was introduced by Raja Ram Mohun Roy. In the words of Tagore, Raja Ram Mohun Roy tried to reopen the channel of spiritual life, which had been obstructed for many years by the sand and debris of creeds that were formal and materialistic, fixed in external practices lacking spiritual significance.

The second was literary led by Sri Bankim Chandra Chattopadhyaya, who with a touch of magic wand aroused Bengali literature from her age-old long slumber. The third movement was socio-political, which gave voice to the minds of the people who were trying to assert their own personality. Of all these movements, the first two influenced Tagore a great deal. But perhaps even more than this, were the influences of the *Upanishad*, the Buddhism, the Vaishnavism and the Baul mystics, which led Tagore to form his own religious views—*The Religion of Man.* This influence was so basic that some expressions like ঈশা, মৈত্রী, করুনা, প্রেম, মনের মানুষ, are spontaneously and frequently used by Tagore in almost all his writings. His monism, his emphasis on the all-pervasive character of god, his assertion of the kinship between man and man, between man and nature, his humanistic approach, all are taken from the *Upanishad* and Buddhism.

Buddhism, like the verses of the *Upanishads* held its own charm for Rabindranath Tagore. He looked towards Buddhism both for its positive and negative prescriptions. Besides, the Buddhistic abhorrence of religious rites and its essential core of altruism, were the two main ideas that Tagore readily incorporated in his own religious views. The magnetic character of Lord Buddha, with his humanistic attitude, love, compassion and self-emancipating teaching had its own impact on the mind of Tagore. Only once in his life, said

Rabindranath, did he feel like prostrating himself before an image, and that was when he saw the statue of the Buddha at Gaya.

In Tagore's family there was a tradition of Buddhist study. In fact, the Tagore family of Kolkata was familiar with Buddhism before Rabindranath Tagore was born. In 1859 Tagore's father, Devendranath Tagore went to Ceylon. In this voyage he took his second son Satyendranath Tagore and Keshab Chandra Sen with him. They returned to India with the living ideal of Buddhism. And from that time Bengal was again interested in Buddhist studies. In 1899, Dwijendranath Tagore wrote আর্য ধর্ম্ম এবং বৌদ্ধ ধর্ম্মের পরস্পরের ঘাতপ্রতিঘাত ও সঙ্ঘাত, In 1901, Satyendranath Tagore wrote *Bauddha Dharma*, which held a special place in Bengali literature. The Theravada Buddhism from Pali *dharma sastra* is accurately described in it. Brahmananda Keshabchandra also after his visit to Ceylon introduced some Buddhist customs in the Brahma Samaj. He even went to Bodhgaya, and then in Calcutta in 1880 he started a religious ceremony called *Sakya Samagam.* Sadhu Aghorenath on instruction of Devendranath Tagore wrote *Sakya muni O Nirvan Tattvaì* in 1882. It was the first literature of Nababidhan Samanvaya Sahitya Mala. Other Brahmo leaders like Protap Chandra Majumdar, Kalishankar Das, Krishna Kumar Mitra, and Binayendranath Sen, etc. followed the Buddhist study started by Sadhu Aghorenath. All these attempts to understand Buddhism influenced Tagore and were instrumental to his interest in Buddhist studies. In 1891, with the help and assistance of Rabindranath Tagore, his nephew Sudhindranath edited and published *Buddha Charit* by Krishna Kumar Sen in *Sadhana*, the historian, *patrika.*

Rabindranath Tagore came into contact with Rajendralal Mitra when he was very young. Rajendralal Mitra was an authority on Buddhism. He had immense influence on Tagore. The poems and dramas on Buddhist episodes composed by Tagore were taken from Rajendralal Mitra's *The Sanskrit Buddhist Literature of Nepal.* Tagore always kept with him the *Hastasar* by Dharmaraja Barua. The English poet Edwin Arnold had an important role in creating interest, curiosity and love for Buddhist literature in Bengal. When Tagore went to Bodhgaya he took with him Arnold's *The Light of Asia* and we see the influence of Arnold in the poem 'Bidaye' of *Kalpana Kavyagrantha.* I cannot resist myself from quoting a portion of it.

এবার চলিনু তবে
সময় হয়েছে নিকট এখন বাঁধন ছিঁড়িতে হবে।
তুমি ঘুমাইছ নীমিলনয়নে
কাঁপিয়া উঠিছ বিরহ স্বপনে
প্রভাতে জাগিয়া শূন্য নয়নে
কাঁদিয়া চাহিয়া রবে
সময় হয়েছে নিকট এখন বাঁধন ছিঁড়িতে হবে। অরুন তোমার তরুন অধর
করুন তোমার আঁখি
অমিয় রচন সোহাস বচন
অনেক রয়েছে বাকি
পাখি উড়ে যাবে সাগরের পার
সুখময় নীড় পড়ে রবে তার...
মহাকাশ হতে ঐ বারে বার, আমারে ডাকিছে সবে।
সময় হয়েছে নিকট এখন বাঁধন ছিঁড়িতে হবে।

Tagore composed more than 50 dramas. The themes of all those dramas ranged from *Puranas, Mahakavyas,* and *Bauddha Jataka Kathas.* But maximum number of dramas were based on episodes of the Buddhist period. I am trying to give a list of these dramas:

1. মালিনী 1896, from মহাবস্তু অবদান, 2. রাজা 1910 from কুশাজাতক of মহাবস্তু অবদান, 3. অচলায়তন 1912 from দিব্যঅবদান মালা 4. নটীর পূজা অবদানশতক 1926, 5. চণ্ডালিকা 1933 from শার্দুলকণাবদান, 6. শ্যামা 1939 from মহাবস্তু অবদান।

'Nagar laksmi' from 'Kalpadruma avadana', 2. 'Mulya prapti' from 'Avadanasataka' 3. 'Abhisara' from 'Bodhisattavadan Kalpalamala' 4. 'Shrestha viksa' from 'vastravadan of Avadanasataka' 5. 'Mastaka vikraya' from 'Mahavastu avadana' (Ajanta Kaundilya Jataka) 6. 'Samanya ksati' from 'Shyamavati' of 'Divya avadanamala'. The poems of Katha Kavygrantha

নগরলমী 2. মূল্য প্রাপ্তি 3. অভিসার from বোধসত্ত্বাবদান কলপলতা।

Rabindranath Tagore took the basic idea from the Buddhist

Kathas and made many experiments on these themes. For example, he made changes in the drama 'Raja' four times. The poem 'Parisodh' took the shape of dance-drama 'Shyama' after 40 long years. Tagore had a natural liking for *Bauddha Kahini.* The *Maitri, Karuna, Mudita, Upeksa,* the self-teaching *Atmodipobhava* message of the Buddha, the humanistic attitude of Buddhism, the compassion, equality, rationality and women's emancipation attracted him most and became the main theme of many of his dramas and poems. In these poems and dramas we have a feeling that we are swimming in the Buddhist era. Our mind walks in Mathura *nagari* where Sanyasi Upagupta is lying on the street, the public woman Vasavadatta going for her nocturnal tryst, the Varuna River in Kasi Baranasi, where the queen Karuna is going for recreation with her maids. Our mind flies like birds in the palaces of Sravasti, Magadh. When we read these creations we feel the beats of revolutions in society, in religion, in state, but transcending these revolutions we feel in our heart the victory of humanity, power of compassion and feel the grace of the Buddha. Tagore took the basic ideas from the *avadanas* but with his peerless literary talent and imagination changed the simple stories into aesthetic forms.

This paper is a humble attempt to compare some of Tagore's dramas and poems where women characters are highlighted, where women's emancipation and equality of human race are depicted.

Rabindranath wrote the poem 'Pujarini' in 1899 and after 27 years, transformed it into a dance-drama called 'Natir Puja'. 'Pujarini' is a poem of *katha* 'Kavyagrantha' based on an episode of Buddhist period. The rites and rituals of Buddhism, the nature of prayer and worship, devotion and love to Buddha, dedication and sacrifice and the interaction between Brahmanyadharma and Buddhism are pictured excellently in the poem and drama. The theme of 'Pujarini', 'Natir Puja' is taken from *Avadana Sataka.* The story goes like this: Raja Bimbisara receiving the knowledge of truth from the lord, had built a big stupa in his palace over the lord's nails and hairs and his maid cleaned the place everyday. When Ajatsatru obtained the throne by patricide, he prohibited the females to sweep the stupa on pain of death. Srimati, a female slave, caring not at all for her life, washed it neatly, and lighted it with a row of lamps. The king in great rage, ordered her to the place of execution. After her death, she as a *Devaputri* appeared before the Lord in the bamboo grove and clearing the mountain of human misery by the thunderbolt of knowledge, obtained all that is desirable.

Tagore changed the last portion of it and the drama ends with Srimati's death. In history we find the names of many women who dedicated their lives for country, for *dharma*, but for prayer, for worship women can sacrifice their lives touched Tagore's heart. 'Natir Puja' is not only a story of sacrifice it is also a story of revolution that started in ancient India centring on Bauddha *dharma*. This dance-drama was a favourite of Tagore. He himself took part as Upali, a *bauddha sramana*, when it was staged at Calcutta.

In 'Malini' also we find a picture of confrontation between *Brahmanya dharma* and *Bauddha dharma*. When Tagore was in London, he was invited by his friend Tarak Nath Palit to stay in his house at Primrose. There he had a dream and then he found a similar situation in one of the episodes of *Mahavastu-avadana*. The story goes like this:

A Pratyeka Buddha entered the city of Varanasi for alms, but got nothing. A girl finding his alms bowl empty brought him home, and gave him a hearty meal. When he died, a stupa was erected on his remains, and the girl decorated the stupa everyday with flowers and aromatics. She desired that she may be born with a garland of flowers in every one of her future existences. Her desire was fulfilled. In her next existence she was born as *devakanya* with a garland of flowers around her neck. From heaven she descended on earth, and was born as Malini, the daughter of Kriki, king of Varanasi. Malini invited Lord Kashyapa and his retinue and entertained them with a sumptuous meal. The brahmanas numerous and influential at the court of his father, taking umbrage at her conduct induced the king to order her banishment. Malini humbly begged for a week's respite, which was granted. During those seven days, five hundred of her brothers, the ministers and the officers of the Bhatta army, and the citizens were all converted to the Bauddha *dharma*. The converts regarded Malini as the saviour of their souls. Angry at the wicked machinations of the Brahmins, they proceeded into a body to remonstrate them. The Brahmins took refuge with the king. They revoked the sentence of Malini's banishment but induced the king to send ten armed men to kill Kashyapa, the root of all their woes. The great sage easily converted these armed men. They next deputed a large number of men, but with the same result, they saw that by sending armed men they only added to the already overwhelming number of converts. They, therefore, determined to despatch the business themselves. Armed with clubs and other weapons they marched in martial array to the hermitage of Kashyapa. Kashyapa invoked the goddess Pritha and desired her to show her powers against these Brahmins. She uprooted a stout palm tree, hurled it at the Brahmanas, and crushed them to death.

Tagore took only the basic idea from *Mahavastu avadana*, rejected completely the last portion and projected it in a different way. He kept the ideal of Buddhism intact in 'Malini'. The concept of Maitri and Karuna took shape in Malini and Supriya. In the *Mahavastu avadana* there was no reference of Supriya and the affair between Supriya and Malini. This is poet's imagination. In this drama the poet showed the greatness of *Ksamadharma*—forgiveness, compassion over other qualities. In 'Malini', the concept of love was expressed in a different way.

আজ আমি জানিয়াছি
ধর্ম মোর হৃদয়ের বড়ো কাছাকাছি।

Supriya, the disciple of Ksemankar, the representative of the Brahmins, loved Malini and realized that Malini's new religion, humanism, is the true religion, which is near to heart. For many years he had studied *Sastras* and performed *yajnas*, but he had not achieved what he was searching for. In Malini's religion he discovered *Amritattva*. He found that the whole world is full of evil-suffering, hatred, treachery, jealousy, but still,

তবু সমুজ্বল তব শান্তি, তব প্রীতি, তব সুমঙ্গল
অম্লান অচল দীপ্তি করিছে বিরাজ - সর্বোপরি।

This peace, this love and joy seemed to be more important to Supriya than worldly name and fame and he embraced death. But Ksemankar's (the leader and representative of the Brahmins) strong personality also attracts our attention. He very bravely faced the death sentence, and when he was going to be executed Malini cried and begged for Ksemankar's life. **ক্ষম ক্ষেমঙ্করে**

This last word of Malini is the ultimate message of the drama compassion, forgiveness, renunciation. It is a unique expression of *Dhamma padas*' famous verse.

অক্কোধেন জিনে ক্কোধং অসাধুং সাধুনা জিনে
জিনে কদরিয়ং দানেন সচ্চেব অলীক বাদিনং।

Tagore in his heart accepted the Buddhist ideal of compassion, forgiveness, and love to all beings. That ideal he has picturised in 'Malini'. It reminds us of Tagore's most favourite *sloka* of Meghasutta in the *Sutta Pitaka*:

মাতা যথা নিয়ং পাত্তং-
আয়ুসা এক পুত্তমনুরকখে-
এবমিপ সর্বভূতেকু-
মানসং ভাবয়ে অপরিমানং।

Rabindranath wrote the poem 'Parisodha' in 1899, then after 40 years from this poem he composed the dance-drama 'Shyama'. The basic theme of this drama was taken from *Mahavastu avadan* and *Kanaba Jataka*. Here there are no major differences in these two *granthas* regarding the theme, but minor differences are there.

Once Lord Buddha was asked by his devotees why he deserted his wife Jasodhara. As answer to this question Lord Buddha narrated this story of his previous life: There was a horse dealer in Taxila named Vajrasena; on his way to the fair at Varanasi, his horses were stolen and he was severely wounded. As he slept in a deserted house in the suburbs of Varanasi, the policemen caught him as thief. He was ordered to the place of execution. But his manly beauty attracted the attention of Shyama, the first public woman of Varanasi. She grew enamoured of the man, and requested one of her handmaids to rescue the criminal at any cost.

By offering large sum of money, she succeeded in inducing the executioners to set Vajrasena free, and execute the order of the king on another person, a banker's son, who was an admirer of Shyama. The latter not knowing his fate approached the place of execution and faced death. The woman was devotedly attached to Vajrasena. But her inhuman conduct to the banker's son made a deep impression on Vajrasena's mind. He could not reconcile himself to the idea of being in love with the conspirator of such a crime. On an occasion when they both set on a pluvial excursion, Vajrasena gave her wine and when she was almost senseless, smothered her and drowned her. When he thought she was quite dead, he dragged her to the steps of the *ghat* and fled, leaving her in that helpless condition. Her mother who was at hand, came to her rescue, and by great assiduity resuscitated her. Shyama's first measure after recovery was to find out a *bhikkhuni* of Taxila and to send through her a message to Vajrasena, inviting him to her loving embrace. Lord Buddha was Vajrasena and Jasodhara was Shyama .

Tagore transformed the last of the episode and brought the concept of compassion in it. In portion *Mahavastu avadana*, Vajrasena left Shyama at the bank of the river and never came back. In Tagore's 'Shyama', Vajrasena is also suffering from guilt feeling, the feeling of committing sin, and at the last part compassion overshadows his guilt feeling, and he repents for his lack of *karuna* (mercy).

ক্ষমিতে পারিলাম না যে
ক্ষম হে মম দীনতা, পাপী জন শরন প্রভু-
মরিছে পাপে মরিছে লাজে প্রেমের ক্ষমাহীনতা
জানি গো তুমি ক্ষমিবে তারে
যে অভাগিনী পাপের ভারে চরনে তব বিনতা
ক্ষমিবে না ক্ষমিবেনা আমার ক্ষমাহীনতা //

This feeling of compassion leaves an impression in our mind. The whole episode transforms itself into an emotion of feeling of repentance for absence of compassion.

Tagore composed *Chandalika* from an episode of *Sardulakarnavadan.* Tagore retained the basic idea of the episode, which was to prove the meaninglessness of caste system and to establish the equality of all human being.

Buddhism believed in the supremacy of human being over and above the rites, rituals, wealth and caste. *Chandalika*, the most popular dance-drama of Tagore in India, is represented as the story of the emancipation of an outcaste Chandalkanya. Prakriti was born in an untouchable family, and from her early girlhood it was ingrained in her through the behaviour of other girls and members of the society that she is untouchable. Her mother accepted the truth, but there was something in Prakriti that revolted against this custom and system. One day, Ananda, the most favourite disciple of the Buddha was passing through that village. Thirsty Ananda asked Prakriti for drinking water, which she refused saying that she is untouchable. But Ananda told her "যে মানব আমি, সেই মানব তুমি কন্যা" (Both of us are human beings), and took water from her.

This was a new message for Prakriti, the message of equality of human beings. This was her rebirth. Now she started thinking that she is at par with others in the society. Ananda left the place but Prakriti couldn't forget him. She loved him; she wanted to see him again. She wanted her mother to help her in bringing him back. Her mother knew witchcraft. Her mother first refused her and said to her that as a Chandalkanya her place is in her own society. But Prakriti didn't accept this. She said I hate that religion which teaches people to hate others. I accept that religion which accepts me. Here through Prakriti we can see the revolutionary self of Tagore whose religion was the the religion of man. At last Ananda comes. Here we see Tagore differs from *Sardulakarnavadan.* There we find that Lord Buddha, by his supernatural power, came to know about the witchcraft and uttered a mantra by which Ananda was saved from desire and evil. But in Tagore's *Chandalika,* Ananda comes to Prakriti. But this Prakriti is not the same girl. There was a metamorphosis within her. When she saw Ananda, she could not bear the fall of her beloved saint Ananda. She falls at down his feet and begs pardon. Ananda utters "কল্যাণ হোক তব কল্যাণী" This is a story of emancipation not of an untouchable woman of society, but the story of emancipation from lust, desire and passion. It is story of victory, of goodness, of compassion over human desire.

The theme of *Samanyaksati* was taken from the story of *Shyamavati* in *Divyavadanamala.* King Brahmadatta of Varanasi had five hundred wives. One day these ladies had gone to a garden for recreation. Bathing in an adjoining river they felt cold and the chief queen, seeing a hut on the bank, ordered her maid to set fire, so that they have a good blazing fire to warm herself. The maid reported that the hut belonged to a hermit. But the queen did not care for this, and insisted upon her order being carried out, and her companions supported her. The hut was accordingly burnt. The hermit escaped from the hut, and rising in the air blessed the maid Malati, whereupon the other women all begged that they might be duly punished for their sins, but after that they may obtain the absolute knowledge.

Tagore took a small portion of this *Shyamavati* episode and recreated the theme in his own way. The *Shyamavati* episode had all characteristics of a *Jataka Katha.* This is also a story of Lord Buddha's previous life. The misdeeds of queens, their repentance, and at last the attainment of real knowledge is described here. Tagore in his poem *Samanyaksati* names the queen Karuna. Instead of 500 wives, the king had only one wife, and Karuna the queen had one hundred maids. In *Shyamavati* we see one hermit's hut was burnt, but in the poem the queen's maids burnt all huts of poor people of the village. They destroyed the village and enjoyed the warmth. In comparison to the queen's wealth, she thought poor people's loss is a little loss. The next part of the poem is Tagore's own creation. The king himself knowing the fact punished the queen. He took the justice wand in his own hand, took off the queen's special dress from Karuna and gave her a beggar's cloth. He banished her from the palace and ordered her to beg for one year. She was also asked to reconstruct all the huts she destroyed. He gave her one year's time for realizing the quantity of loss done by her. This treatment gives an ethical dimension to the poem. Tagore was a worshipper of humanity and love. He found these qualities in the Buddhist literature and transformed these episodes into classic dramas and poems. Like an expert gardener he coined the best flowers of Indian consciousness touched by Lord Buddha.

NOTES

1. Arnold, Edwin, *The Light of Asia*, London, 1885.
2. Barua, B.N., *Studies in Buddhism*, Calcutta, 1974.
3. Davids, Rhys, Hibbert Lectures, 4th edition.
4. Mitra, R.L., *Sanskrit Buddhist Literature of Nepal*, Calcutta, 1882.
5. Radhakrishna, S.S., *Philosophy of Rabindranath Tagore*, London, 1948.

8

Buddha in Rabindra Literature

Bhabatosh Datta

No Bengali thinker was more dominated by Gautama, the Buddha than Rabindranath Tagore. Ever since he wrote in 1888 that he had not the slightest doubt about the historic existence of the Buddha, his reverence for him never waned. Even towards his last days when he was in Kalimpong in the midst of local devotees of the Buddha, he read a poem expressing his deep admiration for this 'greatest among men' as he used to refer him.

It may sound curious that there may be a shade of doubt about the Buddha's existence. We do not know if there was any doubt ever. In the early centuries of our recorded history his advent left an unforgettable stamp in the human civilization. His religion had almost disappeared from India but the Buddha, the man remains as glorious as ever. After several hundreds of years the Buddha was made an avatar or incarnation of Hindu God Vishnu. Jayadeva in the 12th century composed his famous *Gitagovinda* extolling him as an incarnation, though we have no clear indication of the Buddha having left any impact in our daily life. On the other hand, the Hindu society with Puranic background and tradition continues to exist. We have Shiva, Krishna and Ramachandra with no historical basis. Krishna might have been a cowherd boy. Ramachandra might have been a prince of Ayodhya but their identities are lost in the hoary past. They are dehumanised and made gods. Consequently, they cannot be the ideal for us—the ordinary men. Buddhadeva was not a mythological figure. We have his dates and activities historically established. He stands as the extraordinary personality for all time. Rabindranath was drawn by his personality more than by Krishna or Ramachandra. We may recall that Bankim Chandra Chattopadhyaya his great predecessor, had been working to establish Krishna as a historical personality. His *Krishnacharitra* was published in 1886 in which he had carried on painstaking research.

But Rabindranath was not sure of Krishna's historical existence. We note this in his essay on Bankim's *Krishnacharitra.* Some of Krishna's activities may appear to be morally inappropriate and so to take him to be an ideal man remains open to question. Buddha's teachings are free from such apprehension. The life of the Buddha is one of sacrifice, suffering and meditation leading to ultimate realization of Truth. He made us aware of the hard fact of life, the ignorance which gives rise to sorrows and sufferings. He neither talked of gods nor talked of practising any rituals of any kind. He had no mystical way to attain *Nirvana.* His whole emphasis was on the proper conduct of man, conducts that purify man. Buddha's teachings are compiled in the text called *Suttapitaka.* The *Dhammapada* is a part of *Khuddaka Nikaya* contained in that pitaka. About the *Dhammapada* Rabindranath says:

জগতে যে কয়েকটি শ্রেষ্ঠ ধর্মগ্রন্থ আছে 'ধম্মপদ' তাহার একটি। বৌদ্ধদের মতে এই 'ধম্মপদ' গ্রন্থের সমস্ত কথা স্বয়ং বুদ্ধদেবের উক্তি এবং এগুলি তাহার মৃত্যুর অনতিকাল পরেই গ্রন্থাকারে আবদ্ধ হইয়াছিল।[1]

Dhammapada is one of the greatest of all religious scriptures. According to the Buddhists all the teachings contained in the *Dhammapada* are the utterances of the Buddha himself. These were compiled in a bookform sometime after his death.

The book is a compilation of ethical aphorisms in verse, suitable for all men to follow, irrespective of caste, creed and religion. These aphorisms have no communal or religious predilection. It is its universality, which impressed Rabindranath.

Rabindranath, of course, did not try to go on with professional scholarship of Buddhist scriptures. He had the easy insight of getting into the core ideas of the Buddha. In 1903, he described Buddhadeva as follows:

ভারতবর্ষে বুদ্ধদেব মানবকে বড়ো করিয়াছিলেন। তিনি জাতি মানেন নাই, যাগযজ্ঞের অবলম্বন হইতে মানুষকে মুক্তি দিয়াছিলেন। দেবতাকে মানুষের লক্ষ্য হইতে অপসৃত করিয়াছিলেন। তিনি মানুষের আত্মশক্তি প্রচার করিয়াছিলেন। দয়া ও কল্যাণ তিনি স্বর্গ হইতে প্রার্থনা করেন নাই। মানুষের অন্তর হইতে তাহা আহ্বান করিয়াছিলেন।[2]

Buddhadeva made man great. He discarded all caste divisions and relieved man from the compulsion of observing various rites and *yajnas.* He removed gods from being the object. He declared the power of the Self. He refused to beg mercy and welfare of man from heaven and invoked it from within man's own self.

Historically, it is admitted that the Buddha's teachings were a reaction to highly complicated Vedic rules and regulations known as *Karmakanda.* The Vedic people used to perform sacrificial ceremonies with the hope to please the gods. Even in the *Bhagavad Gita* Sri Krishna says:

यामिमां पुष्पितां वाचं प्रवदन्त्यविपश्चितः ॥
वेदवादरताः पार्थ नान्यदस्तीति वादिनः ॥ Ch. 2/424

The undiscerning who are engrossed in the letter of the Veda, O Partha, and declare that there is nothing else speak flowery words.

Disregarding Vedic *Karmakanda* Buddhadeva has said that man need not look to gods for help. Man is the master of his own fate. आत्मदीपो भव. Be your own light as he said. This confirms Rabindranath's view about the Buddha. The same advice was given by Lord Krishna to Arjuna:

उद्धरेदात्सनात्मानं नात्मानमवसादयेत
आत्मैव ह्यात्मनो बन्धुरात्मैव रिपुरात्मनः Ch. 6/5

Let a man raise his self by his self, let him not debase his self; he alone indeed is his own friend, he alone his own enemy.

Rabindranath's contention is corroborated by Radhakrishnan's exposition of the Buddha's teachings as collected in the *Dhammapada.*

'As a man acts,' says Radhakrishnan, 'so shall he be.' We are forever making our own moral world for good or for ill. Every thought, feeling, and volition counts for something in our personal development. Mankind is forever fashioning itself. The thoughts and acts of a remote and invisible past have actually produced the contents of our earth. The Buddha sees life as beneath the sovereignty of infinite righteousness. We can never escape the consequences of our deeds. Suffering of every kind, disease and loss, failure and disappointment, the wounds of affection and the prostration of purpose are all charged with moral significance and determined by the principle of moral causation.[3]

If man be the architect of his self what should be his way to achieve it? Rabindranath refers to the Buddha's way. He says, to adopt the way of conduct or *sheela* is the way to liberation. In his essay on *Brahmavihara* he refers to these *sheelas* elaborately and explains that these take you to *mangala* or ultimate good. Rabindranath also explains his concept of good in line with Buddhadeva. Thus, whenever he spoke of the Buddha he stressed on his concept of *maitri* or love.

Buddhadeva's love for suffering humanity was unbounded. He sacrificed his whole life to find out the path for man, which would liberate them from sorrow and suffering. A Mahayani Buddhist would like to think that the Buddha himself willingly passes through many births only to share the suffering of man. His own nirvana or salvation becomes secondary.

The specific characteristics of Hinayani and Mahayani ideals were clear to Rabindranath. In his essay on *Bauddhadharme Bhaktivad* (1911) he made his own observation. He was for Mahayani ideal of universal love. He emphasised that truth and love were identical. His concept of truth was rooted in the Upanishad and so he says:

> মানুষের প্রকাশ সত্যে। এই সত্য যে কী তা উপনিষদে বলা হয়েছে ঃ-
> আত্মবৎ সর্বভূতেষু য পশ্যতি। স পশ্যতি। যিনি সকল জীবকে আপনার মতো করে জানেন তিনিই সত্যকে জানেন। আপনার মধ্যে সত্যকে যিনি এমন করে জেনেছেন তার মধ্যে মনুষ্যত্ব প্রকাশিত হয়েছে।

In truth man finds himself expressed. The Upanishad teaches us this truth आत्मवत सर्वभुतेषु य पशयति स पश्यति. Only he who knows all creatures in the very way as he knows himself, knows the Truth. Humanity is revealed in one who knows Truth in his own self.

Thus the Truth as declared by the Upanishad is same as the Buddha's concept of love for the *jiva* or animal. *Maitri* is the special term used for love. Rabindranath did not find dissimilarity between the teachings of the Buddha and that of the Upanishad. In *Brahamavihar* (1908) he interprets the philosophy of the Buddha in his own way. In the *Bauddhadharme Bhaktivad* (1911) he gives a sketch of development of Buddhism. Both the essays show his keen understanding and originality of his interpretation.

Rabindranath equates *Nirvana* and *mangala* to be the same. In the essay *Brahmavihara* he explains *mangala* to be the goal of life. He defines also in his own way the concept of *Nirvana* when he says that the goal of life is to attain the good. What does he mean by good? Is it *Nirvana?* Is it *Sunyata?* Rabindranath differs from the Theravadi conception of *Sunyata. Sunyata* or *Nirvana* is not the eternal nothing. The object of life cannot be negative. It must be something positive and that is love or *maitri.* It is the self-satisfying fulfilment. The Buddha's *sadhana* was, according to Rabindranath, for attaining this goal of love. The Buddha became the embodiment of *karuna* and *maitri* himself. One who feels so deeply for a suffering man indeed lives in the state of cosmic consciousness and that is *Brahmavihara.*

Actually Brahma in the *Upanishadic* sense is the ultimate Reality, a formless Being. To attain that Reality has been the object of all seekers of *moksa.* But this is somewhat different from Rabindranath's idea of Brahma. Strictly speaking, Rabindranath believes that liberation or *moksa* is not something away from this world of senses.

> যা কিছু আনন্দ আছে দৃশ্যে গন্ধে গানে
> তোমার আনন্দ রবে তার মাঝখানে

Whatever joy I have out of this world of senses, they bring to me the supreme joy of your presence.

Now, this is not what the Buddha taught. According to him attraction to this world only creates *tanha*—endless sorrow. One has to be free from this attraction. How did Rabindranath reconcile? He resolves it when he says:

> তখনকার বিশ্বাস ছিল এই যে, তপশ্চরণের দ্বারা সমাধিপ্রাপ্তিই ব্রহ্মলাভ। তাহাই চরম সিদ্ধি। কিন্তু যখন বুদ্ধদেব বুদ্ধত্ব লাভ করিলেন তখনই তিনি কর্মে প্রবৃত্ত হইলেন। সে কর্ম বিশুদ্ধ কর্ম কারণ তাহাতে ভয়, লোভ, মোহ, হিংসা নাই; তাহা স্বার্থবন্ধনের অতীত; তাহা দয়ার কর্ম প্রেমের কর্ম।[4]

People at that time used to believe that to attain the supreme state by practising austerity is the ultimate goal. But when Buddhadeva attained Buddhahood he immediately set himself to work. That was pure action, because it was free from fear, greed, jealousy and dotage. It was beyond any selfish interest. It was action purely of love and mercy.

So Rabindranath did not accept that the total extinction of self is the *Nirvana.* On the other hand, to do good to mankind is the urge that must remain.

This great respect for Gautama, the Buddha never declined all through his life. His elder brother Satyendranath Tagore made a study of the Buddha's life and philosophy. His book *Bauddha Dharma* (1903) in Bengali might have created an impression on Rabindranath. But earlier, the book which made an impact on him was Rajendralal Mitra's *The Sanskrit Buddhist Literature of Nepal* (1882). Rabindranath was an admirer of Rajendralal and his book was his constant companion. *The Sanskrit Buddhist Literature* is a descriptive account of various *avadana* stories from which Rabindranath drew themes of some of his well-known dramas and poems.

The first among them is *Malini* (1896), a drama. It is based on the *Mahavastu-avadana* and gives a glimpse of conflict between the Brahmanas and the Buddhists. The same *avadana* provided him the central theme of his poem *Parishodh* (1899) which was later rendered into dance-drama *Shyama* (1939). His another symbolic drama *Raja* (1910 [English under the title *King of the Dark Chamber*]) had also its story taken from Kusha Jataka of the *Mahavastu-avadana.* His *Achalayatan* (1912) had its origin in the *Panchakavadan* of *Divyavandanamala.* This drama was rewritten in 1918 and was titled *Guru.* From *Shardulakarnavadana* he took the story of his poem *Pujarini.* This was later rendered into drama with the title *Natir Puja* (1925). His well-known dance-drama *Chandalika* (1933) had the Harijan Movement of Gandhiji at its background but the story was based on the plight of a low-born woman Prakriti. It is a story taken from *Shardulakarnavadana.*

Most of the poems he wrote with themes taken from the Buddhist literature are collected in his book *Katha* (1900). They are *Abhisara* from *Upaguptavadana* of *Bodhisathwavadana-kalpalata, Mastak-bikraya* from *Ajnatakandilya* of *Mahavastu-avadana, Nagara-Lakshmi* from *Kalpadrumavadana* of *Avadanasataka, Mulyaprapti* from *Padmah* of *Avadanasataka* and *Samanyaksati* from *Makandikavadana* of *Divyavadanamala.* The theme of *Shrestha Bhiksa* was taken from fifty-fifth *avadana* '*Bastram*' of *Avadana-satak.* Evidently, Rabindranath took those themes modifying them or adding to them his own suggestion.

We may also note that when these poems were composed in the early part of the last century, Rabindranath was deeply engrossed in the romantic beauty of the classical tradition of India. He was looking back to the ancient Indian glory and tried to bring them back to his days. He wrote a number of essays on Kalidasa and on *Dhammapada* explaining the ideal of love and beauty as well as the *tapovana* culture. His book of poems *Naivedya* carried the message of ancient *rishis.* His essay on the nature of the history of India (*Bharatavarshe Itihaser Dhara,* 1910) contained his originality in interpreting the history, which attracted the attention of the academic historian. The essay also gives an idea of Buddhist contribution to the Indian culture and history.

Engrossed in the beauty of ancient Indian ideal he tried to bring back those days by introducing in his school at Bolpur the Vedic life and the Buddhist concept of *sangha.* Rabindranath initiated his son Rathindranath in Buddhist studies who translated a portion of Asvaghosha's *Buddhacharita* under the guidance of Bidhushekhar Sastri, a well-known scholar of the Buddha and Buddhism. His

Brahmacharyashrama was modelled in *tapovana* style where students gathered at the foot of their teachers under the wide expanse of nature. At the same time they were taught to live a life in a body of united cooperation, i.e. *sangha*. Rabindranath had in his mind not only the *tapovana* of the Vedic age but the Buddhist *sangharam* also. It was a place where students lived together under the supervision of several teachers bound together by a common ideal of selfless *sadhana*.

That Rabindranath kept in mind the *sangha* concept can be understood from his later reflection. His school grew into a university. He really loved to think that Visva Bharati would develop in the line of great seats of learning like Nalanda, Bikramshila and Taksashila. In his *Vishva Vidyalayer Rup* (1932) he says:

> য়ুনিভার্সিটির প্রথম প্রতিরূপ একদিন ভারতবর্ষেই দেখা দিয়েছিল। নালন্দা, বিক্রমশিলা, তক্ষশিলার বিদ্যায়তন কবে প্রতিষ্ঠিত হয়েছিল তার নিশ্চিত কাল নির্ণয় এখনো হয়নি, কিন্তু ধরে নেওয়া যেতে পারে যে য়ুরোপীয় য়ুনিভার্সিটির পূর্বেই তাদের আবির্ভাব। তাদের উদ্ভব ভারতীয় চিত্তের আন্তরিক প্রেরণায়, স্বভাবের অনিবার্য আবেগে। তার পূর্ববর্তী কালে বিদ্যার সাধনা ও শিক্ষা বিচিত্র আকারে ও বিবিধ প্রণালীতে দেশে নানা স্থানে ব্যাপ্ত হয়েছিল এ কথা সুনিশ্চিত। সমাজের সেই সর্বত্র পরিকীর্ণ সাধনাই পুঞ্জীভূত কেন্দ্রীভূত রূপে এক সময়ে স্থানে স্থানে দেখা দিল।
>
> ভগবান বুদ্ধ একদিন যে ধর্ম প্রচার করেছিলেন সে ধর্ম তদার নানা তত্ত্ব, নানা অনুশাসন, তার সাধনার প্রণালী নিয়ে সাধারণ চিত্তের আন্তর্ভৌম স্তরে প্রবেশ করে ব্যাপ্ত হয়েছিল। তখন দেশ প্রবলভাবে কামনা করেছিল এই
> বহুশাখায়িত পরিব্যাপ্ত ধারাকে কোনো সুনির্দিষ্ট কেন্দ্রস্থলে উৎসরূপে উৎসারিত করে দিতে সর্বসাধারণের স্নানের জন্য, পানের জন্য, কল্যাণের জন্য।

The prototype of a University was first conceived in India when Nalanda, Taksashila, Bikramshila were founded. We are not sure of their dates. It can be presumed that they came into existence before the universities of Europe existed. They originated spontaneously in Indian mind naturally. Before them the exercises in academic learning remained scattered in different parts of India and in different types. These sporadic seats of learning gathered together and came to form centres.

Lord Buddha once preached his *dharma*, which entered deep into people's mind with varieties of philosophical speculations, ways and manners. The whole country earnestly felt that these varieties should be brought to a centre wherefrom the fountain of knowledge would be allowed to flow so that people might be benefitted by ablution and drink.

Rabindranath's dream came true to a certain extent with a number of renowned scholars like Sylva Levi, Bidhushekhar Shastri, Prabodh Chandra Bagchi, Sujit Kumar Mukhopadhay and others meeting at Santiniketan. The Cheena-Bhavan turned out to be a widely-known centre of Buddhist studies. Then came the Department of Tibetan Studies, which we all hope will develop into one of the major centres of such studies in fulfilment of Rabindranath's dream.

He kept the memory of the Buddha fresh to his last days. In 1935, he was invited to Dharmarajika Chaitya at Kolkata on the occasion of Buddhadeva's birth festival. He delivered a long address which began like this:

আমি যাঁকে অন্তরের মধ্যে সর্বশ্রেষ্ঠ মানব বলে উপলব্ধি করি আজ বৈশাখী পূর্ণিমায় তাঁর জন্মোৎসবে আমার প্রণান নিবেদন করতে এসেছি।

I have come here to pay my homage on the occasion of one's birth festival whom I consider to be the greatest of men.

He also travelled to Siam, Brahmadesh, China and Java where he visited the Buddhist temples and monasteries. That inspired him to write several poems surcharged with his deep devotion to Lord Buddha. They are all collected in his later works.

My paper will remain incomplete if I do not refer to Rabindranath's profound admiration for King Ashoka, the Buddha's great follower. When Rabindranath first visited Bodhgaya in 1904, he became full of the spirit of the Buddha and wrote a remarkable essay named *Utsaber Din* (the day of festival). In this essay he described Ashoka as the great bearer of the Buddha's message. He stressed on Ashoka's endeavour to spread the Lord's message in far distant countries not by means of war and conquest, nor by commerce but by the power of goodwill. He sent his mission of goodwill and made friends with the people whom he never saw. What was the message? It was the message of humanism and love. It was not the single occasion when Rabindranath paid his respect to Ashoka. Rabindranath's essays and poems are strewn with references to this great king. In 1940, a lady Hilda Seligman came to Rabindranath. She had written a book *When Peacock Called.* She begged Rabindranath to write a foreword to her book. Rabindranath wrote:

"In an age of fratricide, aided by intellectual dehumanisation in large areas of the world it is difficult to restore the calm air so necessary for the realization of great human ideals. Hilda Seligman has chosen in her book to reveal the organization side of great humanism, which came with King Ashoka of India."

That was his last reference to Lord Buddha and his ideal.

NOTES

1. Rabindranath Tagore, "Prachin Sahitya", *Dhammapada.*
2. Buddhadeva, 1956.
3. S. Radhakrishnan, *The Dhammapada,* Oxford University Press, 1984, Introduction, p. 19.
4. Rabindranath, *Buddhadeva,* Visva Bharti, 1956, p. 38.

9

Buddhist Samgha in the Early Indian Texts

Pranabananda Jash

The history of Buddhism is an embodiment of a vast and complex religious and a philosophical tradition that stretches back over 2,500 years. The religion that was professed and preached by the great Master possesses profound and in-depth implication and common threads connecting diverse traditions of Buddhist thought and practices, like the story of the Buddha, the scriptural tradition of his teachings, the four noble truths, the *ashṭāṅgika-mārga*, genesis of the *Samgha* and the *Vihāra*, monastic and lay ways of life, *karma* and rebirth, ethics, meditation and philosophy. All these aspects of Buddhism are depicted elaborately in the Buddhist texts as well as in the subsequent Indian literature. But the most important and significant aspect of the history of Buddhism is the concept of *Tri-ratna:*

Buddham saranam gacchami
Dhamman saranam gacchami
Samgham saranam gacchami

Thus, the place of the *Samgha* in Buddhism was essential, and Sir Charles Eliot may be right when he comments: "The great practical achievement of the Buddha was to found a religious order which has lasted to the present day. It is known as the *Samgha* and its members are called *Bhikkhus.* It is chiefly to this institution that the permanence of his religion is due."[1]

While concentrating on the formative phase of Buddhism in India, the *Samgha* is considered to have played a vital role for the foundation that has shaped the development of Buddhism beyond India, right from the time of its inception till the present day. A corpus of literature in various Indian languages of the subsequent period is regularly brought out in the realm of the academic world.

The impact of the Buddha and its concept is not confined to Indian language and literature alone, but it delineated a conspicuous stamp on the entire cultural ethos of the Asian people.

It is to be noted that the concept of Samgha (*Samghārāma* in Sanskrit) or the Buddhist monastery, the abode of the *Bhikkhus* (the mendicants) who had renounced the empirical world, is not a new phenomenon in Indian society, but undoubtedly a greater addition and development on the earlier Brahmanical one.[2] The ascetic orders had gained immense influence on the common milieu of the society even before the Buddha, but what the Buddha achieved was to make the order more humane and better organized. In fact, "The greatest genius of the Buddha lay in the organization of the ascetic order and the creation of a code of rules and regulations for the conduct of monastic life."[3]

While tracing the origin of the Buddhist monasteries (*Vihāras*) it may be noted that the Buddhist *monarchism* owes its origin to the Buddhist *Samgha* that has a history of its own. The *Mahāvagga*[4] affords us an interesting account relating to the formation of the Buddhist *Samgha* that afterwards led to the foundation of *Vihāra.* Originally, the Buddhist *Bhikkhus,* known as Sakyaputtiya *Samanas,* were not in a habit of the observance of the *Vassa,*[5] but afterwards being criticized by the Titthiya school[6] the Buddha himself introduced this programme within the activities of his monastic order. Buddhaghosha, the commentator on the *Vinaya text,* explains how this ceremony was performed: "They are to look after their *Vihāra* to provide food and water for themselves, to fulfil all due ceremonies, such as paying reverence to sacred shrines, etc., and to say loudly once, twice, or thrice: "I enter upon *Vassa* in *Vihāra* for three months." Thus they are to enter upon *Vassa.*"[7]

Thus, the custom of staying at one particular place for a specific period ultimately led to the foundation of future *Samghārāmas* and *Vihāras.* We learn from the Pali Buddhist Text *Cullavagga*[8] that the Buddha at the request of a rich merchant (*Setthi*) of Rajagriha in Bihar allowed the following abodes for the monks: *Vihāras, Addhayogas, Prāsādas, Hammiyas* and *Guhās.*[9] We are not sure whether all these abodes were used only during the rainy season or in other seasons too. In course of time, however, the Buddha allowed the use of these dwellings during other seasons; and perhaps, some centuries must have elapsed before the *āvāsa* came to be organized and had a distinct existence. The *Mahāvagga*[10] also speaks of these five types of residence (*pañcalenāni*). Vivid descriptions of these different categories of residence are found mentioned in the *Cullavagga.*[11] Thus, a *Prāsāda* is a storeyed building, often pyramidal in shape, sometimes with a pillared verandah (*alinda*). Some early *Vihāras* had living and sleeping cells for a large number of *Bhikkhus*, but some had accommodation for two or three persons and even for one; these were later on replaced by bigger two-storeyed structure with one or more rectangular courtyards enclosed by lines of cells and other chambers. The definition of *Guhā* is explained differently. *Guhā* usually means a cave, rather a rock-cut cave.

It is generally believed that within the periphery of the *āvāsa*, the lodging houses were known as *Vihāras*, and, in course of time, they developed from the single eremitical to a larger congregational type, from *Vihāras* into monasteries. This development of the Buddhist *Vihāras* all over India can be also traced from the architectural remains. Fergusson has very aptly pointed out this significance: "The oldest *Vihāras* consist of one cell only; little hermitages in fact for the residence of a single ascetic. In the next class they were extended to a long verandah with one cell behind it .... As these had, however, several doors opening outwards, they probably were divided by partitions internally. In the third class, and by far the most numerous class ... the cell expands into a hall, generally, with pillars in the centre; and around this the cells of the monks are arranged."[12]

We should further note in this connection that the process of transition from wandering to settled life was a slow and gradual one, but undoubtedly accomplished early in *Samgha* history, perhaps, as early as the fourth century BC. With this development, the *Samgha* became an organization independent of the wanderers' community; and the Buddhist *Bhikkhus* were by themselves as well as by others distinguished from "wanderers". Moreover, it also marked the beginning of cenobiam among them, and thus in the *Vinaya-piṭaka*, the *Bhikkhu-Samgha* appears not as an institution of the wanderers, but as a settled cenoebitical society.

According to the Buddhist texts, these *Samghārāmas* or the monasteries came into existence as a result of the donations made by the kings, officials of the states, wealthy merchants and even the common people of the society. An elaborate description of the *Samghas* and the *Vihāras* and its activities on various occasions is to be found in the Pali literature, viz., the *Mahāvagga* and the *Cullavagga.* The *Cullavagga* provides an elaborate description about the construction of a *Vihāra.* It is thus proposed that verandah, covered terrace, inner verandahs, overhanging caves, store-rooms, and service-halls gradually came to be built as the number of *Bhikkhus* increased.[13] In its initial stage, the *Vihāras* had no fence; but afterwards the Buddha allowed the *Bhikkhus* to have a fence made of bamboo-sticks, thorns or a ditch.[14] And the *Vihāras* became the permanent abodes of the monks and also possessed a considerable amount of wealth, it became inevitable to protect these fencing round by a wood, brick, or a stone-wall.[15]

The purpose of the *Vihāras* in its earlier stage is "to give *Vihāras* to the *Samgha,* where, in safety and peace, to meditate and think at ease, the Buddha calls the best of gifts. Let then the able men, regarding his own weal, have pleasant monasteries built, and lodge their learned men."[16] Similar objectivity of the *Vihāras* also continued at the time of Fa-hien's visit to Pataliputra (Patna in Bihar).[17] Fa-hien came to this country during the time of the great Gupta emperor, Chandragupta II, the Vikramaditya.

We are also informed from the early literature that the regular business of the monks is to perform acts of meritorious virtue, and to recite their *sūtras* and to sit wrapped in meditation, when stranger monks arrive at any monastery the residents meet and receive them, carry for them their clothes and alms-bowl, give them water to wash their feet, oil with which to anoint them, and the liquid food permitted out of the regular hours. When (the stranger) has enjoyed a very brief rest, they further ask the number of years that he has been a monk, after which he receives a sleeping apartment with its appurtenances, according to his regular order, and everything is done for him, which the rules prescribe.

To have an idea of the life and activities of the Buddhist monk within the *Samghas* or the *Vihāras* we have to deal with the rules and regulations concerning the admission of persons to the monastery and ordination of the monks as recorded in the Pali text—the *Viṇaya-piṭaka.* A monastery was to function within the scope of these laws; and of its existence as an order the *Viṇaya* was the bond. It is possible, therefore, to frame in the setting of the *Viṇaya* laws a picture of *Samgha* organization as it had existed in the early centuries of Buddhism. But the picture did not remain the same in the later period.[18]

Realizing the importance of the *Samgha-Kamma* and the significance of the activities of the *Vihāras* it is imperative to have a brief idea about the procedure by which one could get admission to these monastic orders. The entire procedure of ordination is recorded in the *Viṇaya* text. The *Pabbajjā* and *Upasampadā* ordinations were necessary for every individual to be incorporated as the member of the *Buddhist Samgha.* Of these, the former was the lower form and it denoted only the houselessness of a person. The more solemn form was the *Upasampadā.* The persons who desire such ordination must have "his hair and beard cut off", "must put on yellow robes", "adjust this upper robe so as to cover one shoulder", "salute the feet of the *Bhikkhus*", sit down squatting and say thrice with his folded hands, "I take refuge in the Buddha, I take refuge in the *Dhamma,* I take refuge in the *Samgha*'." Anyone wishing to embrace the monkhood had to approach a teacher of his own choice and request his permission to be initiated; there was no caste barrier; but a minor, a matricide, a patricide, and a eunuch and the like were disqualified for admission to the order of monks. The selected teacher had to get the permission of the *Samgha* and after this he imparted the five precepts to the candidate. Only a *Sthavira* could act as an *Upādhyāya,* and no one could attain the position of a *Sthavira* without spending ten rain-retreats *(Vassa-vāsa).*

It is, however, an enigma to know when and how these rules came to be formulated. These rules were neither drawn up in their entirety in the Buddha's lifetime, nor were they formulated in their entirety after his *Parinibbana.*[19] Some were possibly laid down by the Buddha himself, while some others formulated and incorporated afterwards. Even some earlier rules have been codified with "additions and modifications".[20] This is possibly because of the fact that the life and discipline in the *Vihāras* in its formative stage were very simple but with the growing popularity of this faith among the people in all sections of the society as well as with the foreigners, it became inevitable to formulate or codify more rigid rules and regulations for following the faith of the great teacher in a proper manner.

The changing scenario of the history of the faith and philosophy of the Great Master Gautama, the Buddha, from time to time, age to age, and even region to region, or from country to country, inspired the intellectuals, philosophers and writers in general to compose a corpus of literature in various Indian and global languages in the subsequent period.

NOTES

1. Sir Charles Eliot, *Hinduism and Buddhism*, Vol. 1, p. 237.
2. It was only the goal that differentiated the Buddhist *Bhikkhus* from the *Rshis, Sannyasis, Yatis* and others. The objective of the latter had been to acquire knowledge for them. The Buddhist *Bhikkus* in later times possessed almost similar characteristics when resided in the monasteries and busied themselves with their studies, instead of wandering from place to place.
3. *The Cultural Heritage of India*, Ramakrishna Mission Edition, Calcutta, Vol. I, p. 587.
4. *Mahāvagga*, II, pp. 1-2.
5. *Ibid.*, III. 1.
6. *Ibid.*, The followers of the Titthiya school criticized the Buddhist *Bhikkhus* for wandering even in the monsoon, crushing the green herbs and destroying vegetable and many other small lives. The matter was reported to the Buddha who since then, prescribed that the *Bhikkhus* should enter the *Vassa.*
7. *Mahāvagga*, III, 1fn.
8. *Cullavagga*, VI, pp. 1-2.
9. *Ibid.*
10. *Mahāvagga*, 1.30; III.5, also speaks of these five types of residence (*pañchalenani*).
11. *Cullavagga*, VI.14.1.
12. Fergusson, *The Rock Cut Temples of India* (1964), Introduction, pp. XX-XXI.
13. *Cullavagga*, VI.3.5.6.
14. *Ibid.*, 4.10.
15. *Ibid.*, VI 3.8.
16. *Ibid.*, VI, pp. 1-5.
17. Fa-hien, *A Record of Buddhist Kingdoms*, translated by James Legge, p. 14.
18. I-tsing, *A Record of the Buddhist Religion*, translated by J. Takakusu, pp. 95-107.
19. The *Mahaparinirbana Suttanta*, VI, 3, states that before his expiry at Kushinara, the Buddha had given permission to the monks to dispense, if they liked, with the "minor and very minor precepts".
20. E.J. Thomas, *History of Buddhist Thought*, p.14; I.B. Horner, *Sacred Book of the Buddhist*, Vol. X, part-1, p. XV.

10

Buddhism and Oriya Literature

Bijayananda Kar

I

Buddhist religion, philosophy and culture have great influence on the psyche of Oriyas since centuries. As per the Buddhist sources like the *Mahāvagga* of the *Vinaya Piṭaka*, the two Oriya (Oḍiyā) merchants, Tapassu and Bhallika were made the first two disciples of Lord Buddha near Rajgṛha (Rajgir). Kalinga features extensively both in *Jātaka* and the early Pali texts. After the great Kalinga war (261 BC), Ashoka became *dharmāśoka*, embraced Buddhism in Kalinga and accepted *Dharmarakṣita* as his religious advisor. There were good cultural contacts between Orissa and Ceylon since long, as found evident from the Ceylonese sources like *Dāthāvaṇśa* composed by the poet Dharmakīrti in AD 300. During Ashoka's time, his youngest brother, Tissā remained in Kalinga and dedicated himself for the spread of Theravāda Buddhism in that region.

In order to popularize Bauddha dharma and *darśana*, the Sarvāstivādins developed the doctrine of the *Pāramitās*, which strongly were taken into the very life of a Bodhisattva. Those were greatly respected and were considered as the great source of spiritualization. It is in the *Lalitavistāra* (an important text of the Sarvāstivāda), that there is the mention of six *Pāramitās*: *Dānapāramitā*, *Śilā-Pāramitā*, *Kṣānti-Pāramitā*, *Vinaya-Pāramitā*, *Dhyāna-pāramitā* and *Prajñā-Pāramitā*. It is evident that while the first five mostly deal with moral code and conduct to be followed in general human living, the last one deals with the abstract philosophical *tattva* like *dharma-śūnyatā*. The developed literature, *Prajñā-Pāramitā* was accepted with great zeal by the Mahāyānists. The historians say that the *Aṣṭasāna Prajñā-Pāramitā* is the earliest *Prajñā-pāramitā* literature.[1] On the basis of the *Gaṇḍavyāha* (a work of the AD 300), and the *Lankāvatāra* sources, reputed scholar, N. Dutta holds that Kalinga/Tosali is the place of earliest rise of Mahāyanism (Foreword to *Buddhism in Orissa*). It is

Luipā (AD 669), according to *Pag Sam Jon Zang* source,[16] was from a fisherman's family in Uḍḍiyāna (somewhere near River Prāci). Apart from some of his treatises in Sanskrit language (*Vajra Sattva Sādhana*, and *Buddhodaya*) he is credited also with some treatises in Oriya (like *Tattva Svabhāvadṛṣṭi Dohākośogītikā* and *Luipādagītikā*).[17]

The Tantrayāna, with its esoteric rituals and practices, introduced theism into Buddhism. It was advanced that the Supreme Lord is the Ādi-Buddha. It was further speculated that Ādi-Dharma/Ādi-Prajñā forms a part of Ādi-Buddha and thus constitutes the basis for the whole universe. It is from Ādi-Buddha, five Dhyāni-Buddhas emanate and each Dhyāni-Buddha is to create a Boddhisattva. According to another version, each Dhyāni-Buddha is attached with *Śakti*. Thus, the Dhyāni-Buddha and the *Śakti* together bring forth number of Boddhisattvas for the purpose of both creation and maintenance of the universe. The five Dhyāni-Buddhas are Vairocana, Ratnasambhava, Amitābha, Amoghasiddhi and Aksobhya.

III

The Oriya Vaiṣṇavism which is usually known as propagating *jñāna-miśrā-bhakti* (devotion blended with knowledge), is found to have been propagated mainly by five great Vaiṣṇavites: Achyat ānanda Dāsa, Ananta Dāsa, Balarāma Dāsa, Jagannātha Dāsa and Yaśavanta Dāsa. All these thinkers, despite their allegiance to Vaiṣṇava faith, have been found as remarkably close to Buddhism, specially its doctrine of *Śūnyatā.* Achyatānanda in his *Śūnya-saṁhitā* maintains that *Śūnya* is nothing but Brahman itself (*Brahma-Śūnya*) and the concept of Kṛṣṇa or Rādhā is to be realised as not different or distinct from *Śūnya-Brahma.*[18] Balarām, in his *Brahmāṇḍa Bhūgola,*[19] holds that originally everything was *Śūnya* and the *Śūnya-puruṣa* or Brahman had a desire to create out of Himself, there was the emergence of one *bindu* which subsequently was divided into three parts and then there was the creation of Brahmā, Viṣṇu and Maheśwara. Yaśavanta, similarly in his *Prema bhakti Brahmagītā*[20] refers to the concept of *Śūnya* and mentions four kinds of *Śūnya.* Jagannātha, though has not discussed about *Śūnya* in detail, has referred to the Lord Buddha with clear sense of adoration. He holds that Lord Jagannātha has appeared in the world as Buddha to establish the *nirguṇa-tattva.*[21] All this reveals that Bauddha dharma has never been felt as antagonistic to the age-old Vedic concept of Brahman or *Paramapuruṣa.* Attempt has been made to assimilate Bauddha dharma and *darśana*. The Vedic gods and goddesses are found to have been incorporated in the Buddhistic faith and practices, especially in different forms of Tantrayāna. The Oriya literature, during that period, is found to have accepted the reconciliatory move and it popularizes this trend among the masses by means of composing devotional treatises consisting of *bhajanas, jaṇāṇas* and *gīti-kāvyas*.

One of the important formulations of Tantrayāna is Sahajayāna. While in Vijrayāna, *Śūnyatā* is identified with *Vajra*[22] and *Kālacakra-yāna* is found to have given special emphasis on esoteric practices (*Gupta Sādhanās*) and holds that creation is possible due to the co-operation and union between Kāli and Buddha, Sahajayāna is mainly found to have been propounded by Laksmīkarā, the sister of Indrabhūti. She has the support from Jalandharipāda and his disciples Virupācārya and Kṛṣṇacārya/Kāhṇupāda. All these Sahajayānists hold that the whole universe (*Brahmāṇḍa*) is within the body (*Piṇḍa/ Śarīra*). As such, great importance is given to human body, for it is viewed as the microcosm of the whole universe. That body is the abode of all gods has been clearly indicated by Sāraladāsa in his *Mahābhārata*.[23] Balarāma Dāsa similarly has held that *Brahmāṇḍa* is revealed in all *Piṇḍas*.[24] According to Yāśovanta, both *Piṇḍa* and *Brahmāṇḍa* are essentially one and the same.[25] Similar is the view expressed by Achyutānanda Dāsa.[26]

The Buddhist Sahajayānists have given emphasis on the culture of body (*Kāyā-Sādhanā*) through a peculiar esoteric process (*haṭha-yoga*). According to this yogic practice, the *Sahaja* nature of supreme bliss is realisable through the union of two main side nerves near the spinal cord *Iḍā* (left side) and *Pingālā* (right side) by means of the middle nerve (*Suṣumnā*). In the *Sāralā Mahābhārata* and also in the Oriya Vaiṣṇavite literature, there are found to be a number of references about the *Kāya Sadhana* by the adoption of different poetic imageries and comparisons. In the *Sāralā Mahābhārata*, culture of the body is said to have been explained by the goddess *Kāmākṣā* to Bhīma and Arjuna.[27] Achyatānanda Dāsa compares *Iḍā* as *Candra* (moon) and *Pingala* as Sūrya (Sun).[28] It is further described that the meeting place of the three nerves *Iḍā, Pingalā,* and *Susumnā* is *trikuṭa* or *triveṇi*. Achyatānanda Dasa has taken up the *Sahaja* and he has moved to the extent of advising Rama's disciple to practise *Sahaja-Sādhana*.[29]

Tantric Buddhism, in Orissa, has not only adored the general theistic temper but it is also interesting to note that gradually it has assimilated within its fold the strongly rooted religious cult of Jagannātha. Jagannātha at Puri is never found to have been identified with any particular Vedic/Purāṇic god/goddess. Different Vedāntacāryas who visited Puri have read their own meanings so far as the image of Jagannātha is concerned. It is an image without any definite shape or size of any being. It is the symbol *of nirākāra nirguṇa parā* Brahman of the Upanishads and, in the same way, it is also the symbol of indeterminable *Śūnya* to which no categories (*Koṭi*) can be applied. That is how the Vaiṣṇavites, the *nirguṇa* Advaitins, theistic Viśiṣṭādvaitins and others have found no hesitance in adoring the deity. Both theistic and transtheistic convictions are somehow found to have been integrated here because of the unique point of confluence. Both the Mahāyānists and the Tantrayānists have found no difficulty in such attempt of synthesis and therefore, have come forward not only in accepting the deification of the Buddha but also the corollary suggestions like reincarnation of the Lord at the hour of need. The Buddha is accepted as the ninth *avatāra* (incarnation) of the Lord by Jayadeva, the famous poet of Orissa, AD 1200. Indrabhūti, the famous Vajrayānist of AD 800 has prayed to Jagannātha in the very first verse of his famous treatise *Jñānasiddhi*[30] besides referring to his name on many occasions in the entire text. It is said that *Buddha, Dharma* and *Saṁgha*—the three jewels of Buddhism—are represented in the Jagannātha cult which is the trinity of Balarāma, Jagannātha, and Subhadrā (one female in between two males, i.e. said to be the symbolic presentations of *Prajñā, Upāya* and *Saṁsāra* of the Buddhistic fold.[31] Sāralā Dasa has held that Jagannātha, the Lord of the universe has been reincarnated as the Buddha to destroy the evil and to establish the good.[32]

It is worth noting that when one particular set of socio-moral rules and conduct is emphasised beyond its normal limit and is too much stressed upon, there is the gradual rise of discontentment against such radicalism and an opposite move is introduced and it gets the popular support. In the name of imparting discipline in social order and dhārmic set-up, when a lot of emphasis is laid upon rites and rituals and consequently the human noble element is scarified by the introduction of violent procedure like *Vali Prathā*, the reaction of both Jaina and Buddha is quite relevant. So also, in the name of attaining absolute cessation of suffering and attaining absolute bliss, while there is the prescription for total dejection of the worldly living with all its minimum comfort and peace, there is the obvious reaction from the other side. And, for that, there is the natural support from the mass. The early Buddhist emphasis on *anātmvāda* and complete *niḥsvabhāvatā* do not appeal to the common man; because of his/her expectation to prolong further gets frustrated. So the idea of permanency (*nityatva*) is favoured more.

Further, the theistic outlook which is deeply rooted in human psyche on account of man's feeling of wonder and helplessness cannot easily accommodate the abstract doctrine of non-theism, non-creationism, whatever, rational profundity it may have. Thus, the early Buddhist emphasis on pragmatism (in the worldly sense) has not satisfied the imaginative urge based on some form of optimism. Too much discipline and celibacy have not been tolerated and there then the easy path (*Sahaja Mārga*) has been introduced even in Buddhism that initially is well-known to have been against any sort of deviation of socio-moral lapse. The idea of *ātma-śuddhi* (self purification) in the form of avoidance of bodily comfort has been rejected and *Kāyā-Sādhanā* (as hinted before) has been introduced. Absolute bliss is thought to be accomplished not by the rejection of *Śarīra* but by full care of it. In that way esoteric sexual practices are found to have been acclaimed in *dhārmic-sādhanā.* Laxmikarā, for instance, has held that any kind of self-torture in the name of self-purification is not needed; no worship of supernatural god or goddess is necessary and the image-worship is based on blind faith. All that is needed is to take care of the body where all gods reside and to desire maximum pleasure (*Mahāsukha*) from it through all kinds of sensual pleasures.[33] Even Kālacakrayānists move ahead in those direction to declare that sacrifice of animal at the sacred fireplace is not unsocial and pernicious if it brings the fulfilment of Tantra-Yogic excellence.

The impact of such Buddhist tāntric rites, rituals and practices are noticed in the writings of literary figures of the then Orissa. They have introduced such ideas in their poetic works with the motive of preserving the socio-religious excellence. *Parakīyaprīti* (extra-marital relation) has been encouraged in the name of Divine love between Rādhā and Kṛṣṇa by Jayadeva. The futility of image worship has been held by the Vaiṣṇava poets like Dvārikā Dāsa[34] and the Mahimā poet like Bhīma Bhoc.[35]

In the modern Oriya literature, there is noticeable reference to

Bauddha dharma, darśana and Sanskṛti. One of the pioneers of modern Oriya literature, Fakir Mohan Senapati has composed the kāvya, *Buddhāvatāra.* Padma Charan Pattanayak, in his poem *Dhauli Pāhāda* has offered an imaginative heartfelt account of Ashoka's change of mind at Dhauli Pāhāḍa where the great Kalinga war was fought. Surendra Mohanty in his popular song "Sārīputta" has dealt with the Buddhist view of life. He has ended the story with a life-affirming note. The present writer has written some essays on the Buddhist concepts of *karma* and *anātma.*[36] Dr. N.K. Sahu has written an informative and scholarly book on Buddhism.[37] There is one compilation of scholarly essays by fifteen noted writers, belonging to diverse fields of enquiry, which have dealt with Buddhist religion and culture in Orissa.[38]

But one thing is notable in this connection. Though there is strong influence of Buddhistic metaphysical speculations concerning *Śūnyatā,* deification of Lord Buddha along with its theistic diversifications, some fundamental ideas of Buddha tantrayāna, the degenerated tendencies noticed in some Tāntric beliefs and practices like too much emphasis on sex-based yogic practices which are definitely unethical and unsocial are intelligently rather avoided. Only those ideas and concepts which are human and socially relevant, are taken up and are properly utilized in the literary sources to impart a meaningful message to the common mass. The critical look against pernicious prejudice regarding caste-rigidity, the support for the theistic spirit being kept intact without the background of image-worship, the avoidance of all sorts of yājic sacrifices like animals and men are some of the notable steps which are found to have been well focussed in the Oriya literature. And, in that way, the Oriya literature, in general, has worked well towards socio-moral stabilization.

NOTES

1. N.K. Sahu, *Buddhism in Orissa,* Utkal University Publication, p. 68.
2. According to Hieun Tsang, Nāgārjuna's monastery is called Po-lo-mo-lo-ki-li which is identified as parimalagiri by the historian, N.K. Sahu, *op. cit.*
3. Vide Bhupendranath Dutta, *Mystic Tales of Lāmā Tāranāth,* Calcutta, 1941, p. 49.
4. Vide S.K. Chatterjee, "Arta Ballava Mohanty Memorial Lectures" (1st series, 1964), p. 30, Dr. K. Kar's *Āścarya Caryācaya on the Caryāgītis* published by the Orissa Sahitya Academy, Bhubaneshwar. In *Caryāgītikās,* there is found to be a special style and form of presenting ideas

(*Sandhyābhāsā* or as B. Battacharya says, twilight language) signifying dual meaningone pointing to surface (light) and the other to deeper (dark) meanings. Such language resembles to a great extent language of Oriya (Oḍiya). Vide, for instance, *gītikā*, attributed to Kāhnupā *Māria Sāsunaṇadahare śālī māmāria kāhmu bhagila kabālī,* "māria sāsu naṇada ghare śali māā māria Kāhnu bhaila Kabālī." Its outer meaning is: Kāhnu became a *yogi* by killing mother-in-law, his sister, wife's younger sister and mother in home; and its deeper meaning is: Kahnu became a *yogi* by renouncing all sorts of craving for pleasurable sensations and passions, caused due to ignorance and falsity. Quoted by Dr. S.C. Rath, "Oriya Sahityare Bauddha dharma" in *Odiśāra Bauddhadharma O. Sanskrti* (ed. B. Panda) Bhubaneshwar, 2000, p. 156.

5. Commentary of Munidatta on *Caryāgīti,* 50.
6. His *Śānya Samhītā* (in Oriya), Cuttack, 1955.
7. His *Virātogītā* (in Oriya), Cuttack, 1976.
8. His *Prema Bhaktigītā* (in Oriya), Cuttack, Praici Series, No. XVII.
9. *Viṣṇugarbha Purāṇa* (in Oriya), Praci Series, No. XII.
10. His *Brahmanirūpaṇagītā* (in Oriya), Pracī Series, No. IV, Cuttack, 1935.
11. *Tāranatha's History of Buddhism of India,* by Lāmā Chimpā and Aloka Chattopadhyaya (Ed. D. Chattopadhyaya), Shimla, 1970, p. 8. Saraha was also known as Śaroha, Sakahapāds, Rāhulabhadra.
12. Ed. Rahul Samkrtyāyana, Bihar Rastrabhasa Parishad, Patna, 1957.
13. *Kurukullā* is known from Tibetan source as a goddess of Uḍḍiyāna.
14. S.N. Moharana, *Tāntric Buddhism,* Delhi: Aryan Books International, 2001, p. 165.
15. *Ibid.*
16. *Pag Sam Jan Zang,* Index, p. CXV.
17. Dr. Bhagavan Panda (ed.), "Bauddha Tantra" (in Oriya) in *Oḍiśāra Bauddha Dharma O Sanskrti,* Kedarnath Gavesana Pratisthana, Grantha Mandir, Cuttack, 2000, p. 66.
18. Vide his *Śūnya Saṁhitā* (in Oriya), 7th chapter, Cuttack, 1955.
19. *Brahmāṇḍa Bhūgola* (in Oriya), Cuttack, 1976.
20. *Premabhakti Bhahmagītā* (in Oriya), Praci Sries, XVII.
21. Vide his *Bhāgavata* (in Oriya), Skandha-V.
22. Vide "*Śūnyatām Vajramucyate*"-*Adyaya Vajra Saṁgraha* compiled by MM. Pt. Haraprasad Shastri, Baroda, Oriental Institute, 1927, p. 37.
23. Vide *Ādiparva of Sāralā Mahābhārata.*
24. *Brahmāṇde Sarvaghaṭa thāi,* Brahmāṇda Bhūgola, *op. cit.,* Ch. XXXI, p. 51.
25. Vide his *Ksitisuddhā* (in Oriya), Cuttack, 1935, p. 11.
26. Vide his *Garudagītā,* Chapter-I, Cuttack.
27. *Op. cit.,* Chapter-I (*Sabhāparva).*
28. Vide his *Brahmaśānkuli O Aṇākāra Saṁhitā* (in Oriya), *Kalpa* (III), Praci series, no. VI, Utkal University Pub., 1970, p. 6.

29. Vide his *Brahmaśānkuli O Aṇākara Saṁhila*, Kalpa X, *op. cit.*, p. 26.
"*Sahaja ātmāra Śādhanā*
Rāma e bhāve Sādhakinā"
30. *Pranipatya Jagannātham Sarvajinavarā ccitam Sarva Buddhamayam Siddhi Vyā pinam gajanopaman*—Jñānasiddhi.
31. Vide S.B. Dasgupta, *Obscure Religious Cults*, Calcutta, 1976.
32. His *Mahābhārata, Madhya Parva, op. cit*, p. 296.
33. B. Bhattacharya, *An Introduction to Buddhist sotericism*, Varanasi, 1964.
34. Vide his *Paracegītā* (in Oriya), Chapter-X, Praci Series, no. XV.
35. Vide his *Stuti Cintāmaṇi* (in Oriya), Praci Series, no. III, Utkal University Edition, 1961.
36. Vide his book, *Bauddhikea Saṅkaṭa*, Cuttack, Santosh Publications, 1992.
37. Vide his *Oḍisāre Bauddhadharma*, 2nd edn. Bhubaneshwar, 1980.
38. *Oḍiśāre Buddhadharma O Sanskrit* compiled by Dr. Bhagavan Panda, Cuttack, Grantha Mandir, 2000.

11

Impact of Buddhism on Oriya Fiction

Manoranjan Pradhan

Like many other states of India, Orissa also has been an ancient seat of Buddhism. For propagation of Buddhism many institutions and inscriptions were set up in the 2nd and 3rd centuries BC. The impact of Buddhism on the public life of Orissa can be easily traced from the Buddhist *Pitaka* and *Jatakas.* Many litterateurs have propagated Buddhism through literature. From the very ancient period the impact of Buddhism on the heritage and culture of Orissa has been determined by eminent scholars. The Oriya fiction deserves a special study for the very conspicuous impact of Buddhism.

The impact of Buddhism is very clear on Oriya literature from the early period. The evolution of Buddhist religion and philosophy can be noted from the 11th century. The literature of the 16th century was mainly ornamental and the Buddha was transformed into Jagannath in this period. So we can see many poetic works are based on *Vaishnava* religion in which Lord Jagannath has been worshipped as Radhakrishna. Consequently, the importance of the Buddha was diminished. But the glory of Buddhism reoccurred again in all the forms of modern Oriya literature.

It is found that the philosophy and message of the Buddha find direct expression in modern Oriya poetry. Whereas in drama these are presented symbolically. But modern Oriya fiction is replete with Lord Buddha, Buddhism and his philosophy. In certain cases the authors do not hesitate to depict its dark side also. The philosophy of Buddhism is presented in plot, characters, style and point of view. Perhaps it has been convenient to present the philosophy and teachings of the Buddha with the authors' interpretations in fiction where the story serves as its supporting background.

The renowned novelist Kalindi Charan Panigrahi (1901-1991) propagates the philosophy of Buddhism in his novel *Amarachita*[1] through the hero Subhakanta who also leaves his palace and kingdom as Buddhadev himself. Discarding the luxurious life he advocates for justice and truth. He believes in *Karma* (deeds) and rebirth and has strong conviction that the ultimate end of religion is *Nirvana.* He realizes that the world is full of sorrows and desires. In this way he accepts the paths preached by the Buddha. But in this fiction Subhakanta is the only character that has been partly influenced by Buddhism. No other characters, aspects or plot has been so influenced.

Abhimatara Abhisara [2] (The love tryst of Abhimata) is a successful story by the eminent novelist Surendra Mohanty (1920-1991) which is based on Buddhism. The author has emphasized on the futility of salvation and has emphasized through the leading character Upa that persons devoting their life to human service will get rebirth. Upa is a great follower of Buddhist philosophy, still he says, "You are wrong Kisa, if life is full of delusion then *Nirvana* is only an imagination. So I am in favour of rebirth." Here we find a different picture of *Nirvana* and rebirth.

Two opposite concepts of Buddhism are presented in two different stories—*Sariputta*[3] and *Ambapalli*[4] of Surendra Mohanty. In the story *Sariputta,* the love of the mother for his son Sariputta and in *Ambapalli* the eagerness of the heroine to be a mother has been portrayed with an intellectual as well as emotional fervour. Rupasree, the mother of Sariputta, does not want her son to be a Buddhist Shramana, because she wants to live as a worldly human being with family bondage, pleasure, worries, love and affection. On the other hand, Ambapalli wants to preach Buddhism to her son. The story *Madhumatara Ratri* [5] (The Night of Madhumata) combines worldly pleasure with renunciation. The Buddhist thought and theory have been propagated through Upaka, the main character of the story, but it deviates a little from Buddhism. Nilottapal and Madhumata accept the family bondage and worldly pleasure, which is upheld by the Ajivika sect not Buddhism. Though the characters are from the Buddhist texts, the writer values worldly life more than salvation. So the tone of the stories contradicts Buddhist philosophy. The presentation style, rich language and poetic appeal are unique.

Gautama Buddha had established Buddhism on moral ground. In fact, its foundation was laid on cessation. Human being will be animalized if they thoroughly follow the path of worldly life. Therefore, Buddhadev had formulated ten rules of moralities (*Dasa-sila*) for his followers, the Shramanas and Shramanies. But these ten rules of moralities were not based on religious or spiritual virtues.

These were only to be practiced in their normal day-to-day life. In course of time, the ten rules of moralities were modified slightly which created a conflict between old and new followers of Buddhism. When the restless, insatiated Buddha alone was wandering in search of knowledge, he had spent some time with the Ajivak sect of Makhahali Gosala.[6] But the restraintless undisciplined life of the Ajivak sect having idleness and fatalist mentality could not attract Buddhadev for long. For which Buddhadev quit the Ajivak sect and went alone in search of knowledge again. Therefore, the Ajivaks not only went against Buddhism but also did not hesitate to portray the Buddha as an immoral person. The Ajivaks were against Buddhism, his ten moralities and cessational way of life. They believed that Buddhist institutions would be ruined within a century of the Buddha's death because his idealism was misconstructed on cessation. According to the author there is nothing to be astonished that the fall of Buddhism created feeling of happiness among the Ajivaks. The central theme of the novel *Ajivakar Attahas*[7] (The roaring laughter of Ajivaks) depicts immense change in Buddhism with attractions for world pleasure and lust, after the Buddha's death. The novelist Surendra Mohanty actually was in favour of the ideology of Buddhism but has stressed its change and downfall in his unique pieces of fictions.

Basabadatta[8] (1967) is a collection of short stories comprising twelve stories by Surendra Satapathy. All the aspects of Buddhism such as emphasis on salvation, non-violence, pity towards the animal world are the themes of the stories. Buddhism became very popular within a short period due to its humanitarian outlook. Without any discrimination of caste, sex and religion it embraced all sections of people. Ambapalli, the prostitute, Prakruti, belonging to the lowest caste of the society, Bimbisara and Prasenjit, the two emperors, and Angulimala, the robber, each and every character is endowed with the tender and compassionate touch of the Buddha. They became devotees of the Buddha and followed the way of cessation and salvation. Buddhadev says one becomes noble by deeds and not by birth. His ideology and thought were against the racial customs of that period. This thought finds reflection in the story *Patitara Priyatama* (The beloved of the prostitute). In another story a Shramana called Ananda drank water from a lower caste woman emancipating her from mental slavery which she was suffering from. These ideologies and sayings of the Buddha had influenced his disciples immensely. This was somewhat like a social revolution which could give social justice to the deprived community. We get many examples of such socially-deprived persons becoming Buddhists. Like the barber Upali, many of them could occupy very high positions in the Buddhist organization. Ambapalli, the prostitute of Vaishali, Padmabati of Ujjain, Basabadatta, the city-dancer of Mathura, Prakruti, the lower-caste woman, Angulimala, the ferocious dacoit, could get the supernatural touch of *Nirvana.* This universality was a remarkable magnanimity of Buddhism. The stories like *Ambapalli, Basabadatta, Patitar Priyatama,* etc. are based on this ideology. The greatest teaching of the Buddha was to destroy one's desire and to remain away from worldly pleasure and lust. But the story *Sei Duiti Akhi* (That pair of eyes) asserts that it is too difficult to keep oneself aloof from worldly attachment and desires. Buddhadev realized the truth that desire is the cause of sorrow and sufferings. The story *Gopa O Bhikkhu* (Gopa and ascetic) is based on this philosophy, and gives a pathetic picture of a compassionate mother. Many of the stories glorify Buddhism whereas stories like *Astaraga* (The glamour of sunset), *Sramanara Chitanala* (The pyre of an ascetic) present the causes of degradation of Buddhism. In this collection *Bana Mallira Itihas* (The history of wild jasmine), *Prayaschita* (The penance), *Jayasankha* (The conch sound of victory) and *Dantapurara Itihas* (The history of Dantapura) portray affection, kindness, humility, honesty and forgiveness upheld by Buddhism.

Chandra O Champa[9] (1968) (The moon and champak flower) is an imaginary novel based on the dark history of Buddhist period. The author has written this novel with the help of historical data and superb imaginative power. Buddhists had accepted some principles of Brahmanism at the time of their decline. It happened within the 5th century. But the novelist Bamacharan Mitra (1915-1975) puts the incident after the 5th century, which is a historical error. Binita, a character of the novel, tries to bring into practice the idol worship and woman worship. She introduced transgression and adultery in Buddhism for the purpose of spread and propaganda.

Chandra O Champa represents Buddhist and Brahmanic religion. Chandragupta Maurya, Helen, the Greek beauty and Bimbisara are most famous and memorable characters of history. The author could not neglect them as they were Buddhists. As there is no historical truth behind this theme, the author has highlighted the vain glory of religious persons. Instead of human values the religious sentiment has been emphasized in this novel. *Salabati*[10] (1977) by Basanta Kumar Samal is a romantic novel as *Amrapalli.* But the romance presents a historical fact and glorifies Buddhadev. It has two parts. The first part presents the romance of Bimbisara and Salabati and the other part the philosophy of stoicism and sanctimonious life of the Buddha. The story is based on the sorrowful life of Salabati, the matchless beauty and courtesan dancer. The aim of this novel is not to describe the romantic love affair between Salabati and Bimbisara. The intention of the author is to establish the impermanence of worldly existence. Therefore, the first part of the novel is based on the romantic life of Salabati and it ends with the destruction of desire on the realization of *Nirvanatatwa.*

Bimbisara is a symbol of worldly life whereas Buddhadev is the wide horizon of detachment and sacrifice. Both the paths, enjoyment with Bimbisara and renunciation with the Buddha were open to her. She conquered the bondage of illusion and the allurement of the materialistic world and became a Buddhist.

This novel presents the then political, social and religious picture of Buddhism in India. The author's aim is to free each and every person from all kinds of bondage and to establish a true human civilization. The novel repeats again the eternal message of the Buddha that desire is the sole cause of sorrow and sufferings.

The novel *Buddham Saranam Gachhami*[11] was written in 1983 by Santilata Mohapatra. The pitiable life of the helpless prostitute and the devotee Amrapalli are still now in the memory of public. Mohapatra has applied her imagination for a little change in the plot to strengthen its inner significance. But she is very conscious of the history. All the historical characters like Bimbisara, Ahikanta, Umananda as well as the Buddha and his disciples' activities as well as characters are sketched from historical point of view.

Amrapalli, the paragon of beauty of Vaishali, became a prostitute according to customs but her soul was holy and pure. The Buddha accepted her hospitality and convinced the people of Vaishali about her repentance and purity of her soul. Buddha told them that if man commits any sin in ignorance and repents for it then no other expiation can equal this. Buddhadev accepted Amrapalli as his disciple at her request and the prostitute became the famous first woman disciple (Bhikkuni) and sang with joy *Buddham Saranam Gachhami.* According to some historians acceptance of Amrapalli in Bauddhasangha was one of the main reasons behind the downfall of Buddhism. However, from this, one can see Buddhadev's sympathy for the deprived class of the society.

Karuvaki [12] (1992) by Brajamohan Mohanty is a novel based on historical events following the Kalinga war. It also includes and allows play of imagination. As tradition goes, being bewitched by the beauty of Karuvaki, the queen of Kalinga, the conqueror Ashoka tried to win her. But Karuvaki offered him a condition that Ashoka must be initiated to the Buddha and try for its propagation. In this way it was Karuvaki who turned Ashoka into a Buddhist. Though many historians do not accept this as a historical fact, still they have not completely avoided it. Obviously, when history is silent this legend supplies an interesting explanation to Ashoka's miraculous change. The great historian of Orissa, Harekrushna Mahatab treats this as a historical fact. According to him, "There is an interesting tradition prevalent among the fishermen community of the coastal regions of Orissa, regarding the conquest of Kalinga by Ashoka. This tradition is so popular that it has led the Telegu scholars to write literature in the past. The tradition runs that Karuvaki was the princess of the fishermen community and she was famous for her beauty and valour. Moved with her beauty and valour, the Kalinga prince at last married her and made his queen. Name and fame of Karuvaki spread far and wide and at last it tempted Ashoka who invaded Kalinga at the instigation of his minister Radhagupta. In his Kalinga war the king of Kalinga and the prince were all defeated. Karuvaki fought against Ashoka in this battle and was taken away forcibly to Magadha by Ashoka after her defeat. At Magadha, Karuvaki was persuaded by Nyagrodh and Upagupta to marry Ashoka, but she refused to accept the proposal unless Ashoka was converted to Buddhism. After this event Ashoka accepted Buddhism and married Karuvaki. Thereafter she requested Ashoka to sculpture in the Ranigumpha cave and Udayagiri hill near Bhubaneshwar, the events depicting her fight with Ashoka and how she was carried away to Magadha.

The sculpture in relief on the wall of Ranigumpha in Udayagiri hill near Bhubaneshwar appears to have some congruity with the above legend. But the real historical truth of the scene has not yet been determined to warrant universal acceptance. From epigraphical source it is known that Ashoka had a queen whose name was Karuvaki. She was the second queen of Ashoka and she had a son named Tuvara. In the Buddhist literature description relating to the achievements of Ashoka do not mention the above tradition and the name of Karuvaki. In support of the above legend no direct evidence has yet been available except some facts that indirectly lead to accept the above as plausible with much probability. There is a fisherman caste in the name of Karuvaki still existing in the coastal region of Orissa. They now maintain a tradition that Ashoka renamed Kalinga as 'Cheti'. All these traditions are very interesting though they appear incongruous from the standpoint of historical study."[13] The novel *Karuvaki* has very sincerely followed the above legend especially in characterization of the heroine.

From the above discussion it is evident that Oriya fiction based on Buddhism and Buddha's life is quite rich. Some authors like Surendra Mohanty have composed a good number of stories on the subject with considerable success. The stories by other writers are also quite popular. Certainly the interesting stories of the Buddha and his associates have attracted attention of these authors. They also might have considered particularly getting rid of desire—the message of the Buddha—as a suitable theme in this present society deep drunk with desire and lust. Some short stories on Buddhist themes have been popular in view of the superb style of the authors. Surendra Mohanty is a bright example of it. While presenting Buddhist anecdotes he succeeds in creating the atmosphere of that age by using Buddhist terms, and recreations of the life of the Buddhist *sanghas* by his powerful imaginative skill. The story of Karuvaki is supposed to have a special appeal for the writers as well as the readers of Orissa. On the whole the Buddhist literature, especially in the form of fiction in Orissa, provides ample material for scholars to study.

NOTES

1. Panigrahi, Kalindi Charan, *Amarachita,* 1933.
2. Mohanty, Surendra, *Kabi Ō Nartaki,* 1975.
3. *Ibid.*
4. *Ibid.*
5. *Ibid.*
6. Buddha-Bhasita Saman Phala-Sutta.
7. Mohanty, Surendra, *Ajivakar Attahas,* 1987.
8. Satapathy, Surendra, *Basabadatta,* 1967.
9. Mitra, Bamacharan, *Chandra Ō Champa,* 1968.
10. Samal, Basanta Kumar, *Salabati,* 1977.
11. Mohapatra, Santilata, *Buddham Saranam Gachhami,* 1983.
12. Mohanty, Brajamohan: *Karuvaki,* 1991.
13. Mahatab, Harekrushna, *History of Orissa,* Vol. I, 1959.

12

Buddhism as Reflected in Early Tamil̲ Literature

C. Muthiah

The first three centuries of the Christian era of the Tamil̲ country is sometimes called the *Caṅkam* age, because it is believed that the *Caṅkam* poems were composed during this period. Besides, the Tamil̲ Academy, which is called by the popular name *Caṅkam*, also flourished during this period.

The *Caṅkam* literature can be treated as an authentic literary representation of the culture of the Tamil̲s of that epoch. The *Caṅkam* literary works, which are broadly assignable to the period between *c.*200 BC and *c.*300 AD, are found classified in the form of two anthologies, viz., the *Eṭṭutokai* (eight anthology) and the *Pattupāṭṭu* (ten poems). The *Eṭṭutokai* works are: 1. *Nar̲r̲iṇai* 2. *Kur̲untokai* 3. *Aiṅkur̲unūr̲u* 4. *Patir̲r̲upattu* 5. *Paripāṭal* 6. *Kalittokai* 7. *Akanānūr̲u* 8. *Pur̲anānūr̲u.* The *pattupāṭṭu* works are: 1. *Tirumuru-kār̲r̲upaṭai* 2. *Porunarar̲r̲r̲upaṭai* 3. *Cirupāṇār̲r̲uppaṭai* 4. *Perumpāṇār̲-r̲uppaṭai* 5. *Mullaippāṭṭu* 6. *Maturaikkānci* 7. *Neṭunalvāṭai.* 8. *Kur̲incippāṭṭu* 9. *Paṭṭinappālai* 10. *Malaippaṭukatām.* Together they contain a total number of 2381 poems, of them 102 are anonymous and the rest have been composed by 473 poets. Tolkāppiyam—the grammatical treatise—is also considered to have belonged to this period. The *Caṅkam* poems furnish us with several evidences for the reconstruction of the history of early Buddhism in the Tamil̲ country.

We shall now proceed to examine what information is available from the classical Tamil̲ works of this period regarding the position of Buddhism in the Tamil̲ country. The classical works *Eṭṭutokai* and the *Pattupāṭṭu* do not contain any direct reference to the religion of the Buddha, but certain terms occurring in the poems lead us to believe that Buddhism had secured a firm place in the society of the Tamil̲s and that it had begun to influence the activities and behaviour of the people.

The term *Caṅkam* itself is an important word from the Buddhistic point of view. It might have been derived from the Buddhist term *Saṃgha*, i.e. one of the three jewels (*triratna*)—*Buddha, Dharma,* and *Saṃgha.* The word *Saṃgha* in the Buddhist tradition means the assembly of monks. *Caṅkam* is also a Sanskrit word, meaning gathering. Here it is used in the sense of the gathering of Tamil̲ men of letters, a learned assembly, as academy or even what we now understand by the term university. According to Tamil̲ tradition, there were three *Caṅkams*[1] in the Pāṇṭiya kingdom. The commentator of *Ir̲aiyanār Kaḷaviyal* is the first writer to give an elaborate account of the three *Caṅkams.* Aṭiyārkkunallār, the commentator of *Cilappatikāram* (the first Tamil̲ Epic) repeats the same tradition in his commentary on *Cilappatikāram.*[2] It may be said that the Tamil̲ *Caṅkam* is an imitation of the Buddha *Saṃgha* and there is warrant for this assumption since we know that the Buddhists had entered South India and Ceylon during the early centuries of the Christian era to which date is assigned the Tamil̲ *Caṅkam.* Hence the existence of an association of poets modelled on the Buddhist *Saṃgha* for the promotion of Tamil̲ literature can be easily explained as due to the influence of Buddhists who had by that time settled in South India and particularly in the Tamil̲ country.

There are many *Caṅkam* poets whose names are related to Buddhism in some way or other. There are names such as *Cāttan̲* and *Cāttan̲ār,* which we come across in *Akanānūr̲u,*[3] *Pur̲anān̲ūr̲u,*[4] *Nar̲r̲iṇai,*[5] and *Kur̲untokai.*[6] This is supposed to be the Tamil̲ized form of the Sanskrit word Sāsta, which is one of the attributes of the Buddha. There is a poet of the name *Iampōtiyār,* which literary means the man of the young bōdhi—the sacred tree of Buddhism. The name Pālaikkautaman̲ār, a poet of the *Caṅkam* anthology *Patir̲r̲uppattu,* means the Gautama of Pālai (theme).[7]

There is a poem in *Pur̲anān̲ūr̲u,* which according to tradition, was composed by one Pāṛtiya king of the name *Kaṭaluḷ māyinta Iamperuvaḻuti.*[8]

Uṇṭālamma ivvulakam; Intirar
Amil̲tam iyaivatāyinum, in̲iten̲at
Tamiyar uṇṭalum ilarē; mun̲ivilar;
Tuñcalum ilar, pir̲ar añcuvatu añci
Pukal̲en̲in̲ uyirum koṭukkuvar; pal̲iyen̲in̲;
Ulakuṭan̲ per̲in̲um kaḷḷalar; ayarvilar;

Aṉṉa māṭci aṉaiyarākit
Tamekkeṉa muyalā nōṉtāḷ
Piaṟkkeṉa muyalunar uṇmai yāṉē.

The poet propounds the theory that the world exists because of the existence in it of virtuous men. Their great virtues are detailed in the poem. Even if it be the embrosia of Lord Indhira, they will not eat it alone; they will share it with others. They are free from hatred. They are restless. They prosecute great works without fear. Even at the risk of their lives they achieve objects if they be praiseworthy. Even if the whole world were to be gained, they will not undertake sinful deeds. Restlessly they strive, not for selfish ends but for the good of others. Since such virtuous men live on this earth, the earth, too, exists (It will not exist otherwise). This poem speaks of the concept of Indhira Amiḻtam (Indhira Amṛta) which means the ambrosia of Indhira.[9] According to this poem, this world exists because of the honest and righteous people living in it. They are selfless and live for the sake of others. Even though the ambrosia of Lord Indhira is given to them, they would not take it for themselves; they would share it with their fellowmen. S. Vaiyāpuri Piḷḷai is of the opinion that this concept of the ambrosia of Indhira has entered into the *Caṅkam* literature either due to the influence of Buddhism or Jainism, since there is no such concept that is related to the Brahminical god Indhira. Yet, we are not able to come across this concept much in Indian Buddhism in general. It may be considered one of the distinctive concepts of South Indian Buddhism.

We see references to Buddhism in the collection called *Pattupāṭṭu.* In the *Perumpāṇāṟṟuppaṭai* there is a far-fetched reference to Buddhism.

Pulavuk kaṭaluṭulla vāṉuñ cūṭiya
Malartalai ulakattuḷḷum palar toḻa
Viḻavu mēmpaṭṭa paṭiviraṉ mūtūr

In lines 409-411, in the course of his description of the city of Kāñci, the author Kaṭiyalūr Uruttiraṉ Kaṇṇaṉār says, "that city is superior to others in its glory and in the fact that many men worship there and hold festivals in it." The reference in this passage to many men worshipping and holding festivals in Kāñci is interpreted to mean that representatives of different faiths like the Vaishnava, Shaiva, Jaina and Bauddha lived in that city as they did when Hiuen Tsang visited Kāñci in 7th century AD. Again in the *Paṭṭinappālai* by the same author there is a reference to Jaina and Bauddha monasteries. In the course of his description of Kāvērippūmpaṭṭinam, the author, after describing the sea shore, the large number of boats laden with merchandise anchored near the shore, the beautiful groves, the twin lakes, the lovely ponds and the great feeding houses refers to the "monasteries for (Buddha and Jaina) asceties".

Taṇkēṇit takai muṟṟattup
Pakeṭṭeruttiṉ palcālait
Tavappaḷḷi tāḻkāvaṉ

In lines 51-53, the exact term occurring in the text being "Tavappaḷḷi" which is generally associated with a Buddhist monastery. From this passage, it is evident that in cities like Kāvērippūmpaṭṭinam, Buddhism had attained a permanent status. This is the first time we hear in Tamiḻ literature of settlements of Buddhists and Jains in any city of the Tamiḻ country other than Kāñci. This is corroborated by the latest archaeological finds at Pukār of remains of Buddhist monasteries. Then we come to similar references to Buddhism in another poem of the same collection called the *Maturaikkāñci.*

Tiṇkatir mataṇi yoṇkuṟu mākkalai
Ompiṉart taḻēit tāmpuṇarntu muyaṅkit
Tātaṇi tāmaraip pōtupiṭit tāṅkut
Tāmum avarum ōrāṅku viḷaṅkak
Kāmar kaviṉiya pēriḷam peṇṭir
Pūviṉar pukaiyiṉar toḻuvanar paḻiccic
Ciṟantu puṟaṅ kākkuṅ kaṭavuṭ paḷḷiyum

In lines 461-467, the author Māṅkuṭi Murutaṉār refers to the Buddhist monasteries in Maturai where the Buddhist ladies accompanied by their husbands and children were offering flowers and incense for worship. From this, we are able to know clearly that there was a Buddhist Vihara in Maturai, which was worshipped by people of Buddhist faith in that city.

Vaṇṭupaṭap paḻuniya tēṉār toṟṟattup
Pūvum pukaiyum cāvakar paḻiccac
Ceṉṟa kālamum varūu mamayamum
Inṟivaṭ ṭōṉṟiya oḻukkamoṭu naṇkuṇarntu
Vāṉamu nilaṉun tāmuḻuṇarum
Cāṉṟa koḷkaic cāyā yākkai

Āṉraṭaṅ kariñar ceṟintaṉar nōṉmār
Kalpoḻin taṉṉa viṭuvāyak karaṇṭaip
Palpuric cimili nāṟṟi nalkuvarak
Kayaṅkaṇṭaṉṉa vayaṅkuṭai nakarattuc
Cempiyaṉ ṟaṉṉa ceñcuvar puṉaintu
Nōkkuvicai tavirppa mēkkuyarn tōṅki
Iṟumpūtu cāṉṟa ṇaṟumpūñ cēkkaiyum
Kuṉṟupala kuḻiip polivaṉa tōṉṟa

In lines 475-488, the author when speaking about the different religious cults prevailing in the city of Maturai mentions the Jaina and Buddhist ascetics. From this reference we understand that the Jaina and Bauddha ascetics resided not in monasteries but in gardens. The Cāvakar or Jaina householders were worshipping in their temples with painted walls with flowers and incense. They understood the past and the future as well as what occurred in the present and explained them to people. They also knew what passed on in the three worlds. Even though they were practising ascetic habits they had unfading bodies. They carried in many threaded loops small-mouthed pots looking as if they were cut out of stone. They lived in gardens full of wonderful flowers.

The same poem (*Maturaikkāñci*) is composed in Kāñcittiṇai, a poetic theme that speaks about the transient nature of the earthly things including the humans. After giving a graphic description of the splendour and the luxurious life of Maturai, the poet exhorts the king as follows: "O King! don't develop excessive attachment towards these pompous and beautiful things as well as towards the victories, which you got in battles. All these things are not permanent but impermanent. They are just like a dream and hence impermanent and illusory." What is significant to note here is that the theme Kāñci is somewhat alien to the spirit of the ancient Tamiḻs, who were very materialistic in their attitude towards life. There are several reasons to presume that this theme might have entered into the literary tradition of the Tamiḻs due to the influence of either Buddhism or Jainism. *Tolkāppiyam* speaks about poetic themes (tiṇai) in its poruḷatikāram,[10] in Puṟattiṇai of which there are seven subdivisions, viz., Veṭci, Karantai, Vañci, Kāñci, Uḻiñai, Tumpai and Vākai. Among them, Kāñci is a theme suitable for reflective poem, which dwells on the transient nature of life. If we attribute pre-Buddhist origin to *Tolkāppiyam*, then there are possibilities to say that this theme might have entered into the text of *Tolkāppiyam* in a relatively later period.

Another *Caṅkam* poem *Neṭunelvāṭai*, which is traditionally attributed to Nakkirar, speaks about *piṭakam*.[11] In this poem, the poet uses the *piṭakam* in the sense of basket. This word *piṭaka* is a Buddhist technical term which is seen both in Pali and Sanskrit forms such as Sutta-piṭaka, Vinaya-piṭaka, Dhamma-piṭaka and Tripiṭaka. Here again it is used in the sense of box or basket. From this, we can say that the Buddhist term *piṭaka* was very popular among the Tamil̲ people during the *Caṅkam* period.

Recently, S. Sathiamūrthy has referred to the influence of some Buddhist thoughts in *Caṅkam* literature.[12] He has also mentioned Iḷampōtiyār, Ciṟuveṇṭēriyār and Tērataraṉas Buddhist poets of the *Caṅkam* period.

Regarding references to Buddhism made in the *Caṅkam* literature, we can say that these poems provide us only with scanty details. We may say that from about 3rd century BC to the 3rd century AD, there had been kingdoms in the Tamil̲ country, viz., the Cēra Cōl̲a and Pāṇṭiya. The war-like aristocracy occupied the highest stratum of the social hierarchy during the above period. Consequently, this period is called the heroic age.[13] Since the literary works that had flourished in this period reveal the heroic spirit, they are also called the heroic literature. During this period, the Tamil̲s were mostly interested in secular things rather than the religious matters. That is why these poems have not shown abiding interest in religion in general and Buddhism in particular. But other evidences, which we have already seen, establish with certainty that Buddhism was deeply rooted in the Tamil̲ country, though it had not then enjoyed an extensive sway over the people of the land at large.

NOTES

1. *Iṟaiyaṉār Kaḷaviyal urai* (9th century AD).
2. *Cilappatikāram*, Aṭiyārkkunallār Commentary.
3. *Akanānūṟu* poem No: 53, 134, 229, 306, 320.
4. *Puṟanānūṟu* poem No: 59.
5. *Naṟṟiṇai* poem: 36, 127, 339.
6. *Kuṟuntokai* poem: 154, 349.
7. *Naṟṟiṇai* poem: 72.
8. *Puṟanānūṟu* poem: 182 (colophon).
9. S. Vaiyāpuri Piḷḷai, *kāviya kālam* (The Epic Age), Cheṉṉai, 1962, p. 40.
10. *Tolkāppiyam*, Poruḷatikāram, Sutra 79.
11. *Neṭunelvāṭai*, line 39.

12. S. Sathiamūrthy, Impact of some philosophic thoughts in *Caṅkam* literature, *Āyvukkōvai,* Intiyap Palkalaik Kaḻakat Tamiḻāciriyar Maṉṟam, Mūṉāvatu Karuttaraṅku, 1971, p. 69.
He quotes the 131st poem of *Kalittokai*: in the words of lady maid consoling the heroine that hero will come and marry her soon. To reveal his kindness, she uses an implied simile. Even the beautiful attracting flock of birds living in his littoral region is so kind that they do not kill anything for their prey. They only prey upon their fishes killed by the clash of the waves.
13. S. Vaiyāpuri Piḷḷai, *Kāviya Kālam* (The Epic age), Cheṉṉai, 1962, p. 17.

13

Buddhism as Reflected in Tamil Authors of Pali

Bela Bhattacharya

Buddhism spread not only to different regions in India having their distinctive language and literatures but also spread to remote global areas. As for Buddhism, as dealt with in different languages and literature in India, almost every leading language and literature treated the entire gamut of Buddhist Pali literature. As such it appears to be a stupendous task to discuss the theme of Buddhism as reflected in all these languages and literatures. I, therefore, propose to confine my discourse to one language only and that is, Tamil.

In his exhortation to the disciples, the Buddha highlighted the need for coming in close contact with all sections of people and preach his doctrines. In addition he emphasized on preaching the religion in the vernacular of the people so that the common people not versed in a chaste language like Sanskrit could grasp the essence of his doctrines. The preachers, untiring in their efforts, reached far-flung areas of the country including what is at present known as Tamil Nadu. We can trace the beginning of Buddhism in Tamil country to Ashoka's 'Dhamma Vijaya' as early as in 3rd century BC. Rock Edict II mentions amongst others, names of dynasties like Cola, Pantiya, Satya Putra, Kerala Putra, etc. Of these Cola, Pantiya and Kerala Putra are the Tamil dynasties (*Girnar... Yatha Codā Pādū Satiyaputo ketalaputo ā lamvapamnī amtiyoko...*).[1] Rock Edict XIII mentions the places in Ashoka's territories where the missionaries were sent to propagate Buddhism.[2] The five missionaries including Mahendra were sent by Ashoka to different places to preach the *Dhamma.* It is presumed these monks visited Tamil Nadu also enroute to Ceylon. The *Mahāvaṃsa,* however, does not mention the visit of these missionaries to Tamil country.

The Chinese monk Yuan Chwang, however, mentions that near the capital Kāñci there was a big monastary. In addition to *Vihāra*, there was a high Stupa also. It is interesting to note that a few *Cankam* poems refer to the Maurya dynasty to which emperor Ashoka belonged. As for example, *Akānanūru 251* makes reference to Moriyan. The same reference mentions a place in *Akānānūru 261* and *Pūranānūru 175*. The period from 3rd century BC to 2nd century AD goes by the name of *Cankam* age. It is during this period *Cankam* poems were composed. *Maturaik Kāñci*, composed by Mankuti Marutan, one of the *Cankam* poets portrays a day's activity of the city of Maturai where a family pays a visit to a Buddha *Vihāra* with flowers, etc. as offering to the Buddha. Thus from this it is evident that there was a *Vihāra* in Maturai. *Netunalvatai*, another *Cankam* poem, supposed to belong to Nakkirar, speaks of Pitakam. The Pitakam is a Buddhist term occurring in both Sanskrit and Pali. There are a few *Cankam* poets whose names are derivable from Buddhism. The classical poem *Manimekhalai* composed by Sittalai Sattanar is accepted as one of the five famous *Kāvyas* in Tamil literature and is attributed to the Samgam period (2nd century AD). This marvellous epic poem giving earliest information on Buddhism bears testimony to the existence of Buddhism at Kāñci. Way back in 2nd century AD Manimekhalai, the central female character of the work, was accommodated in the south-eastern region of the city in a grove named Dharmadavana. Here she fed a large number of needy persons regularly. As a gesture of appreciation of her benevolent work, she had been given a *Vihāra* to stay in and a Buddha seat was erected with a special *Chaitya* for the purpose of enshrining of the Buddha's footprints. In Kāñci she got an opportunity of getting herself acquainted with the most authoritative doctrine of Buddhism under the tutelage of Aravana Adigal who was at that time a prominent personality in the intellectual circle of Kāñci. Adigal was instrumental in making her embrace a life of asceticism and perform the missionary assignments. Its merits mention here that consequent on being completely inundated by the sea, the old Chola capital Kāveripumpattinam ceased to exist and its inhabitants shifted to Kāñci and adopted Buddhism.

Here it may be added that the *Cankam* literature does not provide ample details of Buddhism. The reason is traced to the fact that most of the literary activities in *Cankam* literature are secular in nature and do not therefore shed much light on religious matters.

The period from the fourth century AD in the Tamil country met with some social changes and political upheaval. This state of affairs continued till 6th century AD. However, Buddhism in this region gained some momentum as a result of the patronage from different sources during the 4th century AD. Earlier, the first Pallava king Skandavarman who had thrived before the fourth century is known to have espoused the cause of Buddhism. After him, as stated above, the Dark Age, often referred by the scholarly persons as 'The Kalabhra Interregnum' set in. The Kalabhras were in power (4th to 6th century) and are condemned as 'barbarians' and 'enemies' of the civilization. It is interesting to note that modern researchers do not consider the Kalabhras as evil rulers. They are denounced because of their leaning towards Buddhism and the Brahmins could not just tolerate it and hence hurled all derogatory remarks at them. Some scholars are of the opinion that Buddhist monasteries and authors were the recipient of royal favour from the king Accutavikkanta whom Tamil Buddhists remembered for a long time. *Yapparungalam*, a Tamil composition in the eleventh century AD, was composed by the poet Amitasagarangar. During the Kalabhra reign, lasting for about 300 years, Buddhism flourished considerably in Kāñci and at the places in the vicinity of Kāñci. In this period several scholars and Buddhist monks earned celebrity for themselves amongst which names of Nāgaguttanar who composed *Kundalakesi Buddhadatta*, Dhammapala, Buddhaghosa, the Pali commentators deserve to be mentioned. The so-called 'Dark Age', which it is not surely, also marks the prosperity that the Tamil literature gained. The so-called dark period saw great literary activities and most of these works, termed as eighteen minor works, were composed during this period including *Silappadikaram*, and many of the writers were the devotees of the 'heretical' group, i.e., religion other than Hinduism. Evidence of royal patronage is almost absent in the succeeding period of the Chola.

While dealing with the subject matter, I now intend to dilate on the literary luminaries that enriched the Tamil literature profoundly and are related to Buddhism.

Āryadeva (or DEVA)

Āryadeva (2nd–3rd century AD) who appeared during the period 2nd and 3rd century was the foster son of a Sinhalese king. He succeeded Acharya Nāgārjuna who was perhaps the contemporary of the Sātavāhana king Yajnasrī Gautamiputra and propounder of the Mādhyamika (Śūnyavāda) sect of Buddhist philosophy. Āryadeva besides serving as a Professor of Nālandā University, after Nāgārjuna, stretching for a long period, made significant contribution as an ecclesiastical author adding a radical colour to the doctrine he preached. Incidentally, *Catusataka*, the masterpiece of the writing and of exquisite literally splendour, in Sanskrit, is of permanent value. Candrakirti (6th century), a student of Dhammapala, wrote a commentary on Āryadeva. Hiuen-Tsang considered him one of the "four suns that illuminated the world". The other three are Nāgārjuna, Aśvaghosa and Kumāralabdha. Āryadeva was one of the earliest scholars of Nālandā. He was the author of three works, all of which are introduced to Tibet in its own language. His last work, known as *Mādhyamaka-bhramaghātanāma*, was actually written by him at Nālandā at the request of Hdsambudhi-glin-gi-rgyal-po (Jambudvipa Raja) Sukhāchārya, and was translated into Tibetan by Upadhyaya Dipankara Srī-Jnāna.[3]

List of works by Āryadeva:

Caryā-melayana-pradipa

Citta-āvarana-viśodhana, *Catuh-pītha-tantra-rāja-mandala-upāyikā-vidhi-Sārā-Samuccaya*, *Catuhpitha-Sādhana*, *Jñānadākini*, *Ekadrumapanjikā* and doubfully also *Pradīpa-uddyotana-abhisamdhi-prakāśikā-vyākhya-tīkā*.

These apart, to Āryadeva are attributed the following works:
Ārya-prajnā- pāramitā-mahāpari- pṛccha-nāma,
Hastabāla-prakarana-ṇāma,
Vṛtti on above, *Catuhśataka-śāstra-Kārikā*,
Skhalita-pramathana-yukti-hetusiddhi,
Jnāna-Sāra-samuccaya and
Madhyamaka-bhramaghāta,

Āryadeva in the last span of his life settled in Kāñci.

BUDDHADATTA AND BUDHAGHOSA

Buddhadatta and Buddhaghosa, both of them were the products of the 5th century AD. They were reputed Buddhist monks and hailed from the Tamil country. Buddhadatta was born at Uragapuram but the exact birthplace of Buddhaghosa has not been ascertained authoritatively. Moranam near Kāñci is sometimes mentioned as his birthplace. According to Buddhaghosuppatti, Buddhadatta had been to Ceylon to study Buddhism. Having completed his studies in Ceylon he was returning to India by ship, which crossed another ship carrying Buddhaghosa to Ceylon. At this time they got introduced with each other and exchanged pleasantries. Buddhaghosa asserted that the doctrines of the Buddha were available in Ceylonese language and that he wanted to translate those into Magadhi. In reply to that Buddhadatta said that in spite of remaining in Ceylon for a long time he had not been able to finish the job. He requested Buddhaghosa to send copies of the commentaries when compiled and Buddhaghosa complied with the request in due course. On return from Sri Lanka Buddhadatta stayed in a Vihāra at Kaveri Pattanam. While residing there, he wrote *Madhurattha Vilāsini*, a commentary on the *Buddhavamsa*. His other creation was *Abhidhammāvatāra*, which is the summary of Buddhaghosa's commentaries on the *Abhidhamma-pitaka*, and this he did on being requested by a Bhikkhu named Sumati. Another work of his is *Vinaya Vinicchaya* which happens to be the summary of Buddhaghosa's commentaries on the *Vinaya-pitaka*. Another work supposed to be penned by Buddhadatta is the *Uttara Vinicchaya* while he was staying at Anuradhapura. He wrote also *Rūpārūpa vibhāga*.

Buddhaghosa, the contemporary of Buddhadatta, as said earlier, contributed to Buddhism to a large extent in the Tamil country. He wrote a commentary on the *Majjhima Nikāya*, namely, *Papancasudani* on request by the Thera, Buddhamitta. This work was done when both of them were staying at a *Vihara* at Mayuram, as it is now called. Two Theras, Jotipala and Cumati at Kāñci urged him to write *Sārātthapakāsini* and *Manorathapurani*. Kāñci, it may be reiterated, was the foremost of the centres of Pali Buddhism. It is to be noted here that at the time Buddhaghosa appeared at the centre stage, Pali Buddhism was declining in India. It is at this juncture Bodhgaya monks refused to budge from their stand in adherence to Pali. It was under their guidance that Buddhaghosa took pains to study Buddhism. To get himself acquainted with the Ceylonese commentaries he set out for Sri Lanka during the time of King Mahanama and reached *Mahavihāra* at Anuradhapura. During his stay there, he wanted to translate the commentaries from Sinhalese to Pali and after he satisfied the Bhikkhus that he was capable enough to render the job, he was provided with all the facilities to do so. In addition to *Visuddhimagga*, he wrote commentaries on the *Vinaya Pitaka*, *Pātimokkha*, *Dīgha-Nikāya*, *Anguttara Nikāya*,

Khuddakapātha, etc. All these are of immense value to those who are desirous of probing into the Buddhist doctrines deeply. It is immaterial whether by birth he was a Tamilian but the fact cannot be denied that he stayed in Kāñci for some time.

DHAMMAPĀLA

Dhammapāla was yet another scholar in Pali in Tamil Nadu who lived in the 6th century AD and was from the city of Tanja. He is reported to have been born at Kāñcipuram. He wrote the *Nettipakarana* commentary. His famous work is *Paramātthadipani*, which is an exposition of the *Khuddaka-Nikāya.*

DIÑNĀGA (AD 450–520)

Ācharya Diñnāga, called in Tibetan *Phyogs-glan* and who was born near Kāñci, studied *Tripitaka* in Hinayāna deeply and afterwards, under the guidance of Vasubandhu. He had an in-depth study of all the *Pitakas* of the Mahayāna and Hināyana. Although some scholars are inclined to place Diñnāga in the fifth century AD, it is more likely he flourished in the first half of the sixth century AD. While Asaṅga and Vasubandhu enriched the university, Diñnāga appeared as a saviour when the fame of the university was at the lowest ebb. He had to win over the controversialists again and who hurled all unpalatable remarks at him. But he never faltered. Diñnāga was a *Yogacarin* and a *Vijñāvādin.* Diñnāga is truly thought to be the father of medieval logic. It was during his time, logic was treated as completely different from philosophy. Some consider Diñnāga belonging to the *abhidharma* system. Hiuen-Tsang also points out Diñnāga's faith in Hinayāna. Diñnāga's system may be summed up as realistic logic or a system of transcendental realism or critical philosophy. *Pramāṇa-Samuccaya* is a magnificent work by Diñnāga written in Sanskrit but the original one is lost. What is now available is its Tibetan translation. As regards his contribution to logic, mention may be made of his work, the *Nyāyapraveśa.*

A list of the works by Diñnāga is given below:

Miśraka-stotra (Mātṛceta and Diñnāga),

Guṇāparyanta-stotra-ṭīkā (Commentary on Ratnadasa's *Guna paryanta-stotra-ṭīkā*),

Guṇaparyanta-stotra-pada-karika,
Eka-gāthā-ṭikā,
Ārya-mañjughosa-stotra,
Ārya-prajñā-pāramitā-samgraha-kārikā,
Yoga-avatāra,
Samantabhadra-caryā-pranidhānārtha-samgraha,
Abhidharmakośa-vṛtti-marma-pradipa-nama,
Pramāṇa-samuccaya,
Pramāṇa-samuccaya-vṛtti (Col. Auto-commentary),
Ālamban-parikṣā,
Ālambana-parikṣā-vṛtti (Col. Auto-commentary),
Trikāla-parikṣā,
Nyāya-praveśa-nāma-pramāṇa-prakaraṇa,
Nyāya-praveśa-nāma-pramāṇa-śātra,
Hetu-cakra-damaru.

BODHIDHARMA

Bodhidharma is recognized as an extraordinary Indian missionary to China. After he joined Buddhist Sangha, he was initiated in Buddhism by the reputed teacher of *Dhyāna* (meditation) by Prajñātārā. It was through him and as a result of his meditation school, what one finds as Ch'an Buddhism in China which is known as Zen Buddhism amongst the Japanese Buddhists.

DHARMAPĀLA

Dharmapāla was a great philosopher, academician and an outstanding Buddhist scholar. He was a native of Kāñci and born in the seventh century AD. He was the only South Indian to chair the high position of the Vice Chancellor in the world famous Nalāndā University. Dharmapāla was also the Chief Professor of Vijñānavāda there. He belonged no doubt to an older generation, for Hiuen-Tsang calls him a Bodhisattva. We have some detailed information about his early life and conversion. It is difficult to say how far they are really biographical, for Hiuen-Tsang reproduces them from a legend heard by him. It is stated in the legend that Dharmapāla happened, in his boyhood, to witness a grand marriage feast given by the king, but the pomp and circumstances of it prompted in him only the thought of the world's 'vanity of vanities'. The thought preyed upon

ANURUDDHA THERA

Anuruddha Thera was a well-known scholar of Pali and Buddhism. He spent major portion of his life at Kāñci. Apart from other places, he visited Ceylon also where he did some missionary work during the reign of Vijayabahu II. His most reputed work *Abhidhammattha-Sangaha* (manual of psychology and ethics) served as an introduction of *Adhidhamma* philosophy, which continues to be very popular in Burma and Sri Lanka.

DIPANKARA BUDDHAPIYA THERA

Dipankara Buddhapiya Thera too was a prominent Pali scholar. He lived in the twelfth century AD. He wrote the Pali grammar *Rūpasiddhi* while at Ceylon. In the colophon he mentions that he was born in Chola country. Another work of his is *Pajjamadhu* (Nectar of verses), which embodies many excellent poems in praise of the Buddha.

KASSAPA THERA

Another Buddhist monk also from Chola, who lived in the 12th century AD is Kassapa Thera. He wrote a commentary on the *Abhidhamma,* called *Moha Vicchedani*, and a commentary on the *Vinaya Pitaka,* called *Vimati Vinodani* and the *Anāgatavamsa.*

DHAMMAKITTI THERA

Dhammakitti Thera too was from Chola. He went to Sri Lanka and was busy with literary activities. He authored the first part of *Culavamsa,* a continuation of *Mahāvamsa,* the well-known chronicle of Sri Lanka. It is held by many that *Dāthāvamsa* (Tooth relic) was also composed by him.

Of the Buddhist works available still now, mention may be made of *Vira-Coliyam,* a Tamil grammar treating five aspects: *eluttu* (letters), *col* (words), *porul* (poetic content), *yappu* (metre), and *ani* (poetic figures) in 180 verses divided into 10 chapters called *Patalams.*

From the reference appearing in commentary on *Civanana cittiyar* by Nānappirakaras, we get acquainted with two works, namely, *Cittantattokai* (an exposition of Buddhist texts) and *Tiruppatikam.* The first one is in praise of the Buddha's path and the second one is in praise of the Buddha himself.

I have tried to give an outline on the topic of Buddhism, its reflections on Tamil language and literature in concise form. While doing so reference to a few outstanding personalities of Tamil Nadu who were closely associated with Buddhism but not directly concerned with Tamil literature have also appeared here for obvious reasons and I suppose this will not be construed as a digression.

REFERENCES

1. D.C. Ahir, *Buddhism in South India*, Sri Satguru Publications, A division of India Book Centre, Delhi, India, 1st edition, 1992.
2. C.R. Srinivasan, *Kanchipuram Through the Ages,* Agam Kala Prakashan, Delhi, 1979.
3. K.A. Nilkanta Sastri, *The History and Culture of the Tamils*, Firma K.L. Mukhopadhyay, Calcutta, 1964.
4. R. Nagaswami, *Art and Culture of Tamil Nadu,* Sundeep Prakashan, Delhi, 1980.
5. *Studies in Tirukkural*, A Publication of the Tamil Department, Calcutta University, 1996.
6. *Encyclopaedia of Tamil Literature*, in 10 Volumes, Institute of Asian Studies, Thiruvanmiyur, Madras, 1990.

NOTES

1. R.G. Basak, *Asokan Inscriptios*, pp. 5-6.
2. *Encyclopaedia of Tamil Literature*, Institute of Asian Studies, pp. 187.
3. *Taranatha's History of Buddhism in India*, p. 387.
4. S. Dutt, *Buddhist Monks and Monasteries of India*, pp. 290-291.
5. H.D. Sankalia, *The University of Nalanda*, p. 79.
6. Takakusu, *Essentials of Buddhist Philosophy*, p. 85.
7. A commentary on this work called *Pramana-vartika-bhasya* or *Vartika-alankarah* by Prajnakaragupta was published in 1953 by the Jayaswal Research Institute, Patna.
8. Satish Chandra Vidyabhusan, *A History of Indian Logic*, p. 307.
9. 2500 *years of Buddhism*, ed. by Bapat. p. 199.
10. L.M. Joshi, *Studies in the Buddhistic Culture of India*, p. 148.

14

The Influence of Buddhism on Telugu Language and Literature

J. Sitaramamma

Andhras are one among the Indian races who welcomed the gospel of the Buddha and very ardently followed his *Dhamma.* From 3rd century BC for about six hundred years, Buddhism has played a triumphant role in Andhra. It influenced all sections of the people by embracing them into its fold. Andhra Buddhist monks were designated *Andhakulu* (Andhakas). They played a key role in spreading the Buddhanusasana in the South up to Ceylon, in the North-west upto Gandhara, and in the East up to Suvarnabhumi. They carried the cardinal virtues of *Maitri* and *Karuna* to those lands.

Buddhism arose as a response to the challenge faced by India during the 6th–5th centuries BC. It was a period of multi-dimensional conflicts, viz., racial, social, economic and cultural, Aryan vs non-Aryan, Brahmana vs Kshatriya, Brahmana-Kshatriya vs Vaisya-Sudra, and finally rural collectivism vs urban individualism.

Buddhism sought to resolve these conflicts by evolving a synthesis of the contemporary conflicting systems of thought and practice. By advocating the middle way, i.e., avoidance of the extremes like too much self-indulgence and too much self-mortification, made great appeal to people. It is a known fact that Buddhism had spread more rapidly among the Dravidian peoples of Eastern and Southern India.

The Aitareya Brhamana (800 BC) mentioned the Andhras for the first time as a trans-Vindhyan people, classified them with the non-Aryans such as the Sabaras and Pulindas, whereas the other Brahmanical literature is unequivocal in castigating them as Mlechchas. This maybe one of the reasons for Buddhism to enjoy wide popularity with the Andhras as attested by innumerable Buddhist sites that have been discovered and are being discovered all over Andhradesa. The *Vatthugatha* of *Parayanavagga* of the *Suttanipata* made a mention of the advent of Buddhism into Andhradesa during the lifetime of the Buddha. The disciples of Bavari who were residing at a hermitage near the banks of the river Godavari paid a visit to the Buddha and got the opportunity to hear directly from the Buddha, Buddha Vacana; some disciples have attained even arhathood. Some disciples returned to Asmaka region, i.e., Andhra Janapada to meet his teacher Bavari and conveyed the doctrine of the Buddha. The seeds of Buddhism were implanted into Andhra Janapada for the first time by the disciples of the Bavari.

By the time of the advent of Buddhism, Andhras appear to have been divided into several tribes and on the authority of Megasthanese (300 BC). Quoted by Pliny (AD 100) we may say that the Andhras possessed thirty walled towns and commanded together a large army, next only to that of the imperial Mauryas in strength and equipment. We may not be wrong if we infer from this account that the Andhras at that time were passing through the early phase of urbanization and were divided into a number of tribal republics or city-states. The *Paramarthadipani* commentary on the *Mahavastu*, says that Mahakatyayana, one of the foremost disciples of the Buddha, had converted the king of Asmaka into Buddhism.

Prakrit was the language of early Buddhism and Emperor Ashoka made it the lingua franca with the pious hope of achieving cultural unity of the country. The Satavahanas followed his example. The new Buddhism adopted Sanskrit that gradually replaced Prakrit even at the court. The domination of politics and religion by Prakrit and Sanskrit drove the language of the people into disuse. The existence of proto-Telugu, the language of the Andhra during the time of the Satavahanas, is attested by the bilingual coins of the Satavahanas and the *Kathasaritsagara*, which calls it *desi*, the local language (as against Prakrit and Sanskrit which were *videsi* or non-local). The earliest inscriptions from Bhattiprolu and Amaravati show that the people out of their love for Buddhism preferred Prakrit and Sanskrit names. Very rarely we come across *desi* personal names like Pulomavi, Ehuvala, Anikki Eli, Chaliki, Adi and Bapi et al.

The Andhra Buddhist monks became masters of Prakrit and carried on doctrinal discussions in it. During the early centuries of the Christian era the collective intellectual efforts of the parivrajakas and upasakas resulted in the enormous quantities of Sutra literature like *Prajnaparamita, Ratnakuta, Nava Vaipulya Sutras*, and others.

Acarya Nagarjuna who was probably the first to adopt the Karika style which includes the verse and commentary by the same author, later the same style was followed by (other Buddhist philosophy like) Aryadeva, Buddhapalita, Bhavaviveka, Dinnaga and Dharmakirti, who had associated with Andhradesa. Proving that non-conformity is a sign of intellectual vitality, the contributions of these philosophers for the growth of Indian logic in particular and Indian philosophy in general is illumined as unparalleled even by their hostile critics.

Andhra kings patronized and adopted Prakrit languages for a period of 800 years, i.e., from 4th century BC to 4th century AD from pre-Satavahana times to Pallava times. The numismatic evidence proves that at the time of Vasistiputra Pulamavi, one of the Dravidian languages was prevalent in Andhra. In the coins, the script used was *desi*, the word written was 'Arahana'.

The local Andhra language influenced by Prakrit language, which was used to spread the Bauddha Dharma, was named by the Buddhists of Andhra as Andhaka language. Buddha Ghosha in his *Papancha Sudani* clearly stated that the Andhras and the Tamilians had translated the Pali Tripitakas in their own vernaculars, but he felt that the translation was not so adequate in conveying the true meaning. The Andhaka literature was mainly used for missionary purpose. That maybe the reason why the kings used the traditional Prakrit language in all their inscriptions. As a result we find exceptionally a few inscriptions, which were in Sanskrit after 2nd century AD.

At the end of the 6th century and by the beginning of 7th century AD, there was a religious revival movement in Andhra. In that Buddhism was replaced by Shaivism and to some extent Jains were able to withstand and prove their presence here and there in Andhra. Along with Buddhism, the Buddhist language of Andhra, Andhaka was also wiped out from the scene. But one interesting aspect here is that though the religion and its language were not in vogue, the terms and its impact on the Andhra would not completely disappear. Therefore, the terms used in Andhaka language figured in later literature. Although Telugu poets forgot the Buddhist language, it remained in usage in the local vernacular of the commoners and to some extent in the inscriptions. Gradually this Andhaka language had been transformed as Andhra language. Pali is one among the Prakrit languages, but Pali virtually is not a name of a language. The meaning of 'Pali' in Pali language was 'hammanusasana'. The South Indians first used the word 'Pitaka Pali' for Pali Tripitakas. Buddha Ghosa said that the scholars called the language of the Pitakas as Mulamagadhi. Some scholars disputed this view. But there is no doubt that it is a kind of Magadhi.

Here in this paper, I have made an attempt to trace out some of the Pali words in the Telugu language and literature. There are certain Pali words which directly entered into Telugu. The most significant word is *Tanha* on which the entire Buddhist philosophy rests. Tanha means (skt) Tṛṣṇa, i.e., desire. The same word Tanha has gradually been evolved as 'Tanivi' in Telugu. The word *Amsa* (Amsi) of Pali means a boarder, in Telugu it is *Amchu. Amchu* also means boarder in Telugu. *Akkosa* is a Pali word which means scolding, showing disrespect, humiliation, etc. In Telugu it is Akkasu, anger, or Akkasamu. *Akkhara* is a Pali word, its Sanskrit form is *Aksara,* and in Telugu it is *Akkaramu,* it denotes the same meaning. *Aggi* means fire, this word directly entered into Telugu in the same form. For fire the Telugu word is *Aggi.* It is in common usage. *Acchibandha* is a Pali word, which means a square-land. In wetland cultivation the same word is used as Achhukattu (Vinayapitaka 1287). *Acchi* is the Pali word; *kattu* is a local term. By the admixture of both the Pali and Telugu terms, the word *Acchu Kattu* has been derived. Another very popular word in Pali is *Acchera: Acchariya* (Milinda Panha 28) means *Ascharyamu* in Telugu, i.e., amaze. The very same terms *Accheriyamu* and *Accheruvu* were used as a synonyms of *Ascharyamu* (Krisna Kavi: *Sakuntala Parinayamu*).

Amma in Pali means mother. Not only for mother, for any woman to show respect it is used either as a prefix or as a suffix. In ordinary usage and even in literature term *Amma* is used in Telugu for mother. In other South Indian languages Tayi talli, etc. usages were there. It indicates the close relationship between Pali and Telegu. *Allika* is another Pali word, which means intertwined. The same word *Allika* is used in Telugu with the same meaning. *Agu* in Pali means wrong deed, or misdeed, etc. Even in Telugu it is used with the same meaning. The Pali word *Agu* had become *Agadamu* in Telugu which denotes the same meaning. It is generally used for the children who are mischievous. Another Pali word, which is similar to the Telugu word, is *Anatti* which means order or proceedings. A similar word in Telugu in *Anati* and it conveys the same meaning as an order. *Ada* in Pali and *Ada* in Telugu conveys one and the same meaning, i.e., income. In Telugu it is popularly used as *Adayamu. Asa* is a Sanskrit word, it is *Asa* in Pali, which means greed (Vinaya 1.255). Even in Telugu it is used as *Asa* to convey the meaning of greed. Another very popular word, which was directly derived from Pali, is *Ettaka.* It means burnt brick (in Vinaya 2-121). In Telugu it is *Ituka.* Linguists are of the opinion that the word has been derived from the Pali *ettaka* instead of the Sanskrit form of *Istaka. Ithi* in Pali means woman. In Telugu for woman *Inti* is generally used which is close to Pali usage. *Unni,* another Pali word, made its appearance in Telugu also. *Unni* means the skin of a sheep. In Telugu the material weaved with the hair of a sheep is called *unni.*

Uddara is a Pali word which denotes debt (Jatakamala 2.341). In one of the Telugu-speaking regions, i.e., Telangana region, the same word is used to convey the same meaning of indebtedness, i.e., *uddara* in Telugu. But it is not very popular as it is in Pali. *Aettavata* is a Pali word which denotes examining the things finished till now. In Telugu the same word is used to convey the same meaning.

Kamsa in Pali represents a particular metal, i.e., bronze (Milindapanha). The same usage is there in Telugu also for bronze as *Kamchu.* The vessel made of that metal is popularized in Telugu as *kamcham.* Kakkaru in Pali means one type of creeper as mentioned in the *Jataka* tales (6.536). It bears fruit also. The word *Kakara* of Telugu may be derived from the same *kakkaru* of Pali. *Katta* in Pali and *katte* in Telugu means a wooden stick (Samyuttanikaya 1-168). The wooden sticks used as fire to prepare food is also called *katte* (firewood). *Kattari* is a Pali word for scissor. The same word is used in Telugu as *kattera* to denote the same meaning, i.e., scissors. This word is mentioned in the *Jatakas* (3.298). *Kappura* is a Pali word which is used as *kappuramu* in Telugu. It is a kind of incense menthal offered to god. It is *karpura* in Sanskrit. *Kammara* in Pali, *Kammari* in Telugu means the metal worker. They were called *kammara* in Pali (Dighanikaya 11.126). Directly from Pali the word *kammara* has been taken into Telugu. Gradually, this word was confined to the iron workers only. *Kalebara* is a Pali word and *kalebaramu* is a Telugu word. The word *kalebara* indicates body or dead body also (*Jataka* 2-437 and *Jataka* 3-180). In Telugu, the word *Kalebara* is used to convey the dead body only. *Kudda* in Pali means a wall made of bricks, stone or wood. With the same connotation this word is used in Telugu as *goda.* Linguists are of the opinion that there are more chances to derive this word from Pali (*Kudda*) than from Sanskrit (*Kudya*) as *goda. Kuni* of Pali and *kuni* of Telugu indicates the curved piece of land. This word is very popular among the agriculturists. *Kuddala* is a Pali word from which the Telugu words such as *Guddali, Goddali* and *Kodavali,* etc. were derived into Telugu. The word *kuddula* means an implement used to cut the roots and nuts and to dig land. The term *nagali* in Telugu means plough. It also entered into Telugu through Pali. *Kulla* in Pali and *gulla* in Telugu is used for food items which are hollow and not so hard. The fully ripen tamarind is called *chintagulla.* So also *gullamurugulu, gulla kante,* etc. are words which are very popular in Telugu. *Kusi* in both Pali and Telugu is used to show the edge of the joint where the two wooden pieces are fit in. In Pali *kura* is used for any cooked eatable item; in Telugu it is confined only to English curry. *Kotta* in Pali and *kottu* in Telugu is used for granary. The word *kotta* is used (Petavattu vyakhya 126) in Telugu for a storeroom. In Pali, *chira* and *chivara* are synonyms (Vinaya 1.305). The *Bhikkhus* used the word *chivora* for their robes. Because of the impact of the *Bhikkhus* the Telugu people adopted *chivara.* In the earlier stage the robes of both male and female are called *chira.* There are many words derived directly from Pali into Telugu. A few are mentioned here.

This list of equivalent words in Pali and Telugu so far discussed is not exhaustive. A symposium is organized under the aegis of 'Telugu Ghosti' wherein they had put an effort to study the impact of Pali on Telugu language and literature. The fruits of their labour was brought out in a publication entitled '*Telugulo Pali Padalu*' (Pali words in Telugu). Some examples are given below which show the impact of Pali on Telugu languge:

Pali	Telugu	English
Amma	Amma	Mother
Chaṇaka, Canaka	Senaga	Gram (yellow gram)
Chijhi	Chinchi	Cut into pieces
Jūta	Judamu	Gambling
Joti	Joti	Light
Mariyada	Mariyada	Respect
Mānika	Mānika	An implement to measure
Naya	Nyayamu	Method of right system
Thana	Ttana	Open place
Takkara	Takkari	Thief (Taskara in Sanskrit)
Parikkhati	Parikinchu	To inspect, to investigate
Palugga	Pagulu	Breaking (of the following)
Pallala	Pallamu	Low-level land
Punna	Punnamu	Full moon day (punnmayam)
Pudhavi	Pudami	Earth
Pela	Pella	A rice ball
Sukka	Chukka	Star
Bila	Bila	A hole den, *ahde,* a portion
Vaddi	Vaddi	Interest on principal amount
Vikata	Vikata	Bad manner

These are some of the Pali words found in Telugu and remained in the usage of the common people. *Chunna* is a Pali word; by adding 'Mu' to it as suffix the same word would become *Chunnamu* in Telugu, which means calcium. There are many Telugu words derived from Pali just by adding du, mu, vu, lu at the end of the Pali word.

BUDDHIST LITERATURE IN TELUGU LANGUAGE

The earliest Telugu work which makes a mention about Buddhism was *Panditaradhya Charitra of the Buddha.* There are more than five biographical histories written by Palkuriki Somanadhudu. Among the biographical histories of the Buddha in Telugu language, the earliest is *Buddha Charitrames* written by Tiru Poli Venkatee Yamu. Another work is *Buddhist as Buddha Bhagavanunicharitra* written by Charla Ganapati Sastri, Lalita Press, Hyderabad, 1977, and *Siddhartha Charitra* by Chilakamarti Lakshim Narasimham, Ananta Press, Rajahmundry, 1964. Another work which deals with the account of the Buddha is entitled as *Mahabhinishkramanamu* written by Siddhayyakavi, Hyderabad, 1969, the life history of the Buddha and his great departure (*mahabhiniskramanam*) in poetry (Padyakavyam) *Buddha Puranam* Penmats written by a Rajamraju published by Vasudevasraman, Chodavaram, 1983. In this book the entire life history of Buddha is very lucidly described in the poetic form (Padyakavyam). There was one Telugu work entitled *Sakyasimha* which also gave biographical accounts of the Buddha. Another biography is entitled *Visvantara,* written by Amancharla Gopala Rao. The work of that period was *Saundara Nandamu,* written by Pingala Lakshmikantham and Katuri Venkateswara Rao. Pingala Kantham has written a *Kandika* consisting of three poems entitled *Buddha Devudu.* Dharmanand Kosambi's *Buddhas* was translated into Telugu from Marathi by Puttaparti Narayanacharyulu and entitled it as *Buddha Bhagavanudu.* It was published by the Anand Buddha Vihar, Secunderabad. The following Buddhist scholars have written the biography of Buddha for the purpose of college students: P. Venkata Chalapati Rao in 1915, Palaparti Ramamurthi in 1915 and P. Nanjuo Kanchanapalli Kanakamba in 1918.

Similarly, Basu Narayana Rao has written a playlet known as *Buddha Natakamu.* Besides this he also has a notable work entitled *Buddhaniti* (1908), which deals with the ethics of Buddhism. Nori Narasimha Rao has written *Khema bhikkuni.* Similarly, Karuturi

Satyanarayana has written a book on *Amrapali.* Another writer Jnanananda Kavi has written a book on *Amrapali.* Sri Raja Vasireddy Sadasiveswara Bahaddur, the Jamindar of Jayanti Puram translated *Dhammapada* into Telugu in poetic form later; Kala Prapurna Chilukuri Narayana Rao has transcreated it into Telugu.

In Modern Andhra, the teachings of the Buddha were written in the form of dramas (Natakamulu) and were used to perform on the stage. Panuganti Lakshmi Narasimham who was depicted as Andhra's Shakespeare has written a drama called *Buddha Bodha Sudha.* The first Andhra writer who attempted to transcreate the *Jatakas* into Telugu was Kilambi Rangacharyulu. He also wrote an article on *Ambatta Suttam.* Later Sannidhanam Suryanarayana Sastri, by putting all his efforts, made the *Jataka* tales as heart-touching episodes in Telugu literature. This book was entitled *Jataka Katha Guchcamu.* Finally Swami Tallavajjula Siva Sankara Sastri translated all the *Jataka* tales in four volumes entitled in Telugu as *Jataka Kathalu,* and these works were published by Andhra Pradesh Sahitya Academy, Hyderabad.

Scholars from various walks of life have done some research on Acarya Nagarjuna. Kodali Lakshmi Narayana has written a book on the historical accounts of Nagarjuna entitled *Nagarjuna Charitra.* Vemuri Venkata Ramanatham has written as (poetic drama) Geya Natika form on *Nagarjuna Konda* dealing with the biographical accounts of Acarya Nagarjuna from his childhood to Mahaparinirvana. It was published in 1978 at Hyderabad by Sheshachalam and company. Sri Duggirala Balaramayya's contribution to Buddhist literature (in Telugu) is immense. Therefore, he got the title *Bauddha Vajmaya Brahma.* Under this literature some are poems; some are songs. The songs composed by Balaramayya on Buddhism were published separately as *Ajanta Sundari, Asoka Samrajyam,* etc. Another significant work on Buddhist literature was a translation of Asvaghosa's *Saundara Nandamu* by Pingala Lakshmikantham and Katuri Venkateswara Rao. Later, has written a *Khandika* consisting of three poems entitled *Buddha Devudu.* Katuri Venkateswara Rao has written on 'Nagarjuna Konda'. Later Dasarathi Narayana Reddy had written a *kavya* entitled *Mahabodhi.* Buddhist scholars acclaimed and admired it as a masterpiece. The same author had written another noteworthy *geya kavyam* entitled *Nagarjuna Sagaram.* Tirumala Ramachandra, an eminent scholar in many languages, a versatile researcher, a journalist and an author of many works, translated the *Lalitavistara* into

Telugu. Tirumala Ramacandra, a polymath, has edited an anthology of articles on different aspects of Buddhism entitled *Buddhudu-Jivitam-avagahana,* published by Jayanti Publications, Vijayawada (reprint 1997). *Tathagatudu,* written by Ratanbabu, is also a biographical account of the Buddha published in 1985. Ambedkar's *Buddha and his Dhamma* was also translated into Telugu by the Buddhist Society of India, Andhra Pradesh branch, Hyderabad, 1988.

Besides the biographical data of the Buddha, there are some works in Telugu which deal exclusively with the doctrines of the Buddha. Among this category, the noted works were *Dharma Chakram* written by Nanduri Ramakrishnamacharya, published by Triveni Publishers, Machilipatnam, 1960. It was written as a drama describing the first sermon of the Buddha. Many ardent Telugu Buddhist scholars had translated the compendium of Buddhist ethics, the *Dhammapada* into Telugu by Narayanacharyulu and entitled it as *Buddha Bhagavanudu.* It was published by the Anand Buddha Vihar, Secunderabad. The following Buddhist scholars have written the biography of the Buddha for the purpose of college students: P. Venkata Chalapati Rao in 1915, Palaparti Ramamurthi in 1915 and P. Nanjudappa in 1916, Kanchanapalli Kanakamba in 1918; Sri Basu Narayana Rao had written a book in 1908 on Buddhist ethics titled *Buddhaniti.* Later Sri Raja Vasireddy Sadsiveswara Bahaddur, the zamindar of Jayaniti Puram, translated the Pali *Dhammapada* into Telugu and Kala Prapuran Chilukuri Narayana Rao has transcreated it into Telugu prosody.

Most of the Buddhist novels which deal with various aspects of Buddhism of Rahul Sankrityayan have been translated into Telugu. Some of his works in Telugu were *Buddhacarya, Vismruta Yatrikudu, Simhasenapati* and *Jayayaudheya.* So also two of his Buddhist philosophical works *Buddha Carya* and *Bharatiya Tattvasastram.* Similarly, some of the works of Acarya Nagarjuna were also translated into Telugu, for example, some parts of the *Mula Madhyamaka Karika, Vigrahavyavartani, Ratnavali* were transliterated into Telugu by an eminent scholar G.V. Krishnarao. *Suhrillekha* was translated into Telugu by Vavilala Subbarao—it was written in the poetic form by Gajjela Mallareddy. Another work of Krishnarao, which is prescribed for the graduate students as Telugu textbook is *Bomman atchindi*—it deals with a Buddhist theme. *Sunyata saptati,* another work of Acarya Nagarjuna was translated into Telugu by M.

Rajagopalarao, *Vajracchedika* was also translated into Telugu by Bodhacaitanya. Malayasri has translated Asvaghosa's *Vajrasuchi* into Telugu. Santideva's *Bodhicaryavatara* was also translated into Telugu by Bodhacaitanya, it was published by Ananda Buddhavihara, a trust in Hyderabad, in 2001. *Milinda panha* was also translated into Telugu as *Milinda prasnalu* by Bodhacaitanya. The same author has written *Vajrachedika Prajnaparamita* and *Jayamangalam.* Chouduri Upendra has written a small booklet on Pali entitled *Pali basha puttu purvottaralu,* and the philosophical discussions in *Dighanikaya.* All these books were published by Ananda Buddhavihara, Hyderabad.

Another significant work in Tamil literature, *The Manimeghalai* was also translated into Telugu as *Kalyana Manjeeralu.* A noteworthy work *Ksemendra's Avadana Kalpalata* was also translated into Telugu by Tirumala Ramachandra, reprinted in 2000 by the Ananda Buddhavihara, Hyderabad. This trust has published more than sixteen books on different aspects of Buddhism. Finally, one tantric work entitled *Navanatha charitra,* written by Gauranamatya during the fourteenth century was published by the Andhra Pradesh Sahitya Academy, Hyderabad, in 1984. Sri Tummapudi Koteswararao revised it.

All this shows conclusively how the Telugu language and literature is enriched to a great extent with the impact and interaction of Buddhism over the centuries. In modern Telugu literature we see many works which are dealing with the social problems resorting to the discussion of doctrines of the Buddha and his *dhamma.* As discussed earlier, all the Buddhist literary works in Telugu in the form of poetical compositions, novels, plays (including one-act plays), street dramas like *Burra-katha,* which is a corrupt form of Buddhakatha, and dance-dramas, translations, essays, critical descriptive and reflective and research work and all other writings on arts and customs and travels, constitute a steady stream, flowing full with contribution.

15

Buddhism and Hindi Literature

Angraj Chaudhary

I do not think that there has been a great impact of the Buddha on the Hindi poets that I am going to consider in this paper. What I mean is that those who have written on the Buddha have not been greatly influenced by his teachings in that they have not made the Four Noble Truths or *tilakkhaṇa* (three characteristics of things and *dhammas* of the world) as the subject of their writing,[1] nor have they made in all sincerity the social philosophy of the Buddha as the theme of their literary works except perhaps one or two who clearly saw through his great purpose in making no distinction between one man and another on the basis of their birth in a particular caste which is nothing but a social organization and raised their voice against it as Kabir did. Nor have they made the Buddha's Eightfold Path, which is the surest and the most unfailing means of ending misery, as the theme of their works. However, there is no denying that some of them have been greatly influenced by the magnetic and majestic personality of the Buddha where compassion and wisdom meet.

Jai Shankar Prasad, one of the great Hindi poets expresses his deep faith in the great ascetic of all times who forsaking all worldly pelf and pleasures, caring little for the warm love of his beautiful wife, paternal love of his father and desire to fondle the son born to him, made the Great Renunciation in the prime of his life for finding out the path to end not only his own suffering but that of the entire humanity. He prefers the quiet bank of the Varuṇā River to magnificent mansions.

अरी वरुणा की शांत कछार,
तपस्वी के विराग की प्यार।

O, the quiet banks of Varuṇā
Beloved of the ascetic who is non-attached and free from cravings.

He also brings to light what the salient features of his teachings are. The world is burning, burning and burning with the fire of *rāga* (craving), *dvesha* (aversion) and *moha* (ignorance) as the Buddha expounds it in the *Āditta pariyāya sutta* and his message of annihilating craving and aversion is the only way of becoming cool, quiet and calm and to reach *nirvana* where there is no burning. Prasad also puts his finger on the central humanitarian message of the Buddha. Man is great. He can make or mar himself. He can break the wheel of birth and death without depending upon any god or 'God' with a capital 'G'. This humanitarianism, which is the hub of the Buddha's philosophy, finds expression in these lines of Prasad:

देवकर से पीड़ित विक्षुब्ध-प्राणियों से कह उठा पुकार।
तोड़ सकते हो तुम भव-बंध, तुम्हें है यह पूरा अधिकार।

Human beings thought they were troubled and tormented by gods. The Buddha exhorted them and said they are free and capable of breaking the fetters that bind them to the wheel of birth and death.

He exhorted men who believed that their suffering is caused by gods to break the cycle of birth and death and work out their own salvation and said they are fully competent to do so.

He also clearly understood the Buddha's philosophy inasmuch as he says that suffering is caused by man's action and it can be ended only by his action. He also speaks here of the middle path followed and prescribed by the Buddha. The middle path consists in avoiding the two extremes of hedonism and asceticism.

छोड़कर जीवन के अतिवाद, मध्यपथ से लो सुगति सुधार।
दुःख का समुदय उसका नाश, तुम्हारे कर्मों का व्यापार।

Avoid the two extremes of hedonism and asceticism, and follow the middle path. It's your actions that cause you suffering and it is they that put an end to it.

He concludes his poem with an impressive visual image when he says that the Buddha was the living embodiment of the consciousness of the suffering world.

Sumitranandan Pant's small poem entitled बुद्ध के प्रति (To the Buddha) brings out his great praise of the Buddha's right thought, his practice of meditation to see through things as they are and his discovery of the path walking on which man can make his life happy and free from suffering. He sings his praise to the Buddha who was like the golden pinnacle (स्वर्णिम शिखर) in the dark world of troubles and tribulations, and the embodiment of all great values.

नव भावी स्वप्नों से विस्मित जब मैं विस्तृत
सिंह दृष्टि डालता विगत के धूमिल पट पर,
सबसे स्वर्णिम शिखर तुम्हीं दीखते अतन्द्रित।
मुझे तथागत-भास्वर सुन्दर निःस्वर, निर्जर
युग के गौरव शिखर जहां मन मुक्त विचर कर
आर-पार कर ध्यान निरीक्षण सम्यक चिंतन
शतियों में विस्तीर्ण मध्ययुग के करता दिग्दर्शन।

Nirālā is deeply influenced by the Buddha's spiritualism which contrasts significantly with modern materialism marked by great scientific achievements which easily provide us with creature comforts, but do not tell us to turn our face from them and take to the path leading to *nirvanic* happiness.

Nirālā seems to have understood the values the Buddha stands for and realizes their importance in the world, which, dominated by materialism, stands on the brink of destruction. It is true we have made great strides in the field of science, which has given us faster means of movement and has made several discoveries to add to our creature comforts. It has not only given boost to gross materialism which is like a ghost with an ugly face but also has developed in us the desire to have more and more and become more selfish than ever. The sad result is that we have forgotten to turn our face from *preya* to *sreya*, to forsake rather than possess and to give rather than take. When the world was torn by these conflicting values, and there was darkness of ignorance, Tathāgata came shedding light and glorified renunciation and not possession of material things. His walking on the Eightfold Path enabled him to put his finger on the cause of man's suffering and also discover the way to root out its cause. With his realization there came a light in the world, which went a long way in dispelling darkness. It was so strong that spiritual pragmatism got over material pragmatism and his teachings spread far and wide in the world, which ennobled the heart of different peoples of the world.

आज सभ्यता के वैज्ञानिक जड़ विकास पर, गर्वित विश्व नष्ट होने की ओर अग्रसर स्पष्ट दिख रहा
हंसते हैं जड़वाद ग्रस्त, प्रेत ज्यों परस्पर, विकृत नयन-मुख, कहते हुए अतीत भयंकर था मानव के लिए एक मात्र सत्य के लिए, रूढ़ि से विमुख, रतकठिन तपस्या में, पहुंचे लक्ष्य को तथागत
फूटी ज्योति विश्व में...
फूटे शत-शत उत्स सहज मानवता-जल के, यहां वहां पृथ्वी के सब देशों में छलके
छल के बल के पंकिल भौतिक रूप अदर्शित हुए तुम्हीं से, हुई तुम्हीं से ज्योति प्रदर्शित।

This is a good tribute to the Buddha as Nirālā says that the Buddha showed light, but he does not seem to have understood the importance of the middle path propounded by the Buddha who did not put a premium on austere penance. Nirālā seems to wrongly glorify it.

Maithilisharana Gupta does not directly deal with any Buddhist subject as such, say, *aniccatā* (impermanence) or *dukkhatā* as it is dealt with by the poet of Telakatāhagāthā who in about one hundred verses muses on nothing but death, impermanence and sorrow, nor does it exclusively deal with other Buddhist subjects like change as we find it dealt with by the Theri Ambapali who stands disillusioned when her blooming youth faded and gave way to old age. In her verses she poignantly describes how all her limbs, which were incomparably beautiful when she was young, lost beauty and what a disappointing change had come upon her. But this poignant observation of change in her does not make her sad and sorrowful, instead she finds how true are the words of the Buddha which describe reality and girds up her loins and makes effort after truly understanding the nature of reality, develops non-attachment *(nirveda)*, strives for ending her misery and ultimately attains *arahathood.*

Yasodhara of Maithilisharana Gupta is written with the purpose of bringing to limelight Yasodhara's character as the poet felt that she was neglected by poets and writers in the same way as Urmila, Laxman's wife, was neglected both in the *Ramayana* and the *Ramacaritamanasa.* Urmila's sacrifice is great. Sita lived with Rama in the jungle, two of her sisters were with their husbands but Urmila, left alone, had to suffer a great deal at the hands of Kamdeo who used to shoot at her his soft shafts of flowers which made her burn in the fire of separation from her husband. As Gupta delineates the character of Urmila in the 9th and the 10th cantos of *Saketa,* so in *Yasodhara* he takes upon himself to delineate Yasodhara's character, her great sacrifice, her duty as a mother in bringing up her son Rahul and at the same time living a life of *sanyasini* without caring for worldly pleasures. No sooner does her husband leave home for leading a homeless life than it dawns upon her that worldly pleasures are fleeting. They are like a mirage which cannot give a lasting happiness and which can never be satisfied. But the poet has shown her as a *mānini nāyikā,* a woman offended at the behaviour of her husband. She is unhappy not because her husband renounced home for leading an ascetic life, but she is offended because he did not consider her worth his trust. She says that it is a matter of pride that he renounced this world to attain enlightenment and seek liberation, but it is a severe blow to her that he reposed no trust in her and left home clandestinely.

सिद्धि हेतु स्वामी गये, यह गौरव की बात।
पर चोरी-चोरी गये, यही बड़ा व्याघात॥
सखि, वे मुझसे कहकर जाते।
कह, तो क्या मुझको वे अपनी पथबाधा ही पाते?

This act of her husband is giving her excruciating pains. She cannot bear the fact that he did not consider her worth his trust. She knows that she would not have proved an obstacle in his path, but that he did not inform her suspecting her to be weak is what sharply stings and stabs her. She feels let down. She complains that although he loved her much, he failed to fully know her, to recognize her and to identify her strengths and weaknesses. She feels like reproaching him, feels like calling him a cruel person, but she does not do so, thinking at the same time that he is not cruel, he is so full of warmth and love that had he seen her crying, he would have found it impossible to bear it, but she sheds tears as she finds herself alone in 'the deep wide sea of misery'. She wishes him well and further wishes that his objective is fulfilled. She is sure that he would bring something incomparable.

It is a praiseworthy literary effort that Gupta has taken up his pen to delineate the character of Yasodhara who had almost been obliterated from the minds of the people. Yasodhara was a sacrificing lady who suffered silently. With strong resolve she followed the path of her husband. Without leaving home (it is not as easy for a mother to leave home as it is for a father), she lived a homeless life, a life shorn of all pleasures and luxuries and a life almost of a *Bhikkhuni.* Lest her long beautiful dark hair should be dishevelled and take her time to comb and arrange it, she decides to get rid of it and resolves living a very simple life with no ornaments and no diamonds on her body. Like a true Indian woman with vermillion mark shining on her head, she considers herself fortunate and wishes that the fire-like red mark on her forehead may render all his troubles to ashes.

बस, सिन्दुर-बिन्दु से मेरा जगा रहे यह भाल,
वह जलता अंगार जला दे उनका सब जंजाल।

There is a great conflict going on in her mind and Gupta has very vividly and powerfully expressed this conflict. The conflict that goes on in her mind is why is it that he did not trust her, why is it that he did not inform her before leaving home. Was she so small and selfish that she would have been an obstacle in his path? When she could give up all comforts and luxuries and live a simple life, would she not have let him go?

हाय स्वार्थिनी थी मैं ऐसी रोक तुम्हें रख लेती
जहां राज्य भी त्याज्य, वहां मैं जाने तुम्हें न देती ?

She says that she would have gladly bid him farewell without obstructing his path. But as he did not inform her, he deprived her of the opportunity to welcome him back. That she is not going to welcome him is considered by her as impolite, but what to do? She did not bid him farewell, how can she welcome him? As a result she feels both shame and anguish.

विदा न लेकर स्वागत से भी वंचित यहां किया है
हन्त अन्त में यह अविनय भी तुमने मुझे दिया है।

But this does not make her weak. Instead, she resolves to become strong. She says that if he considered her a slave of desires, a weak woman, she would prove that she is not so. She decides not to remain a delicate and feeble woman but wants to become tough and enduring. She also resolves to pass the test, which her husband has passed successfully.

अब कठोर हो वज्रादपि ओ कुसुमादपि सुकुमारी।
आर्यपुत्र दे चुके परीक्षा, अब है मेरी बारी॥

It dawns upon her why, of a bevy of beautiful girls, he took only her hand. He did so because he saw in her a suitable companion, a suitable spouse who would help him in his great cause. If she does not prove herself capable of espousing his cause, she would look small in her own eyes. So she makes an effort to prove herself equal to the task.

She asks a question, if a woman is an obstacle in the path of liberation, how can she attain her own liberation?

सिद्धि मार्ग की बाधा नारी, फिर उसकी क्या गति है ?

She musters courage to face reality, understands that her youth and beauty must undergo a change and asks others not to feel pity for her. Instead, she decides to prove herself equal to the task for which she was chosen by him and gladly asks him to work out his own salvation and discover a medicine to end the suffering of mankind. Now she feels no remorse, is happy to remain his servant and asks him to have मुक्ति (deliverance) as his queen-consort. She is ready to bear pangs of separation from him and wishes him success in his endeavour. She knows that when a man practices penance, Sakra sends beautiful dancing damsels *(apsaras)* to interrupt his austere penance and break it. She wishes that he who has taken her hand should have no interruption from them.

तुम्हें अप्सरा विघ्न न व्यापे यशोधरा करधारी।

At one place she says beautifully that as the nature of oil is to burn, of vapour is to rise, of rain to come down, so the nature of our body is to suffer.

जलने को ही स्नेह बना, उठने को ही वाष्प बना
गिरने को ही मेह बना, सब सहने को देह बना॥

This is how she learns to reconcile herself to the adverse circumstances in which she finds herself. Her greatest prayer now is that the fruits achieved by him should be enjoyed by all.

उनके श्रम के फल सब भोगें, यशोधरा की विनय यही।

When Rahul charges his father with leaving his home and leaving them in lurch, she puts up a strong defence for him and says that as his heart is large he is generous enough to make the whole universe his family, to care for each one of the people and not to selfishly think only of his wife, son and parents.

बेटा, घर छोड़ वे गये हैं अन्य दृष्टि से
जोड़ लिया नाता है उन्होंने सब सृष्टि से।
हृदय विशाल और उनका उदार है
विश्व को बनाना चाहता जो परिवार है॥

In spite of all these strengths in her character and also of her great heart full of sincere wishes for his glorious success in his spiritual endeavour, she has been painted as a fatalist.

She considers herself unfortunate. That is why he did not take leave of her, nor her amorous gestures could keep him from renouncing the world.

मेरा हास विलास! किन्तु क्या भाग्य तुम्हें रख पाये?

She gets solace and strength from her belief in fate.

भोगना ही पड़ता है, जो-जो भोग होता है।

This is strong fatalism which is not in tune with the philosophy of the Buddha who says that what a man reaps accords with his deeds. But her character has been painted by a poet who was a devotee of Rama and was hardly familiar with the spirit of the Buddha's thought.

Being asked by Rahul as to why she sheds tears off and on she says she does so because she likes it as it relieves her, eases her pain. Thereupon Rahul asks her not to be under the control of her desires, but control them, but she says that it is tears which produce cathartic effect on her. She likes sorrow and suffering as they bring all suffering people of the world together. In order to prove that she does not shed her tears because she is unhappy, she says peoples' eyes become wet too when they are happy.

दु:ख से भी जाऊं? मुझे उससे है ममता।
बढ़ती है जिससे सहानुभूति समता॥
शोक के समान हम हर्ष में भी रोते हैं।
अश्रु-तीर्थ में ही सुख-दु:ख एक होते हैं।

Yasodhara's pain and sorrow are like a poet's pain and sorrow, not those of a saint. The latter aims to transcend them, the former considers them a very strong bond amongst the suffering people. Rabindranath Tagore eulogises sorrow from this point of view. It is this which unites all labourers of the world. Mahādevi Verma is fond of this because it brings suffering people together and enables them to develop noble sentiments like love and sympathy.

It is true that Gupta does not paint the character of Yasodhara objectively, but even then he paints her as a woman whose sole aim is not to enjoy only sensual pleasures (पर क्या पूर्ति वासना भर की) but as a woman where pride and humility gloriously meet. (दैन्य और दर्प जहां दोनों का बसेरा है।)

It is on record in Pali literature that Yasodhara was ordained and became a nun. She became a nun because she wanted to break the cycle of birth and death, and attain *nirvana,* a state of desirelessness, a state where there is no burning. But Gupta has made her spurn deliverance and say that she likes to come as the sun and the moon and the cloud come again and again in this world to do wholesome actions and enjoy the prescribed pleasure, for isn't the desire for deliverance in itself a desire?

कह मुक्ति, भला, किसलिये तुझे मैं पाऊं?
ये चन्द्रसूर्य निवार्ण नहीं पाते हैं, ओझल हो-होकर हमें दृष्टि आते हैं।
झोंके समीर के झूम-झूम के जाते हैं, जा-जाकर नीरद नया नीर लाते हैं।
तो क्यों जा-जाकर लौट न मैं भी आऊं?
कह मुक्ति भला किसलिये तुझे मैं पाऊं?

The aesthetic that Gupta uses to delineate Yasodhara's character is full of anachronisms. It was the custom of the medieval period that Rajput women used to send their brave husbands to the battlefield equipping them with a shield and a sword. It was not so during the time of the Buddha. Therefore, when Yasodhara says that:

स्वयं सुसज्जित कर के क्षण में, प्रियतम को प्राणों के पण में,
हमीं भेज देती हैं रण में, क्षात्र-धर्म के नाते।

and when Rahul says that he likes the story of Damayanti and advises her mother to make a gander her messenger, Gupta uses anachronistic examples to delineate her character, for the *Mahabharata* containing Damayanti's story and Kalidasa's *Meghadūta* making the cloud a messenger are later works. Similarly, when Siddhartha makes his Great Renunciation, Gupta puts these words into his mouth:

ओ क्षणभंगुर भव राम-राम and
हे राम तुम्हारा वंश जात,
सिद्धार्थ तुम्हारी भांति तात,
घर छोड़ चला यह आज रात, are chronologically anachronistic. It is clear that Gupta has taken liberty with history, but the question is how much liberty can a creative writer take while creating works of art? It seems Gupta has taken more liberty than prescribed by Anandavardhana.[2]

In spite of these drawbacks the way he painted the character of the Buddha has much authenticity. He seems to have understood the central philosophy of the Buddha.

घूम रहा है कैसा चक्र? and
कैसे परित्राण हम पावें? किन देवों को रोवें-गावें?
पहले अपना कुशल सुनावें, वे सारे सुर-शक्र।
खोज रहा है क्या सहाय तू? मेट आप ही अन्तराय।

He exhorts people not to depend on gods for their deliverance but asks them to strive hard and work out their own salvation by breaking the wheel of birth and death.

Mahadevi Verma is another Hindi poet on whom there has been some impact of the Buddha's compassion and his philosophy enunciating the Four Noble Truths of suffering. The Buddha's philosophy is not merely a theoretical philosophy like that of Leibnitz's, but it has a very well-defined realistic action plan. It is a philosophy of action and not of idle speculation.[3] Whatever is propounded here has sprung from his own experience. He realized things at the level of experience, so his realization is the realization of truth. When he propounded the philosophy of ubiquitous suffering, he also made a resolve to end it. He discovered the path by walking on which one can end one's suffering. So in the Buddha we do not find any weakness whatsoever, not an attitude to break into tears in the face of all kinds of troubles that come to men. Instead, he observes *sila*, practices meditation *(samādhi)*, develops wisdom *(pannā)* and makes himself fully able to annihilate all kinds of sufferings altogether, root them out completely. The great compassion that he feels for suffering beings urges him to show them the path he discovered, walking on which one can end one's suffering forever. He feels compassion for suffering beings, but does not cry and shed tears. Instead, he makes a resolve to root it out. His compassion, therefore, is not passive, but it is an active one. His experience of suffering does not make him lachrymose. Instead, he strives to end it.

His compassion for suffering beings drives him to work incessantly. He preaches man to work out his own salvation. So it does not stop him from doing hard work, it does not weaken him but makes him strong. This compassion is born in him the moment he attains enlightenment and because of it he takes upon himself the arduous task of helping others to come out of their suffering. Poetry may be born from a cry, a cry of pain but the Buddha does not cry, although he experiences excruciating universal pain very sensitively. Mahadevi's poetry is born of her cry of pain. The former's experience of pain is that of saint whereas the latter's is that of a poet, a distinction rightly made by Dinkar.[4]

The impact of the Buddha on Mahadevi Verma is rather superficial. Had it been deep, she would not have written only lachrymose poetry. The Buddha never wants suffering to become his companion as Madhadevi does when she says to one whom she worships that he should come to her in the form of suffering. तुम दु:ख बन इस पथ से आना। The Buddha knows why it is caused and he resolves to root it out. He also knows that suffering can be ended. Mahadevi Verma, on the other hand, says that she knows of no human situation or no period in human history when there has been no suffering. So she wants to be friends with it, like Shelley who says, "Misery, we have known each other like a sister and a brother." She likes suffering, because her being lachrymose brings all suffering beings closer and closer. It is true that the feeling of pain does bring suffering people together, but is it to be liked on this account? Is it to be made friends with on this account? Mahadevi's personal life caused her intense suffering, as there was no way out of it, she bore it patiently and expressed it in her poems so artistically that it seems to have become spiritual and mystical. It is like Shelley's "the desire of the moth for the star". Had she understood the Buddha's philosophy, she would have at least visualized that suffering could be ended.

She likes suffering because suffering people come closer to her and feel sympathetic towards her. She has come to realize that suffering will endear her to all. Just as rose blossoms amidst thorns, so she thinks her life will grow and become meaningful amidst suffering. She also brings out the chastening effect of sorrow.

शूलों में नित मृदु पाटल-सा, खिलने देना मेरा जीवन।

She brings out the value of suffering by saying that flowers are to be pierced before they can be made into a garland.

क्या हार बनेगा वह जिसने सीखा न हृदय को बिंधवाना?

She says:

"Suffering is capable of binding all people together. Our umpteen pleasures may not teach us the first lesson of humanity, but one drop of our tears can make our life sweeter and more fertile."

मैं नीर भरी दु:ख की बदली।
रजकण पर जलकण हो बरसी,
नवजीवन अंकुर बन निकली,
पथ को न मलिन करता आना
पदचिह्न न दे जाता जाना,
सुधि मेरे आगम की जग में
सुख की सिहरन हो अन्त खिली
विस्तृत नभ का कोई कोना
मेरा न कभी अपना होना
परिचय इतना इतिहास यही,
उमड़ी कल थी मिट आज चली।

It seems that she has no attachment. That's why she does not have the desire to possess even a small part of the vast universe. This brings her close to the Buddha's philosophy of developing *nirveda.* But has this *nirveda* developed from her realization of transitoriness of all things at the experiential level or has it developed from her frustration of not getting what she wants?

At one place she says, "Man wants to enjoy pleasures alone, but he wants to share his sorrows with others so that his sorrows may become universal sorrow just as a drop of water loses its existence in the vast ocean."

Mahadevi regards sorrow as something permanent. It has always been there in the world. But the Buddha knows how it comes into being and therefore he preaches people to remove its cause to end it.

So far as Mahadevi is concerned, she wants to lose herself, annihilate her ego, has no desire to be remembered by others as Christina Rossetti says in one of her poems:

When I am dead, my dearest,
Sing no sad songs for me
Plant thou no roses at my head
Nor shady Cyprus tree.

Her personal life is very sad, because of her unsuccessful conjugal life, but she thinks it a blessing in disguise. It may look like a curse to others, but it is not so to her.

शळभ मैं शापमय वर हूं ?
किसी का दीप निष्ठुर हूं
ताज है जलती शिखा
चिनगारियां श्रृंगारमाला
ज्वाल अक्षय-कोष सी
अंगार मेरी रंगशाला
नाश में जीवित किसी की साध सुंदर हूं।

She seems to have been influenced by the Buddha's philosophy of transitoriness at only the intellectual level. All are in a constant state of flux.

न रहता भौरों का आहवान, नहीं रहता फूलों का राज।
कोकिला होती अन्तर्धान, चला जाता प्यारा ऋतुराज
असंभव है चिर सम्मेलन, न भूलो क्षणभंगुर जीवन॥

The call of the bees does not last forever,
Nor does the kingdom of flowers last

The cuckoo disappears after the spring
And the beloved spring also goes away.
Forget not that life is but ephemeral.
and

भुला डालो जीवन की साध, मिटा डालो बीते का लेश।
एक रहने देना यह ध्यान, क्षणिक है यह मेरा परदेश॥

But unlike the Buddha she believes in a permanent soul, which after death goes to its own permanent abode. At one place she says that as she became devoted to the Buddha right in her childhood, so she became familiar with his pessimistic philosophy, rather untimely, rather prematurely. But the Buddha's philosophy is not pessimistic. Mahadevi Verma has not realized the deeper significance of the Buddha's philosophy.

From what she says above it is clear that she is only superficially influenced by his philosophy of transitoriness. She has, however, been greatly influenced by the Buddha's personality:

जाग, बेसुध जाग।
अश्रुकण से उर सजाया, त्याग हीरक-हार,
भीख दुःख की मांगने फिर जो गया प्रतिद्वार।
शूल जिसने फूल छू चन्दन किया संताप
पुन जगाती है उसी सिद्धार्थ की पदचाप,
करुणा के दुलारे जाग।

From all this it becomes clear that Mahadevi has been influenced by the great personality of the Buddha who made a great sacrifice by giving up pleasures and pelf, discovered the path by walking on which one can end suffering and quench burning. But the impact of the Buddha on her is only partial, of a superficial kind. That Mahadevi sees in suffering a chastening effect can be said to be the impact perhaps of Jain philosophy which believes that suffering (physical punishment) has a disciplining effect on life. The Buddha does not believe in the cathartic and chastening effect of sorrow, of tears. Mahadevi seems to believe in both.

REFERENCES

1. cf. Telakatāhagātha.
   cf. Verses of Therī Ambapli.
   (See my article entitled 'Buddha's view of Beauty' in *Essays on Buddhism and Pali Literature.*)

2. *Itivṛttavasāyātām tyaktvā'nanuguṇaṃ sthitiṃ/*
Utpreksyāntarābhiṣṭa rasocita katthonnayah// - Dhvanyāloka.
3. See my article entitled 'Buddhism; Where Philosophy and Religion Converge', collected in *Buddhism in India and Abroad,* K.J. Somaiya Institute, Mumbai.
4. Veṇuvana—Dr. Ramadhari Singh 'Dinkar'.

16

Impact of Buddhism in Ajñeya's Works

Bimalendra Kumar

The impact of Buddhism on literature in various Indian languages has been continuous and in the present century, modern writers have shown their interest in the Buddha's life and ideals in an effort to overcome the misery of casteism and violence in one's life. Though there are nearly a score of major Indian languages, discernible Buddhist influence has been only on a few. In this paper there is a humble attempt to throw light on the impact of Buddhism on Hindi literature, specially the works of Ajñeya.

The concepts of non-violence, higher human values and equality for all are also seen in the songs of some devotional saint poets of Hindi as Gorakhanath, Kabir, Ravidas, etc. Some scholars as Hazari Prasad Dwivedi and Pt. Rahul Sankrityayan believed that this was due to the impact of Buddhism. There might also be Vaishnava influence on devotional Hindi poets. From Kabir to Bhartendu there is no trace of Buddhism in Hindi writing. Bhartendu Harishchandra rendered the book *Mudrā Rākshasha* with Buddhist political structure into Hindi, but has also passed satirical comments on Buddhism in his other writings. Rahul Sankrityayan has taken reference from Buddhism in *Volga Se Ganga* and *Sihasenāpati*; Jaishankar Prasad in *Chandragupta, Ajatshatru, Rajyashree;* Maithilisharan Gupta composed *Yashodhārā* (poetry); Acharya Chaturasen Shastri took many references in *Vaishālī Kī Nagaravadhu;* Sacchidānand Hīrānand Vātsyāyan Ajñeya wrote *Asādhya Veeṇā, Āgana Ke Pār Dwār* and *Kitanī Navon Mein Kitanī Bār* in the light of Buddhist philosophy related with life. It is not possible to analyze the works of all modern Hindi scholars in this small paper. I am concentrating my article especially on the works of Ajñeya, having influence of Buddhism.

The teachings of the Lord Buddha are dynamic principles, gradually moving towards amelioration and generation of complete harmony in life as a whole. It is like a raft (*kullūpama*) going from this shore to another of the river full of stormy waves.[1] Here, this shore is the state of suffering; the other shore is the state of happiness alone. The river is the weary life process with attachment and the boat is the *dhamma* as the righteous efforts.[2] Ajñeya in his poem *Ham nadī ke sātha sātha* has expressd symbolically this idea as:

Nadī kā nāva,
Na jāne kaba khula gayī,
Nadī hī sāgara mein ghula gayī,
Hamarī hi gānṭha na khulī,
Dīṭha na dhulī, ham phir lauṭa kar gali gali,
Apanī purānī asti kī ṭoha mein bharmāte rahe.[3]

Nobody knows when the boat got unanchored; the river itself merged with the sea, only our knots did not loose, our eyes could not be washed, we after returning loiter amongst lanes in search of our existence.

The similar idea can also be seen in the first utterance of the Lord Buddha after having got the enlightenment:

Aneka jāti samāram sandhāvissa anivissaṃ,
Gahakāraka gavesanto, dukkhā jāti punappuna,
Gahakāraka diṭṭhosi puna gehaṃ na kāhasi,
Sabbā te phāsukā bhaggā gahakuṭaṃ visamkhataṃ,
Visarikhāragataṃ cittaṃ taṇhānaṃ khayamajjhagā.[4]

The line *hamārī hi gānṭha na khulī* of the poem suggestively underlines various impressions of our chain of births. It also records our passions, which are within us. These are the rootcause of our birth and death cycle and we cannot observe it. Ajñeya adds that it is unfortunate that man fails to realize the reality of the world.

In another poem *Samparāya,* Ajñeya sets forth the impermanence of life. He tells:

Rūpa
rūpāyamāna,
rupāyita,
yon grihit,
pahacānā,
phir isa liye anrit
akānta jhuṭa.[5]

These lines show that this entire visible world is a deception, unreal and momentary. This world is merely an illusion and has no reality.

Ajñeya has also put his philosophical quest in his collections. His collection *Āṅgan Ke Pāra Dvār* is divided into three sections: *Chakrāntaśēlā*, *Antahsalilā* and *Asādhya Vīnā*. In the poem *Maun*[6] the poet seems to hear the music of eternal life force.[7] The following lines explicitly pronounce the merger of individual soul with the eternal silence:

Arī O ātma rī
Kanyā, bholī Kwānrī,
Mahāsunya ke sāth bhānvare terī racī gayī.[8]

Oh virgin, innocent, simple soul, your marriage is to be celebrated with eternal silence.

The same thing appears in the *Brahmanimantikasutta* of the *Majjhima Nikāya* taking a note of a consciousness, infinite and universal in nature. It presents description as:

Viññanaṃ anidassanaṃ anantaṃ,
sabbatopabhaṃ taṃ paṭhaviyā
pathavattena ananubhūtaṃ, āpassa
āpattena ananubhūtaṃ ... sabbassa
sabbattena ananubhūtaṃ ... [9]

There is a consciousness, invisible, infinite, all-pervading, which cannot be reached through the extensity of extension, by the cohesiveness of cohesion ... by the allness of the all Brahmā.

In Theravāda Buddhism, *Nibbāna* is that which is achieved in this very life after total negation of desires together with other polluting factors. *Parinibbana* is that state of freedom, the merger of the individual mundane consciousness into the supramundane universal consciousness and experiencing the eternal bliss after the expiry of the life process of an Arahata. In the poem *Oh Nisanga Mamatar* of Ajñeya, we also find the influence of the concept of *nirvana*. He says:

O vis'va pratima,
ab tū isa kriti sīpa ko apne mein sameṭa le,
yah paridris'ya sokha le,
swāti bunda, cātaka ko ātmleena tu kar le.[10]

Oh image of the world! collect and swallow this shell and absorb all this scene in thyself. Oh drop of swati, assimilate thy lover, the bird cātaka into thee.

The poem entitled *Asādhya Vīṇā* of Ajñeya is a symbolic

representation of self-realization. The musical instrument called *vīṇā* is essentially a symbol of the physical existence of man. The poem unfolds that one, who is the real seeker of Truth (*satya*), eternal silence (*nirvāna*) and the great void (*mahāśunya*) can play upon this instrument. Such music is an expression of eternal truth. The king, the queen and the courtiers are only common people not endowed with the faculty of perceiving the subtle music of that symbolic *vīṇā* expressed through the mortal human frame. Even the seekers of the truth cannot realize and resolve the mystery of creation unless they surrender themselves to the great cosmic power. The poem also says that we all are in chains of *Tanhājaṭā* (tangles of desire) and to disentangle this tangle, one is required to possess morality (*sīla*), concentration (*samādhi*), and knowledge (*prajñā*). In Buddhism, *sīla* curtails the physical-vocal misdeeds and makes them morally sound. *Samādhi* destroys the mental misdeeds and prepares a congenial atmosphere for emergence of the pure consciousness. *Prajñā* removes the darkness of ignorance, penetrates into the nature of reality, makes it understandable as impermanent, subject to suffering and substanceless, helps in uprooting the thickets of attachment and realisation of the supramundane blissful state. These three are the essentials of entire physio-psychic and spiritual life of Buddhist tradition.[11] The poem *Asādhya Vīṇā* has also a practitioner of *sīla* namely, Priyamvada:

Par usa spndita sannāṭe mein,
Maun priyamvada sādh rahā thā vīṇā,
Nahīn, svayam apane ko śodha rahā thā....
bhūl gayā thā keśakambalī raj-sabhā ko....
kambal par abimantrita eka akelepana mein
ḍub gayā thā.[12]

Priyamvada practices *sīla* and *samādhi*, which are essential for entering into a state of eternal bliss. He by his perseverance elevates so high that he feels one with Endless, Infinite, Intransient, Omnipresent, and Omniscient completely by crossing these stages of *paṭhamjjhāna, ekodibhāvanā, upekkhā* and *jhāna*. He utters:

'sunā āpane jo vaha merā nahīn,
na vīṇā kā thā,
vah to saba kucha kī tathatā thī ....
mahāśunya wah mahāmaun
avibhājya, anāpta, adravit, aprameya
jo sabdahīna saba mein gātā hai.[13]

Here, one thing is noteworthy that the truth, which vibrates in the music of Priyamvada's flute, has no relation with time, as it is non-existent. Now, the speech, the speaker and the thought have merged together completely. Priyamavada being guided by the knowledge attains complete calm. That is why he, enjoying the oneness of all substances and realizing Truth in them, comes out with the following philosophic utterance:

Mein to duba gayā thā svayam śunya mein,
Viṇā ke mādhyam se apane ko maine,
Sab kucha ko saumpa diyā thā,
Mahāśunya,
Vah mahāmaun
Avibhājya, anāpta, adravita, aprameya,
Jo sabdahīna
Sabme gātā hai.[14]

The above utterance which defines the one, ascertains *tathagatā* in all substances. Priyamvada too experiences various images and events one by one while he is in a state of meditation. But now he is able to recognise them. He, approaching the state of *samādhi,* moves towards *nirvāna* and feels liberated from this illusory world. He holds:

Mujhe smarana hai, aur chitra pratyeka,
Stabdha, vicarita karatā hai mujhako,
Sunatā hun main
par har svara kampana letā hain mujhako mujhase sokha,
Vāyu-sā nāda bharā main uḍa jātā hun ....
Mujhe smarana hai,
par mujhako mein bhūl gayā hun sunatā hun main,
par main mujhase pare, sabda mein tiyamāna.[15]

Uttara Priyadarshi is another celebrated poetic drama of Ajñeya. It vividly dramatizes the later life experiences of Davānāmapriya Ashoka. Consequent upon the huge devastation and innocent deaths in the fierce Kalinga battle, a great change of heart took place in Ashoka. He became an extemely compassionate man. This change of heart acquired immense significance and meaning after his acceptance of Buddhism as a governing principle of his life. *Uttara Priyadarshi* captures these crucial moments, conflicts and experiences of Ashoka's life and portrays them very intensely. In the Buddhist

17

Buddhism and Sanskrit Drama

Kalpika Mukherjee

In the long history of Sanskrit drama, the *Saugandhikāharanam* is the earliest drama that is said to have been enacted during the lifetime of the Buddha.[1] It was enacted by the two noted disciples of the Buddha, one was Upatissa, a pet name of Sāriputra, and the other was Maudgalyāyana. If this is taken as authentic then it will open a new vista of dramatic literature and dramatic performance in India. Scholars like A.B. Keith are, however, sceptical about this view. He says, 'We see the objection of the sacred Canon to monks engaging in the amusement of watching these shows. Whatever their nature was gradually overcome, and it is an important fact that the earliest dramas known to us by fragments are the Buddhist dramas of Āśvaghosa.'[2] Keith does not mention therefore the *Saugandhikāharanam.* Keith has dismissed the account of the Lalitavistarā that the Buddha was proficient in nātyakalā as legendary.[3] He refers to the legend of a drama being performed in honour of a pair of Nāga kings, and the Avadāna-śtaka, which may place the dramatic performance in India to a remote antiquity. The Avadānaśataka refers to Kuvalayā, an actress of enormous fame, who performed a drama at Rājagṛha under Gautama, the Buddha himself and to another tale in Tibet where the monks represented the life of the Buddha. All these have left their impression on the form of the Saddharma Pundarika.[4] Of course, the dramatic characters of the pabbajitasutta, bhikkhunisutta, theragāthā and therīgātha, ummadanti, padhanasutta, etc. are really dramatic in character.[5]

However, the first extant Sanskrit Buddhist drama is the *Śāriputra-prakarana* of Āśvaghosa in the 1st century AD. We have received the drama in two MSS traditions.[6] The theme of the drama has been drawn from the *Mahāvagga, Vinaya-pitaka* which conforms to the narration of the post Āśvaghosa period, viz., *The dhammapad-aṭṭhakathā* by Buddhaghoṣa (5th century AD). The story describes the conversion of Śāriputra and Maudgalyāyana.

Maudgalyāyana and Śāriputra were born in two respectable Brahmin families in Magadha and were bosom friends since their childhood. They were also known as Kolita and Upatissa after their village names. The place of the drama is Rājagṛha. One day they went to see a colourful festival on the mountain-top. For some time both enjoyed the fun of the festival thoroughly. After some time they felt a sort of discontentment and pondered over the impermanence of the worldly things. In this mental condition, one day, they saw Aśvajit, a noted disciple of the Buddha who was one of the 'pancavaggiya *bhikkhus*', roaming about in the streets of Rājagṛha and seeking alms. They were attracted by his serene appearance. They approached Aśvajit and opened their minds to him. He escorted them to the Buddha and they were ultimately ordained.

It is a *prakāraṇa* type of drama which is the second variety of 'rūpaka'. It conforms to the criteria of a *prakāraṇa* laid down by Bharata, who was either a senior contemporary or a contemporary of Āśvaghosa, in his nāṭyaśāstra. It is a social form of drama where the hero Somadatta and the heroine Magadhavatī are selected from the middle-class society. We have example of this in the *Mṛcchakaṭika* of Śūdraka where the hero Cārudatta is a Brahmin by birth but a merchant (*sārthavāha*) by profession. Here, in the *śāriputra-prakāraṇa,* the hero is a Brahmin by caste and later on a *śramaṇa* by conversion. As in the *Mṛcchakaṭika,* so also here, various types of people always crowd the stage. There is one *vidūṣaka* who is the *ālambana vibhāva* of *hasya rasa* (the sentiment of laughter). The 'duṣṭa' corresponds to Samsthānaka the rogue, in the *Mṛcchakaṭika.* The only diversion from the laid-down criteria of a *prakāraṇa* is the angi-rasa or the predominant sentiment of the drama. In *Śāriputra-prakaraṇa,* the angi-rasa is not *ṣrngāra,* which should be as per rule, but *śānta* for obvious reason. The author has chosen this *prakāraṇa* type since it has a deeper appeal to the masses. It may be noted that this drama has not been translated either in Chinese or in Tibetan even though it is a confirmed and a genuine work of Āśvaghosa like the *Buddhacarita* or the *Saundarānanda.* Dr. B. Bhattacharya thinks that the 'lalita' element of the drama was not accepted by the 'puritanie translators'.[7]

Along with the MSS of the *Śāriputra-prakaraṇa,* fragmentary MSS of two other dramas have been found. There is no other evidence of their authorship than that they are contained in the same place along with other works of Āśvaghosa and that they display some general characteristics of Āśvaghosa's writings. One is an allegorical drama as we get in the specimen of Kṛṣṇa Miśra's *prabodhacandrodaya* later on, having *kīrti* (fame), *dhṛti* (firmness) and *Buddhi* (wisdom) for characters. The Buddha appears with a hālo. The allegorical figures converse with each other. The other is a *hateara* drama where there is a heroine Magadhavati, a hero Somadatta, a *vidūṣaka* named Kaumudagandha. Kieth and other scholars like[8] S.K. Dey, M. Winternitz and the like have accepted it as a separate drama, whereas Dr. B. Bhattacharya, after a detailed scrutiny has said that the *Śāriputra-prarkaṇa* and the *heteara* drama are identical, or to be more precise, the later is a part of the former, and so also the allegorical drama.[9]

Rāṣṭrapāla-nātaka is another drama by Āśvaghosa. We know this from some direct and indirect sources since the Sanskrit original of the drama is not known to us. The entire drama has been preserved in the Chinese translation. The earliest reference is found in fu fa tsang yin yuan chuang of the Chinese *Tripitaka*. This was done in AD 472 by Ci Cia Ye (Nanjio) or Ki Kia Ye (P.C. Bagchi), whom he identifies as Kim Karya, a monk probably from central Asia. In 1958, Dr. Bagchi's article titled the 'Rāṣṭrapāla-nāṭaka of Āśvaghosa' was published in the Sardesai Com. Vol. His article was based on an article of Mr. Vidhusekhara Sastri, entitled 'A New Drama of Āśvaghosa' published in *JGIS*, Vol. 5, Calcutta, 1938. Sastri's observation is based on two references of the *Rāṣṭrapāla-nāṭaka*; one in the *Vādanyāya* of Dharmakīrti, the famous logician of the 6th century AD, and the other in the *Nayāya-mañjarī-granthibhaṅga* by Cakradhara on the *Nayāyamanjarī* of Jayantabhaṭṭa, composed in AD 900. The former reference comes in course of the *Nirgrantha-sthānam* where some portion of the Sanskrit text is quoted by *Dharmakīrti*. This runs as follows:

Nairātmavādinastu tat-sadhane nṛtya-gītyāder api tatra prasangāt. Yathā pratijñābhidhāna-purvakaḥ kaścit kuryāt - nāstyātmeti vayam bauddhā brūmah.

Ke bauddhāḥ?
Ye buddhasya bhagavataḥ śāsanam abhyupagatāḥ
Ko buddha bhagavan?
Yasya śāsane bhadant-āśvaghoṣoḥ pravrajitaḥ
Kah punar bhadantāśvaghosaḥ?

Yasya rāṣṭrapāla nāma nāṭakam

Kīdrśam rāṣṭrapāla-nāma nāṭakam?

Iti prasangam kṛtvā-nāndyante tataḥ praviśati sūtradhāra iti pathen nṛtyed gāyecca.

Prativādi taṁ ca sarva-prasangaṁ nānukartum samartha iti parājitaḥ syāt.

In the *Nyāyamañjarī-granthibhaṅga* quotes from *kaḥ punaḥ* to *nāṭakam* then with a slight variation-*iti prasangaṁ kṛtvā-nāndyante tataḥ pravisāti sūtradhāra-ityādikam paṭhen nṛtyec ca.*

The drama is complete in six acts. In the introductory portion Dr. Bagchi describes Āśvaghoṣa as a poet of high merit and ranks him on the same pedestal with poet Kālidāsa. In this connection the valuable comments of Dr. Bhattacharya may be reckoned with. The scholastic capabilities of the kavi were combined for the vindication of his cult.... Like a true poet he was an embodiment of the harmonious trio of the *kāvyāṅgas*... viz., *pratibhā, vyutpatti*... and *abhyāsa* which the later ālamkārikas prescribed for making a poet.[10]

There is a detailed description of the dramatic performance in the Chinese translation. In this Āśvaghoṣa, a musician preacher played the main role and the performance took place in Pataliputra (Hoa Che), and Lai cha ho lo was enacted for converting the citizens of Pataliputra into Buddhism. From the description it appears that the drama was of an opera type and therefore may safely be placed under an uparūpaka and not *nāṭaka* which comes under rūpaka. The omission of the word *nāṭaka* in the Chinese translation and describing it as a melodrama therefore maybe deliberate. But since the drama was meant for the propagation of Buddhism and the theme was the conversion of Rāstṛapāla, so naturally the sthāyin is *nirveda* depicting the duhkha, sūnyatā and nairātmya of all the samskṛta dharmas.

The same drama is found in the Jain work *Piṇḍa-nijjuti* attributed to Bhadravāhusvāmin. It was also enacted at Kusumapura where thousands of Kshatriyas were converted to Buddhism, after having seen the drama. Then out of grudge, people of Kusumapura burnt the drama. In the *Nyāyamañjari-granthibhaṅga,* however, the name of the drama is not *Rāṣṭrapāla-nāṭaka* but *Rājyapāla-nāṭaka.*

The *Lokānanda-nāṭaka* of Candragomin is also composed for the purpose of propagating Buddhism. The mystery, which veils the identity of the author of the drama, is yet to be unveiled. Candra, the well-reputed author of the *Cāndra-vyākaraṇa* felicitated with the honorific title 'gomin', was a Buddhist. The grammarian must have lived earlier to AD 650 since he has been profusely quoted by Vāmana and Jayāditya in their *kaśikā vṛtti*. Vasurāta, the precerptor of Bhatṛhari was his disciple. Belvalkar fixes the date of Candragomin about AD 470 but M. Krishnamachariar is in favour of putting him to a much earlier date.[11] Since he was a poet of high merit, and composed a *kāvya* known as *Śiśya-lekhā-dharmakāvya*, there is no reason to say that he is not capable of composing the drama *Lokānanda*.

The *Lokānandanāṭaka* is not available in Sanskrit original, but it exists only in Tibetan translation. Dr. Biswanath Bhattacharya has done the reconstruction of the original text in Sanskrit and Prakrit from the Snar-than edition of the Bstan-hgyur, preserved in the Visva-Bharati University library, in consultation with the Tibetan translation by Dr. Michael Hahn. The first act of the drama was posthumously published in the Visva-Bharati Annals, N.S.II, pp. 165-204. After having offered salutation to the Sarvajna Buddha in the nāndī verse, he introduces himself as the son of Jatukarṇa and Devīrajnī which most probably is not a proper name.

Pūrva-pradeśaja-oulan (?) nanu Jatukarnād
Devī-monorathavaśād iha yo hi jajne
(Tib-lha mo rgyal ma yid kyi sin rta las
meaning devi-rajni-manorathāt)
vodhum śaśāka na hi yo guru-rājya-bhāram
tasyās tanuja iti yah su-yaśasca lebhe.

In the next verse he speaks of his knowledge of grammar:

Yasyālamkritipūrna-padya nipuna-khyatipriyah sajjanāh
Tāvanmātraniriūpane vyavasitam ksīnam na jātam khalu
Yena vyākaranaika-deśakam atho (a?) śuddham samāptam kṛtam
Loke yena rajas-tamo-guṇa-gaṇa krāntaś ca śaktyā mahām.

This self-assessment probably throws some light on the authorship of the drama also and there should be no hesitation for ascribing the authorship of Candragomin, the grammarian to the *Lokānanda-nāṭaka*. There is a thematic variation from the dramas of Āśvaghoṣa. It is the story of Manicūda, a vidyādhara prince and Padmāvati, a vidyādharī. The *sṛngāra rasa* ultimately becomes conducive to Śānta.

Next we come to the *Nāgānanda* of Śrīharṣa, who is credited with the authorship of another two dramas of *uparūpaka* type, viz., [illegible] the ten *pāramitās* in both forms. It is true that the author [illegible] of Brahmanism [illegible] because of his proficiency in the Vedas, and he [illegible] all the virtues [illegible] by the Buddhist [illegible] the highest perfection [illegible] may achieve through constant [illegible]. The repeated use of the word [illegible] such as [illegible] and the like seems to be deliberate [illegible] of the [illegible] *Saṃvāhaka*, who had been [illegible] in the house of Cārudatta during the days of his affluence, [illegible] gambling on becoming jobless [illegible] the poverty of the hero and became apathetic to the worldly life and took to the life of a Buddhist monk. The author has also displayed his compassion for the heroine in a dying condition [illegible] a Buddhist monk [illegible]

[illegible]

Even in the 20th century Sanskrit dramas have been composed with Buddhist theme, though their number is very insignificant. One is [illegible] by [illegible] Kumar Bhattacharya and the [illegible] by Dr. [illegible] on the [illegible] of [illegible]

1. [illegible]
2. [illegible] Delhi, 1978 [illegible]
3. [illegible] Calcutta, 1981 [illegible] 298
4. [illegible] A.B. [illegible]
5. [illegible]
6. [illegible]
7. [illegible] *History of Classical Sanskrit Literature* [illegible]
8. [illegible]
9. [illegible]
10. [illegible]
11. [illegible]

18

Influence of Buddhism on Urdu Literature

Aziz Haider

Christmas Humphreys in *The Buddhist Way* has remarked that Buddhism today represents the largest field of thought in the known history of mankind. It is an admitted fact that this system of thought and discipline has always held a special appeal for the intellectuals and the creative writers. The remarkable thing about the Buddha is that he was a man among men who conquered the human hearts by the force of conviction rather than arms or political domination. He is remembered in the entire world by virtue of his deeds and teaching. He dedicated his life to free mankind from pain and bondage. When Arnold treated the Buddha's life and deeds (*Buddhacharita)* in his long poem, he called him 'The Light of Asia'.

It will not be wrong to say that Buddhism emerges as the major theme in world literature. Now the question arises whether it is possible to trace the influence of Buddhism on Urdu language and literature. In order to answer this question, it is necessary to know in the beginning that though a direct impact of Buddhism on Urdu language and literature is not traceable, one can easily notice some evidence of indirect influence of Buddhism on it through the medium of poetry and Sufism.

In his well-known book, *Arab-o Hind Ke Ta-aalluqat* published by Hindustani Academy, Allahabad, Maulana Syed Suleiman Nadui observes that etymologically, the word 'but' is derived from 'Buddha' and it maybe called its Persianized form. Qurratul Ain Hyder has also made this point in her Urdu novel *Kar-e-jahan Daraz Hai.* It is significant to note here that the word 'but' originally meant 'an idol' in Persian and this meaning was taken because of the worship of the beautiful idols and paintings of the Buddha in the monastries and *Viharas* in the regions of Bactria, Khotan, and Timrez until they were conquered by the Muslims about AD 1000. Sir Charles Eliot in his book *Hinduism and Buddhism* (Vol. 3) has written on this point. Later on, the word 'but' passed into poetic usage as a metaphor for the beloved and it is in this sense that the Persian poets like Sa'di, Hafiz and Urfi have used it in their poetic compositions.

Urdu literature is deeply indebted to the Persian literary tradition because Urdu writers follow in the footsteps of the Persian masters. Everybody knows that the word 'but' is used in Urdu *ghazal* very frequently. In addition to this, phrases like 'but-tannaz' (the arrogant beloved) and 'but-e tauba shikan' (continence smashing beloved) are used as metaphors for the beloved in Urdu poetry. The word 'but' in the sense of the all-conquering moon-face was used by two early Urdu poets, Wali and Siraj of Aurangabad. Later on, Mir Taqi Mir made use of this word 'but' to complain of the revishment of his heart by 'idol' (but). The well-known Delhi Sufi poet Khwaja Mir Dard also used this word 'but' in his poetry. The lines quoted below are the two glaring examples in point.

1) *Agar be hajabana vo but miley*
gharaz phir to Allah, Allah hai

[If my idol could meet unveiled
I would praise God with all my heart]

2) *Rabt yeh naz-e butanko hai meri jan ke sath*
Yeh hai vabasta mera unki har ek ān ke sath.

[My life depends on the blandishment of these idols
I relish their coquetry with all my heart]

The word 'but' also appears in the witty poetry of Mirza Ghalib and the following two examples are often given to illustrate this point:

1) *Dekhye āte hain us shokh batoñ se keya faiz*
Ek Brahmni ne kaha hai ke yeh sal achcha hai.

[Let's see what favours the idol grant their lovers.
A Brahmni forecasts it is an auspicious year]

2) *Keyun Kar us but se rakhoon Jan aziz*
keya nahin hai mujhe Iman aziz

[How can I withhold my life from that idol,
do I hold my word of faith light]

Momin Khan Momin, the well-known poet from Delhi is also noted for an excellent use of the word 'but' in his poetry. In the following lines, he shows his unflinching devotion to the idols of flesh and blood:

Umr to sari Kati lshq-e- butaan men Momin
Akhri waqt men kiya khak Musalmaan honge.

[O, Momin, I have spent a lifetime in adoring these idols
How can I turn a Muslim toward the end of my days?]

From the examples quoted above, it is quite clear that the word 'but' etymologically derived from 'Buddh' has been used in Urdu poetry in its Persianized form. Moreover, much of Urdu poetry is deeply influenced by Sufism and this shows a fairly close relationship with the Buddhist philosophy and legends. In his illuminating lecture on Buddhism at the Banaras Hindu University, Professor M. Hasan of Aligarh Muslim University has thrown ample light on this point.

For a more direct, conscious and consistent interest in Buddhism on the part of Urdu writers, it is necessary to make a survey of Urdu literature in the 20th century. When the sacred books of the East were translated in European languages, it stimulated interest in the Indian heritage and the rise of nationalism reinforced within the country. The Urdu writers too were naturally drawn towards this trend and Allama Dr. Mohd. Iqbal wrote a poem each on Shri Ram, Swami Ram Tirath and Guru Nanak. In the following lines, Allama Iqbal refers to the teachings of Lord Buddha and praises his words:

Qaum ne paigham-e-gautam ki zara par ka naki
Qadr pehchani na apne gohar-e yak Dana Ki
Ah badqismat raha awaz-e-haq se be khabar
Ghafil apne phal ki sherini se hota hai shajar
Ashkar usne kiya jo zindagi ka raz tha
Hind Ko apne khiyali Falsafe par naz tha.

[Little heed did the people pay to Gautam's word. They realized not the venue of this perfect pearl. Oh, the ill-fated ones were deaf to the voice of truth. For oft the tree knows not the flavour of its own fruit. He unrevealed the deep mystery of being. Yet his land revelled in its speculative thought.]

A glowing tribute to Gautam has also been paid by the well-known Urdu poet Brij Narain Chakbast in his famous poem *Khake Hind* (The Indian Soil). In this poem Gautam is described as the Enlightened One who bestowed sanctity on this worship-house of ancient days.

Several references to Gautam occur in the poetry of Raghupat Sahai Firaq of Gorakhpur. It is a well-known fact that Firaq Gorakpuri was a reputed Urdu poet and an eminent English teacher. His long poem *Adam Nama* (An Epistle of Man) mentions Siddhartha's renunciation and his belief in the impermanence of the world. In this connection the following lines of Firaq deserve to be quoted:

Dunya men hain Kangal bhi aur ahle dawal bhi
Hai taak men donon hi ke sayyade Ajal bhi
Duniya Ka hai yeh rang to kya Raj mahal bhi.
Raton ko kapilvastoo mein moonh mod chalenge.

[The world holds the pauper and the propertied too. And the hunter Death stalks them ever and alike. That is the way of the world. So what? The palace dwellers turn away from Kapilavastu it at night.]

Firaq's *Hindola* (The cradle) is also a famous poem that traces the evolution of India's glorious civilization and makes several allusions to Gautam. Similar is the case with Ali Sardar Jafri's poem *Dua* (Prayer), Khalilul Rahaman's poem *Nirvan,* Krishna Mohan's poem *Gautam ke piyaro* (The followers of Gautam) and Sikander Ali Wajid's poem on the Ajanta caves.

Among the prose writers of Urdu literature, Qurrat-ul Ain Hyder makes reference to Buddhism in her masterpiece *Aag Ka Darya* (The River of Fire). The fact is that this title is based upon the Buddha's fire sermon and it spans a gigantic time frame from the age of Alexander and Kautalya to the mid-fifties of the twentieth century. The theme of this masterpiece shows the writer's intimate knowledge and creative use of the Buddha's life and philosophy. Her other novels like *Kare Jahan Darax Hai* and *Chandni Begam* also bear specific allusions to Buddhism. Her novelette named *Sita Haran,* which contains numerous Buddhist echoes and allusions, further proves Hyder's interest in Buddhism.

Another Urdu writer Sharvan Kumar Verma is also worthy of notice here. His *Doosra Buddha* (The Other Buddha) published in the silver jubilee number (1978) of the *Tahreek* presents a Buddhist myth in order to portray the suffering and tensions of a school teacher. In the same issue of the *Tahreek* Mehdi Tonki's short story *Ek Aur Nirvan Yatra* (Yet another journey to *Nirvan*) is published. In this story the psychological complex of a brilliant but unsocial scholar has been delineated. The theme of this story is that on the eve of his wedding he quietly goes away at night and like Gautam Buddha he seeks peace and satisfaction in renunciation. Thus, the *Nirvana* motif clearly figures in this story. Another short story of Tonki is entitled *Jandar ki pehcan* (The mark of the living). This story is published in a literary magazine *Shair* of Bombay (July 1984). In this story Tonki mentions Mahatma Buddha when he deals with the nervous breakdown of a factory clerk who is fed up with the pressures and tensions of life. Here again the Buddha's reference to suffering and non-attachment is clearly made by Tonki.

In the light of the above discussion, it is correct to say that Urdu literature of the past and of the present is full of several references to Gautam Buddha and Urdu writers have made artistic use of the literary potential of Buddhist thought and myth in their writings.

19

Buddhism in Tripura: A Brief Account

Sirajuddin Ahmed

INTRODUCTION

Tripura is a small state located in the north-eastern region of India with an area of 10,491 square kilometres. It is a land-locked state surrounded by Bangladesh, Assam and Mizoram with an international boundary of more than 850 kilometres. The word 'Tripura' is a Sanskritized form of 'tui' and 'pra'. 'Tui' means water and 'pra' means near. 'Tuipra' has subsequently been corrupted into 'Tipra'. During the British imperialism in India she was known as Hill Tipperah. The native hill people still call her as 'Tipra'.[1]

BUDDHIST COMMUNITIES IN TRIPURA

There are only four predominant communities in Tripura professing different religious beliefs: Hindus, Muslims, Buddhists and Christians. The Mogh, Chakma and Barua communities are followers of Buddhism. The Chakmas are divided into several groups and sub-sections and found mainly in the subdivision of Kailashahar, Amarpur, Sabrum, Udaipur and Bilonia. The original abode of the Chakmas of Tripura was in the hill tracts of Chittagong in Bangladesh. The Moghs claim that they have descended from the same line of Kshatriyas in which was born Lord Buddha. They migrated from Arakan area of Myanmar (Burma). The Barua community is the smallest group among the Buddhists in Tripura and they have scattered settlements in various parts of this state. The Moghs speak Arakanese dialect, which belongs to Tibeto-Burmese group. The Chakma language has derived from Prakrita (mainly Sauraseni and Magadhi) and belong to the Neo-Indo Aryan Linguistic group of the present Indian subcontinent. But its peculiarity is that it has acquired some loan-words from Tibeto-Burmese and Thai language groups. It also shows some close affinity with Assamese and Chittagong dialects of Bengali. The Baruas generally speak local dialects of Bengali language. Anthropologically all the Mogh, Chakma and Barua communities belong to Mongolian race. Although all of them are Buddhists by religious faith, they have different rituals and customs of their own. The three communities of Tripura mainly believe in the stream of 'Hinayani' Buddhism.

Moghs are taken to be the offshoots of Arakanese and Barua community is a section of Moghs. The enlightened Baruas claim themselves to be the real Rajbansi descent from the Hindu king of ancient Magadha of Bihar.[2]

According to the Census Report of 1991, the total population of Buddhists in Tripura had been 1,28,260.[3] Due to non-availability of community-wise distribution, we can roughly estimate that the number of Chakmas, Moghs and Baruas would be round about 80,000, 40,000, and 8,000, respectively.[4] This includes about 54,000 Chakma migrants who have already returned to their ancestral home in the Chittagong Hills of Bangladesh in 1998. According to the decadal growth rate @15.74% during the years 1991 to 2001, as shown in the 'Provisional Population total of Tripura–2001,'[5] the total figure of Buddhist population in Tripura will come up to 86,000 approximately.

BUDDHISM IN ANCIENT BENGAL AND TRIPURA

It is now widely believed that Buddhism was known in Bengal even before Ashoka's time, but information for this period is rather scanty. A copper plate in Gunaighar village near Comilla in Bangladesh records a land grant in favour of a 'Mahayana' Buddhist Sangha.[6] The grant was issued by Maharaja Bainya Gupta in AD 507-08.[7] Excavations in Mainamati and Paharpur have indicated a flourishing Buddhist civilization in the area of south-east Bengal which borders Tripura. Some Buddhist images have been found in various parts of Tripura, namely, Dharmanagar (North Tripura District), Bishalgarh (West Tripura District) and Udaipur, Bilonia and Amarpur (South Tripura District), but they are yet to be scientifically studied. However, the excavations made so far in Pilak area, under Bilonia subdivision give evidence that Buddhism flourished in Pilak at least in 6th century AD. It is worth-mentioning that the 'Hinayani' Buddhism as now being practised by the Chakmas, Moghs and Baruas has no direct connection with the 'Mahayani' Buddhism prevailing in ancient Bengal and Tripura.

According to Dr. Heinz Bechert, Buddhism spread to the 'Kuki lands' (Eastern India and Burma) during Ashoka's time and after the Turki invasion in Magadha, a large number of monks fled from there to the 'Kuki lands'. Perhaps around that time the Chakmas accepted Buddhism as their religion.[8] Rani Kalindi, the last independent ruler of the Chakmas invited Sangharaja Saramitta Mahasthavira of Arakan to come to her kingdom to head a religious reform movement in 1864. This movement deeply affected the Buddhists in Chittagong as well. In 1956, when 2500th Buddha Jayanti was celebrated, there were 310 Viharas and temples in East Bengal, over 240 in Chittagong alone. Aryamitra Mahathera, the then head of all *Bhikshus* and *Viharas* of Tripura led a revival movement there.[9] The Chakmas belong to 'Theravada Buddhism', which is a sect of 'Hinayana'. After the celebration of Buddha Jayanti Utsava—2521st in 1976—the number of Buddhist monastery and temples in Tripura increased rapidly. In 1991 the number was 280 and it has gone up to 350 approximately in recent times.[10]

RELIGION OF MOGHS AND BARUAS

The term 'Mogh' is a misnomer. According to Dr. Heinz Bechert, the Arakanese are popularly known as Moghs, but they prefer to be called by the name 'Marma'. The Moghs are Buddhists except a very few who profess either Hinduism or Christianity.[11] Their supreme God is 'Phora' or the Lord Buddha. But they also worship Sari (Chini), Kali, Ganga and Baradevta (Chichi). Every Mogh village has a 'Kheyang' or temple of Lord Buddha that is looked after by a priest known as 'Samphura'. The religion of the hill Marmas, writes Dr. Bechert in his *Contemporary Buddhism in Bengal and Tripura*, has been described by Claude Levi-Straus as a syncretistic religion in which some elements of ancient animism prevail.[12]

The Moghs of Tripura speak Arakanese dialect. The Barua Moghs or Baruas also worship Lord Buddha, but they are very close to the Bengalis and speak Bengali local dialects.[13] Both the communities have different rituals, customs and customary laws governing their system of marriage, divorce, social punishment and the law of inheritance. At the time of marriage the Barua brides and bridegrooms wear 'Mangalasutram' from the Buddhist *bhikshu.* On the other hand, the Chakma marriage follows the local Hindu customs and rituals.

RELIGION OF CHAKMAS

Although the religion of Chakma community of Tripura belongs to 'Hinayani' Buddhism, but in the inner phase of their society the system of worshipping prevails in accordance with the Tantras of Buddhism.[14] They have four types of priests in connection with their religious observancy: (1) *Bhikkhus,* (2) Raulees, (3) Ozhas and (4) Gankulies. The *Bhikkhus* are Buddhist monks, the Raulees perform customary rites, the Ozhas propitiate the gods and evil spirits and the Gankulies sing songs of the days gone by and participate in certain religious functions.[15]

The *pujas* and festivals of Chakmas may be classified into four groups. They are (1) family-based, (2) *Gutti* or clan-based, (3) village-based and (4) public or universal based. The family based *pujas* include *Gharchumlang, Ma-Lakki-Ma, Kajaipani* or Ganga, *Dharmakam* or Buddha. Some of the village-based *pujas* are *Thanamana* (Ma-Kaki-Ma, Ganga, Dhaleswari, Bhut Raja, etc.) and *Burpara* (Matya, Ganga, Biyatra, Bajamatti). The *Gutti* of clan-based *pujas* are *Ghuttibhat* or *Bhatdya,* which is a kind of worshipping of Lord Buddha and other gods and goddesses.

It is evident from these *pujas* that the Chakmas still follow the nature-worship cults and believe in animism and evil spirits, which are associated with the 'Tantras'. The Chakmas of Tripura observe some public festivals like cart pulling or chariot pulling, Bizhu festival, Buddha Purnima, Prabharani Purnima (Laksmi or Kojagari Purnima), Kathin Chibar Dan, etc. No marriage ceremony can take place during the period of three months from Ashadhi to Lakshmi Purnima. From 1998 onwards, the Government of Tripura has been celebrating 'Pilak Utsav' every year at the end of January in and around 'Thakurain Tilla'. This place is located in Pashchim Pilak area of South Tripura, where relics of Buddhist and Hindu civilization have been discovered and are still being excavated lately.

BUDDHIST RUINS IN PAṬṬIKERĀ AND PILAK

Buddhism flourished in ancient Paṭṭikerakā or Paṭṭikerā, a place located in south-east Bengal which lay to the east of Brahmaputra.[16]

Extensive ruins of Buddhist monastery have been unearthed in Mainamati Hill, which was a part of ancient Tripura (Tippera). The entire hill was infested with mounds (Stūpas) of different sizes. These have been classified into 18 groups and the Mound no. 5 was the largest among them. A painting of goddess 'Chunda' with 16 arms which was copied in AD 1015 in a Nepali manuscript mentioned the city of Paṭṭikerakā as : *Paṭṭikere Cundāvarabhavana Cundā.*[17] The manuscript is of *Ashṭa-Sahasrikā-Prajña-Pāramitā*" and it is presently preserved in the Cambridge University.[18] A sandstone idol of Chunda with 18 arms has been found in Pilak and it very much resembles the Chunda of Paṭṭikerā.

The terracotta images and the stone and bronze idols found in Paharpur, Mainamati and Pilak areas are similar in nature. They also show strong resemblance with the images and idols of the Gupta and Pala Period.

Pilak is a vast area comprising three parts—Pashchim Pilak, Madhya Pilak and Purba Pilak. Buddhist and Hindu relics have been found in Jolaibari, Pilak, Debdaru and Kalsi. The images and idols of different gods and goddesses are found scattered here and there in this large land. They are the Buddha, Avalokiteswar, Tara, Loknath, Marich, Chunda, Nṛisingha, Mahishamardini, Mahadeva, Surya, Vishnu, Ganesha, etc. The bronze idols of the Buddha (8th century AD), Tara, Avalokiteswar, Loknath, Hariti, Vishnu (all of them belong to 9th century AD) and the ruins of the Buddhist mounds of 10th century AD are the main objects to be seen here.

The very presence of both the Buddhist and the Hindu relics in this area suggests that there had been a cultural synthesis or a peaceful co-existence of pluralism in those days among the two different religious communities. The other noticeable thing is that the nature of erosion of the idols and images compel us to infer about a disastrous flood caused by the Muhuri River.

ORIGIN OF THE WORD 'PILAK'

No inscription or rock-edict has been found anywhere in the Pilak area, but a good number of silver coins inscribed 'Piraka' or 'Beraka' have been discovered in and outside the region. Even no word like 'Pilaka' was found there. The archaeologists have traced one pillar-edict preserved in a Pagoda, which is situated in the Mrohang area of Burmese Arakan. It is established that the edict had been engraved and dedicated by one Ananda Chandra in 8th century AD. The Pillar inscribed the words 'Pilakka Banaka'.[19] One can phonetically reconstruct the word 'Pilak' in this way–Piraka > Pilakka> Pilāka> Pilāk.[20] However, more excavation as well as scientific study is badly needed to trace out the archaeological map of this ancient civilization and the genesis of a great settlement in the entire Pilak area.

BUDDHISM IN TRIPURA: BEFORE AND AFTER ACCESSION

It may be mentioned that the accession of Tripura to the Indian Union took place on October 15, 1949. Maharaja Bir Bikram, the last king of Tripura made a great contribution towards the upliftment of Buddhists in Tripura before its accession. He travelled various countries including China, Japan, Sri Lanka, Myanmar, etc. and collected idols of Lord Buddha and other tokens. He had a high regard for Buddhism and its ideals. A contingent of Tripura Army participated in the Anglo-Japanese War during the World War II. At the time of retreat they brought four *Ashṭadhātu* idols of Lord Buddha and a gigantic bell from a Buddhist Pagoda in the Sendway area of Arakan. They presented these articles to Maharaja Bir Bikram. The king made a land grant to the 'Bhikshu Sangha' to help build the present 'Venuban Vihar', the biggest temple of Tripura at Agartala, near the Kunjaban Palace. The temple was ceremoniously inaugurated with the great and generous patronage of the king on May 4,1947. The four Buddha idols brought by the Tripura Army and one marble idol presented by Maharaja Nalinaksha Roy, the then Chakma king of Hill Chittagong were placed on the altar. Maharaja Bir Bikram along with his royal family members worshipped the deity and Prince Kirit Bikram accepted the 'Panchashil' and on behalf of the king he formally bestowed the Venuban Vihar as a royal gift to the Bhikshu Sangha. In the year 1956, the 2500th Buddha Jayanti was celebrated with great pomp and splendour.[21]

Shri B.P. Maurya, the then Hon'ble Minister of State, Govt. of India participated and delivered a speech during the ceremony.[22] The holy 'Kathin Chibar Danotsav–2000' was observed on November 5, 2000 at the Agartala Venuban Vihar.[23] In between the year 1978 and 1983 Shri Nripen Chakravarty, the then Hon'ble Chief Minister of Tripura extended financial support for reconstruction of several Buddha temples in Tripura. On May 7, 2001, Shri Jitendra Choudhury, the Hon'ble Minister for Information, Culture and Tourism, Govt. of Tripura inaugurated the 2545th Buddha Jayanti Festival at Mainama, a place situated in the Longtarai Valley under Dhalai district of Tripura.[24]

The Buddhist priests have been preaching the ideals of *Maitri*, *Prajña* and *Karuṇa* successfully among all the religious communities of Tripura in the present time. But recently the Buddhist community of Tripura has been at crossroads, as some insurgent groups supported by a few Christian Missionaries and certain foreign powers constantly antagonize them.

NOTES

1. *Tripura District Gazetteers*, 1975, Chapter 1, p. 1.
2. Suren Debbarman, *The Chakmas and Moghs*, Agartala, March, 1987, p. 38.
3. *Some Basic Statistics of Tripura*, 1999, Directorate of Economics and Statistics, Govt. of Tripura, Agartala, p. 13.
4. The number has been suggested by Sri Srutoranjan Khisha, a journalist who happens to be a Chakma Buddhist residing at Abhoyagar, Agartala.
5. *Census of India 2001*, Series-17, Tripura, p. 3.
6. Omesh Saigal, *Tripura—Its History And Culture*, Concept Publishing Company, Delhi, 1978, p. 107.
7. Dipak Bhattacharya, *Pilak Katha*, Akshar Publications, Agartala, 1999, p. 21.
8. Omesh Saigal, *op. cit.*, p. 108.
9. *Ibid.*, p. 109.
10. As informations supplied by Sri Srutoranjan Khisha, Abhoynagar, Agartala.
11. *Educational Miscellany Vol. IV*, Education Directorate, Govt. of Tripura, 1986.
12. S.B.K. Devvarman, *The Tribes of Tripura—A Dissertation*, 2nd Edn., 1986, Special series No. 1, Directorate of Research, Govt. of Tripura, Agartala, pp. 27-28.
13. Suren Debbarman, *op. cit.*, pp. 43, 48-49.
14. Pannalal Majumdar, *The Chakmas of Tripura State Tribal Culture Research Institute & Museum*, Govt. of Tripura, Agartala, 1997, p. 149.
15. S.B.K. Devvarman, *op. cit.*, p. 31.
16. Dipak Kumar Barua, *Vihāras in Ancient India,* Indian Publications, Monograph Series No. 10, Calcutta, 1969. p. 179.
17. *Ibid.*
18. Dipak Bhattachrya, *op. cit.*, p. 36.
19. *Ibid.*, p. 19.
20. *Ibid.*, p. 25.
21. Bhikshu Arya Mitra: "Agartala Venuban Vihar", *Buddha Jayanti Bulletin,*

Published by the Tripura Rajya Buddha Jayanti Committee on the occasion of 2521th Buddha Jayanti, Agartala, November 6, 1976, pp. 4-9.

22. *Ibid.*, p. 11.
23. Booklet published by the 'Kathin Chibar Danotsav—2000' committee, Venuban Bauddha Vihar, Agartala on 5-11-2000.
24. A leaflet published by Sri Mahian Chakma, Secretary, Nirban Nagar Vihar, dated May 7, 2001.

Remarks on Recent Works in Bengali on Buddhist Metaphysics and Pramāṇa Śāstra

Rita Gupta

Buddhist religion and philosophy occupy a central place in Indian spiritual and philosophical traditions. Naturally, they attracted the interests of many savants of Indian spirituality and philosophy in India, including Radhakrishnan and S.N. Das Gupta, in the last century. Many eminent scholars in Bengal, in the last century, were also highly influenced by the Buddhist philosophy and culture. Mention may especially be made here of the important works on Buddhism by S.C. Vidyabhushan, Vidhushekhar Shastri, N. Dutta and Satkari Mookherjee. However, these scholars wrote mainly in English. Many scholars have written short treatises in Bengali on Buddhist literary works and culture in the course of the last sixty years. Many of them have even translated in Bengali some *Theravāda* Buddhist texts like *Dhammapada* from a specifically Buddhist soteriological point of view. I shall leave the task of determining their value to others.

I shall confine myself, in this paper, to a critical appraisal of treatises written in Bengali, on Buddhist metaphysics, epistemology and logic in the last century.

The trend of writing scholarly treatises in Bengali on Buddhist philosophy was set in motion with the publication of the valuable work *Vaibhāshika Darshan* by Ananta Kumar Bhattacharya. In this work the author discusses Buddhist metaphysical notions like momentariness, dependent origination (*pratītya-samupāda*), denial of a creator God, and also Buddhist epistemological and logical notions as found in the works of Nyāyavādi-bauddhas like Dignāga, Dharmakīrti, Śāntarakṣita, Ratnakīrti *et al.*

I shall try to make a critical appraisal of some chapters of *Vaibhāshika Darshan* dealing with metaphysics, epistemology and logic.

CHAPTER IV, *KṢAṆIKATVANIRUPAṆA*

The exposition of the doctrine of momentariness is based on Dharmakīrti's *Hetubindu,* Śāntarakṣita's *Tattvasaṃgraha* and Ratnakīrti's *Kṣaṇabhaṅgasiddhi.* The doctrine was introduced in a logically coherent form by Dharmakīrti. According to him, everything in the phenomenal world is causally efficacious and, consequently, momentary. Dharmakīrti refers to a *reductio ad absurdum* argument: if a thing has causal efficacy and is, at the same time, non-momentary, then it will be characterized by two contradictory characters.

(a) If the non-momentary seed produces the sprout not at the moment1 at which it comes into existence, but at the next moment2, then at moment 1, the seed is *not a producer,* while at moment2 it *is a producer.* In that case, the seed of moment1 must be regarded as different from that of moment2, otherwise we will have to admit that the identical seed is characterized by contradictory properties. Thus a non-momentary thing cannot produce its effect successively (*krameṇa*).

(b) If the seed produces the sprout at moment1 of its coming into existence, then it cannot produce it once again at moment2. In that case, the seed must be admitted to be a producer at moment1 and not a producer at moment2. In order to avoid saying that two contradictory properties belong to one and the same seed, we are obliged to admit that the seed of moment1 is different from that of moment2. Thus a non-momentary thing cannot produce its effect simultaneously (*yugapat*).

The thesis of momentariness was subjected to severe criticism by the Naiyāyikas. Dharmakīrti was aware of some of these and tried to defend the doctrine by several arguments.

In the face of scathing criticisms of the doctrine of momentariness by the Naiyāyika and the Mimaṃsaka, Śāntarakṣita puts up a brilliant defence of Dharmakīrti's doctrine in *Tattvasaṃgraha.* In addition, Śāntarakṣita introduces many a novel argument in support of the doctrine. Mention must be made here of Śāntarakṣita's argument that destruction (*vināśa*) is independent of any extraneous cause (*ahetukī*).

Spontaneous Destruction and Momentariness

Śāntarakṣita argues that whatever is a product (*kṛtaka*) is perishable by its very nature. Why should its destruction then depend on an extraneous cause? If its destruction is independent of such a cause, a thing will be destroyed immediately after securing existence. Śāntarakṣita puts his argument in the form of a syllogism: Whatever is not dependent on others for any special feature always has that feature. [e.g., the assemblage of efficacious causes, that are not dependent on other causes (for bringing about the effect), always brings about the effect.]

Products are not dependent on any causes for being destroyed. Therefore, products are always liable to destruction.

[*ye yadhāvaṃ pratyanapekṣaste tadbhāvaniyatāḥ, yathā-samanantaraphalasāmagrī svakāryotpādane niyatā. vināśaṃ pratyanapekṣaśca sarve janminaḥ kṛtakā bhāvā. TSP, p.167*]

Unfortunately, the chapter on momentariness of the book concerned does not quote the syllogism. The absence of such a quotation fails to present Śāntarakṣita's argument in its sharp logical form. The reader cannot even properly grasp the logical force of the debate, which follows, between the Buddhist and the Mīmāṃsaka and Naiyāyika opponents, after Śāntarakṣita formulates the above-mentioned argument (which is recorded in detail in *Tattvasaṃgraha*). The author presents the main arguments of Śāntarakṣita and his critics only in a tenuous form in the chapter. He does not even bother to refer to the original *kārikās* or the commentary in the *Tattvasaṃgraha-pañjikā*, let alone quoting the Sanskrit originals from text. He does not either cite the quotations from *Hetubindu* while presenting Dharmakīrti's arguments. In the absence of original quotations the reader cannot independently evaluate the arguments.

The chapter in *Tattvasaṃgraha* abounds in referring to the objections to the doctrine of momentariness by Uddyotakara, Aviddhakarṇa, Jaiminī, Kumārila and Yogasena. The author does not refer to them. Yet, such references are vital to the understanding of the debate that raged between the Buddhists and the critics on the issue of momentariness.

Aviddhakarṇa argues that, being an event occurring at a determinate time, destruction must have a cause. Uddyotakara points out that as an uncaused entity, destruction can be either a non-existent like a 'barren woman's son', on an eternal being like *ākāśa.* If destruction is a non-existent chimera, then all existents will be eternal, as they will know no destruction. If destruction is eternal, it will be co-existent with the things destroyed. Yet, this is absurd, as the presence and destruction of a thing are contradictory.

Śāntarakṣita points out two senses of 'destruction'. Firstly, in the Buddhist sense, destruction stands for the momentariness of all things, which, by their own nature, are destroyed by giving rise to other things, at the next moment. And the evanescence of a thing, in the Buddhist opinion, is due to a cause, viz., the intrinsic nature of a thing. In the second sense, destruction is absolute negation, which is an unreality. The many twists and turns of Śāntarakṣita-Uddyotakata polemics are altogether neglected in the concerned chapter on momentariness.

Both Jaiminī and Kumārila point out that the established fact of recognition (*pratyabhijñā*) cannot be accounted for if everything is momentary. Śāntarakṣita, however, argues convincingly, that recognition is not a source of valid cognition. It is not perception, as perception, according to the Buddhist, is non-erroneous; and recognition erroneously apprehends different things as non-different. Moreover, a source of valid cognition, in the Buddhist opinion, must acquaint a knower with a novelty. And yet, recognition is due to the revival of past impressions of things already known. The arguments of Jaiminī and Kumārila, and Śāntarakṣita's rejoinder, elaborately sketched in *Tattvasaṃgraha,* which occupy a position of vital importance in properly grasping the thesis of momentariness, are completely omitted in the discussion on momentariness in *Vaibhashika Darshan.* Yogasena's objections, and Śāntarakṣita's rejoinder to defend momentariness also go unnoticed in that book.

The next phases of the elaboration of the doctrine of momentariness is traceable in Ratnakīrti's *Kṣaṇabhaṅgasiddhi.* Ratnakīrti tries to prove the unreality of non-momentary objects with the help of the following *vyatirekī* (negative) *anumāna*:

1. That which is lacking in successive and simultaneous activity is incapable of bringing about any effect. (e.g. the hare's horn)
2. The non-momentary is lacking in successive and simultaneous activity.

3. Therefore, the non-momentary is incapable of bringing about any effect (and, consequently, it is unreal).* [*Ratnakīrtinibandhāvalī*, p. 83]

The Naiyāyika points out that the subject or locus of reason (*hetu*) must be an existent fact. The *pakṣa* in Ratnakīrti's inference is non-momentary, which, according to him, is a fiction. How can such a fiction, which cannot be known by any *pramāṇa*, function as a subject (*āśraya*) of a reason? The *hetu* of the inference is thus unestablished (*asiddha*) in its substratum (*āśraya*). Ratnakīrti, however, argues that the reason would have been unestablished had its subject, the non-momentary, been a completely uncognised entity. However, the non-momentary is apprehended by the faculty of conceptual construction (*vikalpa*).

The Naiyāyika urges that if a conceptual construct can become the subject of an inference, then there will never be a fallacy of a reason unestablished in a subject, as an imaginary subject can be easily conceived in every case of inference. Ratnakīrti argues that such a fallacy is illustrated in the Naiyāyika's inference, "the self is ubiquitous, because it is apprehended everywhere". Here, a positive reason is predicated of an unreal subject, viz., the self.**

The Naiyāyika objects, at this stage, that nothing can be predicated with regard to an unreal subject, which cannot be known by any *pramāṇa*. Ratnakīrti retorts by saying that a pre-condition of predicating anything to a subject is that the former is somehow cognised. There is no rule laying down that such a cognition must be derived from a *pramāṇa*. Ratnakīrti's debate with the Naiyāyika forms a fundamental part of the developed doctrine of momentariness. The neglect of this debate by the author of *Vaibhashika Darshan* becomes a lacuna in the proper understanding of the doctrine of momentariness.

Pandit Bidhubhushan Bhattacharya has published a Bengali monograph, *Kṣaṇabhaṅgavāda* in 1975. Compared to chapter IV of *Vaibhashika Darshan*, this monograph is disappointing. The author makes no attempt to acquaint the readers with the logical arguments of Dharmakīrti, Śāntarakṣita and Ratnakīrti. Neither does he bother to make the readers conversant with the logical form of the debate between the Buddhist and his opponent. He does refer once or twice to the original texts. Yet, it seems that he sees the doctrine of

* According to the Buddhist, causal efficacy is the hall-mark of the real.

** *Ratnakīrtinibandhāvalī*, p. 85, K.P.J.R. Institute, Patna, 1975.

momentariness generally through the eyes of a Naiyāyika, and specifically from his own personal viewpoint.

II

CHAPTER VIII, *ĪŚVARAKHANḌANAM*

The notion of an ominiscient, omnipotent creator of the universe, advocated by the theists, is an anathema to the Buddhist, who does not admit the validity of the *Vedas,* and attempts to explain the universe by his doctrines of dependent origination (*pratītya-samutpāda*) and *karma.* The author presents the Buddhist antitheistic arguments in the following way.

If an omniscient, omnipotent God is the sole cause of the universe, then contrary to the perceived fact, events and effects appearing gradually in it, will all, perforce, have to appear simultaneously. Moreover, the emergence of effects with dissimilar properties due to the differences of place and time of their appearance will be inexplicable. The same kind of fruits and flowers produced in the eastern or southern regions do not have the same taste, smell and colour as those produced in the east or south. This fact and the fact that specific types of fruits and flowers grow in specific seasons only, become inexplicable on the hypothesis of God being their sole cause.

It may be argued by the theist that God wishes a variety in this creation, and this explains the variety of effects. The Buddhist will ask: is God capable of producing effects, which are produced at a particular place and season, also at a different place and season? If He is capable, and His capacity is independent of other conditions, then there will be no variety in His creation. Since variety is a perceived fact, it must be admitted that God is capable of producing certain effects and incapable of producing certain others. And capacity and incapacity cannot be properties of an identical God.

The theist may argue that even when He does not actually do so, God has the capacity to produce all effects at all times. And this capacity is dependent on its auxiliary conditions for its actualization. A writer has the capacity to write at all times. It is not actualized due to the absence of materials for writing. The Buddhist retorts that the presence of capacity is inferred by its production of effects. The capacity of writing can be inferred in the writer, limited by a specific time, and not at all times. Hence, the theist's argument regarding divine capacity cannot be accepted.

If one has to properly follow the anti-theistic arguments, one has to study them in a systematic form, starting from their original forms in the syllogistic inferences of Dharmakīrti, and proceeding next to the defence of them (against theist's criticisms) by Śāntarakṣita. Bhattacharya has not followed such a procedure. He seems to have reconstructed them only as they are found in the Nyāya critique of theistic arguments. This may be the reason why he has never referred to the original arguments of Dharmakīrti and Śāntarakṣita.

One of Uddyotakara's famous theistic arguments is as follows:

> *Things like Pradhāna, atoms and karma are controlled by some intelligent agent before they produce an effect because they are unconscious.* As for example, an axe[1]

It will have to be admitted that unconscious atoms, *karma*, etc., and the combination of which produce mountains, seas, etc., could not have combined themselves. They can be combined only by the control of an intelligent agent. Since this agent cannot be of limited intelligence, this must be Omniscient God.

Dharmakīrti, however, argues that if Uddyotakara aims at establishing that effects like a pot or a cloth are produced by an intelligent agent (*sakartṛka*), then he is only trying to establish what is already established. If, however, Uddyotakara claims that his argument succeeds in establishing the existence of a disembodied omniscient eternal agent, then the examples like axe, threads, clay, etc., cannot exemplify such an agent. Hence, the argument fails to prove the existence of God.[2]

Dharmakīrti urges that the underlying assumption of the theistic argument is that every effect presupposes the functioning of an intelligent agent. However, we do not, he says, need to admit God for the emergence of effects like pots, clothes, ant hill (*valmīka*), etc., What then are the effects for explaining whether the existence of God is necessary? Perhaps the effects concerned would be mountains, oceans etc. Dharmakīrti, however, comments that once it can be

1. NV. 4/1/21
2. PV 1/12
3. PV 1/13

shown that mountains, oceans, etc., are effects, one may postulate the existence of an intelligent agent who produced them. But the question is, how can we be sure that mountains, etc., are effects? Has anyone ever seen them being produced by an agent?[3]

The Naiyāyika tries to defend his position by arguing that as mountains, etc., have constituent parts (*sāvayava*), they must be effects (*kārya*); and, as they are effects, they must also have been produced by an intelligent agent. Dharmakīrti, however, points out that it is true that mountains, etc., have, like pots, parts which are combined in a particular way so as to yield a specific configuration (*sanniveśa*). But this similarity alone does not prove that mountains, etc., are produced by an intelligent agent. Can we claim that all objects having a whitish (*pāṇḍura*) colour like smoke are, invariably related to fire?[1] Dharmakīrti also points out that if the mere property of being an effect is sufficient for establishing the property of having an intelligent agent, then one can also argue that a potter produces an ant-hill.

Dharmakīrti devotes a number of arguments to show that the notion of creation of the universe is incompatible with the notion of God, the creator, as eternal and unchanging. All the arguments advanced by Dharmakīrti in *Pramāṇavārttika* are traceable in a more convincing form in Śāntarakṣita's *Tattvasaṃgraha*.

The anti-theistic arguments advanced by Śāntarakṣita are discussed in some sections of an anthology of articles written by Balakrishna Ghosh in Bengali, *Vijñānavāda* (published in Calcutta, in 1988). However, the anti-theistic arguments present therein are not always intelligible. They would have been much more intelligible had the author taken the trouble of relating them to their original sources in *Pramāṇavārttika.* To cite an example of unintelligibility, we can refer to Ghosh's Bengali rendering (p. 80) of *kārikā* 77 of *Tattvasaṃgraha,* vol. 1 and Kamalaśīlas commentary on it. The main contention of Śāntarakṣita in the second line of the *kārikā* (*viṣayāyānāṃ kramitvena tajjñāneṣvapi ca krama*) is shown in the following way:

The knowledge of events in the world, which are successive, must arise in a successive manner. If God is the creator of the world, then He must know them in a successive manner. However, an eternal God must have knowledge of all things at one go (*yugapat*). In order to know them successively, He has to abandon His non-changing

---

1. PV 1/14

nature. Ghosh, however, interprets the *kārikā* as trying to present only the argument that if the universe is a creation of an eternal God, then all events in it will be simultaneously present, and the succession of events in the universe would be inexplicable. He thus completely ignores the second line of the *kārikā*.

Ghosh's anthology contains an article on momentariness, as the doctrine is presented only in *Tattvasaṃgraha*. The arguments would have been more intelligible had the author connected them with their original source in *Pramāṇavārttika*. The translation of the *kārikās* of *Tattvasaṃgraha* have not always been satisfactory. Take for example, Śāntarakṣita's proof of momentariness with the help of the notion that destruction is without any extraneous cause, referred to on pp. 216-17. The author's incorrect rendering of the *kārikā* and its commentary (on p. 167) is as follows:

"Whatever is not dependent on other causes for producing anything must be admitted to be eternally connected with that thing, since the thing is produced from the very nature of the producer. Now, just as a thing is independent of others in producing its effect, the whole complex of products is likewise, as far as destruction is concerned." This translation fails to present the logical coherence and precisenesss of Śāntarakṣita's argument as presented on pp. 216-17.

III

Now we proceed to discuss the three chapters on *pramāṇa* in *VaibhashikaDarshan*. These chapters deal with Dharmakīrti's concept of *pramāṇa* (valid source of cognition), *pratyakṣa* (perception) and *anumāna* (inference) as mainly found in his *Nyāyabindu*. The author has occasionally referred to *Tattvasaṃgraha-panjikā* and *Hetubindu* in these chapters. The chapter on *pramāṇa* makes a lucid presentation of Dharmakīrti's concept of *pramāṇa* with special reference to the necessary and sufficient conditions of it, viz., *avisaṃvādakatva* (uncontradictedness[1]), *anadhigatatva* (novelty = unacquiredness[2]), *niyatatva* (necessity) and *arthasārūpya* (similarity with the form of the

1. A source of valid cognition is un-contradicted in the sense that it renewals the object in such form that, the knower is able to successfully attain the object in that form.
2. i.e. it is not already known.

object). The chapter on *pratyakṣa* ably presents Dharmakīrti's definition of *pratyakṣa* as a cognition free from conceptual construction (*kalpanāpoḍham*) and non-erroneous (*abhrānta*). However, the author has failed to make it clear why Dharmakīrti insists that the term *abhrānta* (non-erroneous) must be included in the definition of *pratyakṣa.* Dignāga believed that since all errors are due to conceptual construction (*vikalpajābhrānti*), the inclusion of the term "free from conceptual construction" in the definition is sufficient to distinguish *pratyakṣa* from erroneous cognition. Dharmakīrti, however, points out that errors can also be due to defective sense-organs (*indrayajā-bhrānti*), where no conceptual construction is involved. Defining *prayakṣa* as "free from conceptual construction" is thus not sufficient to exclude all sorts of erroneous cognition from the arena of *pratyakṣa.*

Śāntarakṣita's argument is based on common experience. He cites the example of the common experience of a man witnessing a dance. If, at the same time, when he is thinking about a prize he will offer to the dancer, he is suddenly aware of something moving (e.g. a patch of colour) before his eyes, then the later awareness is a non-conceptual perception. As he is preoccupied with the thought of the prize, he cannot conceptually interpret the object before his eyes by giving it the name 'blue', 'yellow'.

The Naiyāyika may suggest that both the cognition of the name of the prize and the cognition of the thing before the observer's eyes are conceptual cognitions. The two conceptual cognitions are occurring successively. The mistaken idea of their simultaneity is due to the rapidity of succession. For example, the rapid circular movement of a flaming torch produces the wrong impression of a fiery circle.

Sātarakṣita observes that if the rapidity of succession could be an obstacle to the perception of real succession, then we would not be able to apprehend any succession between words like 'latā' and 'tāla', when they are pronounced very quickly. However, in spite of their quick pronunciation, we can apprehend the succession between such words and do not think them to occur simultaneously (*kārikās* 1246-50, *TS*, vol.1). Ghosh, however, wrongly interprets the objection:

Naiyāyika objection: Perception of sights, sounds, smells appear simultaneously to the consciousness of the man witnessing the dance, why cannot many conceptual cognitions be simultaneously present in consciousness?

Śāntarkṣita: Many conceptual cognitions cannot simultaneously occur in a consciousness.

Naiyāyika objection: Perception of sights, smells, sounds appear successively, yet due to the rapidity of their occurrence they seem to occur simultaneously (Ghosh, p. 321).

The Naiyāyika objection is wrongly interpreted here. The opponent is really trying to prove that the thought of the prize and the perception of the patch appear successively.

Śāntarkṣita proves the non-conceptuality of *pratyakṣa* with the help of a brilliant syllogistic proof. Ghosh fails to realize that *kārikās* 1258-61 of *Tattvasaṃgraha* represent such a syllogistic proof (Ghosh, p. 322).

Dharmakīrti's views on *pramāṇa, pratyakṣa* and *aumāna* can also be found in the Bengali translation of *Nyāyabindu* by Satyajyoti Chakrabarty (published in 1994 from Sahityashree, Calcutta). Chakrabarty does not quote Dharmottara's *ṭīkā* on *Nyāyabindu*. The purpose of students and researchers would have been better served had he quoted it. This translation is faithful to the original Sanskrit in most places. In some contexts, however, the translation has not been upto the mark. I quote some examples below:

(i) In the context of asserting that *all forms* of *citta* (consciousness) and *caittas* like pleasure, pain, desire, aversion, volition, are all objects of *svasaṃvedana-pratykṣa* (self-cognising perception). Dharmottara remarks: "*nānyā cittāvasthetyetadāśaṇkā-nivṛttyarthaṃ sarvagrahaṇaṃ kṛtaṃ.*" Dharmottara means to say here that not only *caittas* like pleasure and pain, but all *caittas* (desire, aversion, volition etc.) are objects of self-cognised perception. Chakrabarty, however, translates it as implying: "there is no general knowledge besides pleasure, etc. In order to avoid this misapprehension, it has been said-all *cittas* and *caittas*" (p.16).

(ii) As a species of valid cognition, *pratyakṣa* is evidently *avisaṃvādaka* or non-erroneous. Dharmakīrti's definition of *pratyakṣa* as *abhrānta* or non-erroneous, is accordingly criticized as being repetitive. Dharmottara, in defence of Dharmakīrti, explains that *abhrānta* and *avisaṃvādaka* are not synonymous. *Avisaṃvādakajñāna* really means a knowledge which leads to the successful attainment of the object known. *Abhrānta-jñāna*, however, indicates a knowledge wherein the causally efficacious object impresses its form on consciousness as it really is *(tasmādgrāhyārthakriyākṣame vasturūpe yadaviparyastaṃ tadabhrāntam. Nyāyabindutīkā,* p.10). Thus the *abhrāntatva* of a cognition depends on the exact co-ordination (*sārūpya*) between the forms of object and cognition. Chakrabarty wrongly interprets Dharmottara here as saying: "hence, the meaning of the sentence (*pratyakṣa* is *abhrānta*) is to be understood thus—that *avisaṃvādaka* cognition is called *pratryakṣa,* which is free from conceptual construction and is also *avisaṃvādaka.* No defect will arise here by taking the meaning of *avisaṃvādakat*" (p. 11. Italics mine).

(iii) According to Dharmakīrti, *arthasārūpya* is the cause of the validity of a valid cognition or *pramāṇa* (*arthasārūpyamasya pramāṇam*). A valid cognition is a *niyata*-(specific) *jñāna,* and it is *arthasārūpya* which makes it so. The question arises: if perception is free from conceptual cognition, how can it be *niyata* ? Can it not be the case that it is the determinate judgement, (*adhyavasāya*), which follows from the indeterminate (*nirvikalpaka*) perception is really the *pramāṇa*? Dharmottara contends that the original (indeterminate) sensations differ among themselves as valid cognitions due to their co-ordination with the forms of particular *svalakṣaṇas* of blue, yellow, etc. As a result of this co-ordination they are determined, later on, in determinate judgements. Thus, the determining power of the judgement is really a derivative power. As the real source of this power of determination lies in the original sensations, it is the original sensations that play the role of determiner, and, consequently, that of *pramāṇa.* ['*janitena tvadhyavasāyena sarūpyaṃ vyavasthāpanahetutvāt praṃāṇaṃ siddhaṃ bhavati*'. *Nyāyabinduṭīkā,* p. 20].

Chakrabarty misleadingly translates Dharmottara's commentary here as: "When *adhyavasāya* is produced, a cogntion becomes determined as the cognition of blue due to *sārūpya.* Therefore, it is established that *sārūpya* is *pramāṇa* as the cause of determination." (p. 30). This translation does not make it clear that Dharmottara intends to say that *adhyavasāya* does not have the original power of determination.

Chakrabarty's translation of *Nyayabindu's* chapter on *anumāna* is a better translation than the chapter on *pramāṇa* and *prayakṣa.* The task of making Dharmakīrti's notion of *anumāna* more comprehensive is attempted by Heramba Chattopadhyay Shastri in his monograph entitled *Bauddhacharyasammata Svarthanumner Samkshipta Alochana* (1983, Calcutta). By his comparative study of slightly varying expositions of the same topic in different works such as *Hetubindu*, *Pramāṇavārttika*, *Nyāyabindu* and *Tattvasaṃgraha-pañjikā*, Chattopadhyay makes Dharmakīrti's conception of *anumāna* much more specific and intelligible than that found in the chapter on *anumāna* in *Vaibhasika Darshan*. A Bengali translation of the chapter on *anumāna* in *Tattvasaṃgrahapañjikā* appears in Ghosh's *Vijñānavāda*. Yet, the chapter in *Tattvasaṃgrahapañjikā* is largely a defence of Dharmakīrti's views on *anumāna*. Consequently, Ghosh's translation remains largely incomprehensible to readers not acquainted with Dharmakīrti's arguments.

IV

We would now concentrate on the Bengali works on the Mahāyāna metaphysical doctrine of *vijñaptimātratā* of the Yogācāra-Vijñānavāda school. A valuable translation of *Viṃśatikāprakaraṇavṛtti* of Vasubandhu, dealing with the above-mentioned doctrine of *vijñapatimātrarā*, is made by Professors Sukomal Chaudhury and Prabal Kumar Sen (1991, Calcutta). Both the *Viṃśatikā* and *Triṃśikā* have been translated by Ghosh in his *Vijñānavāda*. Ghosh's translation fails to bring out the proper import of the *kārikās* and their commentaries on a number of occasions.

External objects, according to Vasubandhu, are creations of consciousness. The independence of external objects confronting consciousness is only apparent. A man suffering from an ocular disease sees hair floating before his eyes, and a double moon in the sky. There is no real hair or double moon. Likewise, the so-called external objects are nothing over and above our consciousness of them. The opponent urges that if external objects do not exist, then we cannot explain the spatio-temporal determinations (*deśa-kāla-niyama*) of the objects in a particular space and at a particular time. Neither can we explain the rule (*niyama*) that all people (*sarvasantāna*) and not one person only present at a particular place and time perceive the object present there and then. Even the fruitful activity (*kṛta-kriyā*) which, as a rule (*niyama*), follows knowledge of real objects (as different from mere ideas of them) is inexplicable on the hypothesis that there are no external objects.

Vasunandhu says that the *niyamas* mentioned above do not justify the independent existence of external objects. They are found even in dreams and in hell where there are no external objects.

Even in a dream, a city, a garden, a woman, a man, etc., are seen in a particular place and a particular time. Fruitful activity too results from unreal dream objects. The roaring of a dream tiger causes real fear. Again, all those persons, and not just one of them, who on account of their evil deeds go to hell, see the same river of pus. Hence, it can be concluded that consciousness, the sole reality, manifests itself as a subject and an object.

According to Vasubandhu, the object of perception cannot be *one* whole (*avayavī*) of parts, or many atoms. A whole cannot be perceived apart from its parts. Nor are miniscule atoms perceivable.

Atoms must combine in order to produce gross perceived objects. Yet, their unitary and impartite nature precludes their combination. It is not easy to understand how impartite atoms come into contact with one another, as all contact is of parts with parts. To give rise to perceptible extension, atoms must be arranged side by side. One side would be in contact with one atom, another with another. Yet, that which has sides must have parts.

In *kārikā* 11 of *Viṃśatikā* Vasubandhu argues that the object of visual, tactual and other sorts of perception cannot be *one whole* (*avayavī*). Nor can it be *many* atoms (as separate perception of each atom of a collection of them is not possible). Neither can atoms be such objects in a combined form (as an atom is not established as a real thing).

The above is an English rendering of the Bengali translation by Professors Chaudhury and Ghosh. However, it interprets the *kārikā* rather misleadingly as follows:

The *kārikā* means: a thing is not constituted either by one atom or by many atoms. A thing is not even a combination of separate atoms. The reason is: an atom itself does not have a separate existence (p. 21). Note that the emphasis is given here not on how objects are *perceived*, but on how they are *constituted.*

Vasubandhu anticipates an objection to his thesis: If consciousness is the sole reality, then Lord Buddha would not have, on many occasions, spoken of *rūpāyatana, śabdāyatana,* etc. Surely, as external bases (*bāhyāyatana*) of our colour-perception, sound-perception, the independent existence of colour, sound, etc., must be acknowledged! Vasubandhu contends that Lord Buddha has spoken of *rūpāyatana, śabdāyatana* with a view to instruct disciples of less advanced intellect. Those who believe in permanent *ātman* need to be convinced that the so-called *ātman* is nothing but an aggregate of *rūpāyatana* and its corresponding consciousness, *śabdāyatana* and its corresponding consciousness, etc. Yet, such an instruction will only help them to realize *pudgala-nairtāmya.* The final end of the spiritual progress comes only with the realization of *dharma-nairātmya*—the realization that external objects are essenceless, and that pure consciousness is the sole reality. In order to establish that colour, sound, etc., are manifestations of consciousness only Vasubandhu says:

yataḥ svabījādvijñaptiryadābhāsā pravartate /
dvividhāyatanatvena te tasya muniravravit //

Kārikā 9

The intended meaning of the *kārikā,* according to Professors Chaudhury and Sen are as follows: Impressions (*vāsanā*) in consciousness produce both consciousness of colour and visual perception. Keeping in mind the impressions as the seeds of consciousness, the Lord has instructed about *cakṣurāyatana* and *rūpāytana* of that consciousness. The *kārikā* is literally translated by them as: "consciousness of colour, etc., is produced from its own seed. The said seed and the said consciousness have been expressed by the Lord as the twofold *āyatana* (*ādhyātmika* or internal and *bāhya* or external) of the said consciousness" [pp. 51-52].

The Bengali rendering of the *kārikā* by Ghosh (p. 20) is quite misleading: "Being produced by its own seed, consciousness appears as the direct apprehension of all objects. The reason is: Lord Buddha has said that these appearances of consciousness are due to the twofold *āyatana.*"

Buddhist metaphysical and epistemological doctrines have been subjected to criticisms in Uddyotakara's *Nyāyavārttika,* Jayanta Bhaṭṭa's *Nyāyamañjarī* and Udayana's *Ātmatattvaviveka.* In these works the authors have tried to show inconsistencies in the Buddhist views by interpreting the Buddhist views and technical notions in terms of the specific *Nyāya* technical notions and terminology. As a result, a researcher in Buddhist philosophy will fail to appreciate the real force of the Buddhist arguments in reading only these criticisms of the Buddhist positions. *Nyāyamanjarī* and *Ātmatativaviveka* have been translated (with notes) in Bengali by Panchanan Tarkabagisha (1939-41) and Dinnatha Tripathi (1989). Since the readers will not be able to get the proper perspective of the Buddhist view by studying these books only, I have refrained from making detailed observations on these treaties. Brief outlines of Buddhist philosophy have been produced by scholars like P.C. Bagchi (see his *Bauddha Darshan O Sahitya* 1994, Calcutta). Such works are not meant for serious research scholars of Buddhism.

ABBREVIATIONS

1. NV : *Nyāyavārttika*
2. PV : *Pramāñavārttika*
3. TSP : *Tattvasaṃgrahapañjika*

BIBLIOGRAPHY

Dharmakīrti	:	*Pramāṇvārttika*
Dharmottara	:	*Hetubindu,* edited by E. Steinkellner, Wein, 1967 *Nyāyabindutika,* ed. Chandra Shekhar Shastri, Chowkhamba, Varanasi, 1968.
Kamalaśīla	:	*Tattvasaṃgrapañjika,* ed. Dwarikadas Shastri, Varanasi, 1968.
Śāntarakṣita	:	*Tattvasaṃgraha* as quoted in *Tattvasaṃgrapañjika.*
Uddyotakara	:	*Nyāyavārttika.*

21

Representation of Buddhism in Indian Poetry in English

Niranjan Mohanty

A religion that emanated from and originated with the Buddha, the Enlightened one, could exert lasting impact not only on the minds and hearts of the people of India but also on its literary traditions.

An attempt is made in this paper to study the influence that Buddhism could exert on Indian Poetry in English, more particularly, on the post-Independence Indian poetry in English.

In a perceptive article "Indian Writing in English" included in *Buddhist Themes in Modern Indian Literature,*[1] Prema Nandakumar identified influences on Sarojini Naidu's *To a Buddha Seated on the Lotus,* R.L. Bartholomew's *An episode from Amra* on the Buddha's life, P. Lal's *The Dear at Nara,* Achyuta Bose's *Nirvana,* Motilal Jotwani's *Alien There is None* (1989), K.R. Srinivasa Iyengar's *The Incarnations* (1989), *Sati Sapthakam: Saga of Seven Mothers* (1990), Rabindranath Tagore's *Natir Puja, Candalika, Malini,* Asif Karimbhoy's *Om Mane Padme Hum,* Sri Aurobindo's *The Prince of Edur,* Harindranath's *Siddhartha: Man of Peace* (1956), Masti Venkatesa Iyengar's *The Last Days of Sariputra,* Vimala Raina's *Ambapali* (1962), Raja Rao's *The Serpent and the Rope,* Dilip Kumar Roy's *Hark! His Flute* (*1972*), and Prema Nandakumar's *A Mother Too* (1987). Nandakumar identified those works, which directly celebrated Buddhist tenets or Buddhism's appalling, surging and all-embracing humanism. With Sarvapalli Radhakrishnan's *Indian Philosophy* (1927) and his master lecture at the British Academy (1937), a fresh, insightful look into Buddhism could open up a new philosophical approach. Radhakrishnan described the Buddha as a "reformer of the innovator, and that his silence on the ultimate problems implied neither agnosticism nor atheism but a refusal to speak of the Absolute of which he was aware, because it was not directly relevant to ethical ways of living." Jawaharlal

Nehru's profound realization of the true nature of the Buddha's greatness in *The Discovery of India*, his unearthly power, his detachment, his compassion, his enlightenment, remain quite valid and relevant even today. Nehru wrote:

Seated on the lotus flower, calm and impassive, above passion and desire, beyond the storm and strife of this world, so far away he seems, out of reach unattainable. Yet again we look, and behind those still, unmoving features there is a passion and an emotion, strange and more powerful than the passions and emotions we have known. His eyes are closed but some power of the spirit looks out of them and a vital energy fills the frame.[2]

The post-Independence Indian poets writing in English have taken clues from Radhakrishnan and Nehru for looking at the Buddha, the Enlightened one, and Buddhism, the religion with a difference, the religion that championed the human element so immaculately, rather differently. Jayanta Mahapatra, the celebrated Anglophone poet, who celebrates in his poetry the inviolable connection between the places, the native culture and the creative writer, looks at the Buddha from a different aesthetic angle. Mahapatra, a poet who intends to elevate poetry to *mantric* heights, looks at the meditative Buddha differently. He has been successfully depicting silence as the ultimate delight of the flux of words. The silence that orients the flux of words and directs the movement of this flux of words towards itself as an embodiment or a manifestation of an ideal, is seminally aesthetic. The silence that Mahapatra celebrates is primarily artistic which must have originated from the Buddha's meditative silence. This silence is creative and redemptive for Mahapatra. The way Mahapatra tries to study and examine grief and the causes of grief, the manner in which he depicts multiple dimensions of desire and its effects on individuals can be traced back to the tenets of what the Buddha taught. The willingness to transcend the bounds of mortality and whatever corrupts or corrodes mortality as reflected in Mahapatra's poetry, is due to his aesthetic reading of the Buddha's teaching is the sermon he gave in Banaras after Enlightenment:

Listen ye Bhikshus! He who wants to renounce worldliness should avoid both excess and undue abstinence. On the one hand, he should not be addicted to things, which attract the mind merely through passion, especially through carnal desire. That is the low, vain and worthless life of ignorance fit for none but the blind worshipper of the world. On the other hand, he should not be given to self-mortification. That also is painful, ignoble and useless. There is Ye Bhikshus a middle path between the two, which the

Tathagatha (Buddha) has found. The pursuit of this path opens the eyes and enlightens the mind. This is the way of peace of mind, higher wisdom, illumination and *nirvana*.[3]

The poetics of Mahapatra's creative practice intends to achieve this transcendental quality of *nirvana* by valourizing and unravelling the mysteries of silence. Mahapatra's sensitive understanding of Orissa's cultural and historical past led him to harp on the Kalinga war that brought in transformation in Ashoka who abandoned warfare after victory and accepted Buddhism and became the chief architect responsible for spreading the messages of the Buddha. Viewing the bloodshed Ashoka could realize the fatuity of his pride as a victor and conqueror. In *dhauligiri* Mahapatra limns the fathomless pain of Ashoka:

Afterwards
When the wars of Kalinga were over
The fallow fields of Dhauli
Hid the red-smeared voiceless bodies.
....
The measure of Ashoka's suffering
does not appear enough
The place of his pain peers lamentably
from among the pains of the dead.

(*Waiting* 24)

In another poem *River*, Mahapatra expresses his own grief over the lost Kalinga war, which changed the heart of Ashoka after watching the Daya River turning red with the blood of the brave race of Kalinga. By revisiting history, Mahapatra not only strengthens his ties with his own cultural past, but also suggests the links of a changed Ashoka with Buddhism that taught him that victory over hearts is more enduring than victory over kingdom through warfare, bloodshed and massacre:

And the light stirs, as if to rise,
But is buried under the old papal limbs,
By the river, pain rolls on in the water's unconcern
Where we keep on seeing shapes
Of the way we looked once.

(*Burden of Waves and Fruit* 20)

In yet another poem *Shapes by the Daya*, Mahapatra captures the wounds, the pain of the people of Orissa represented by Daya River on whose banks the Kalinga war was fought:

> A thousand birds fly to grief in these
> Frightened minds, the wounded letters in the stones' arms
> Mirror themselves in the sky.
> ....
> Time rests its terrible quiet on the river.
>
> (*Burden of Waves and Fruit 21*)

Mahapatra's suggestive reference to Kalinga war and Ashoka orchestrates his reverential attitude towards Buddhism which whetted the rough edges of humanism in the most critical juncture of Indian history, when Hinduism was becoming increasingly ritualistic and elitist.

Bibhu Padhi, another significant voice from Orissa, in a poem entitled "Buddha" sharply draws our attention to the distinction between the ideal and the real, the one represented by a creative silence and the other by the wrestle of words, the one timeless and spiritual and the other time-tattered and physical world, of the world of matter. Padhi writes:

> I've lost your world, your weary
> human voice. My eyes are supported by
> a different space, my ears open
> to the sconce of an infinite sky.
> I've known how to pray without a voice,
> See what those eyes don't see;
> I know what new light breaks behind
> The shadows of these mountains.
>
> I've known the hushed migration of the soul
> Into a loving, patient hand waiting
> beyond history and time; I've known
> the course of its simple reverent flight.
>
> Why then do you ask me these questions
> of return? Is there any need to locate
> other homes? Which familiar world can bring me
> this space, what old gestures make me your own?
>
> (*Going to the Temple 41*)

Thus for Padhi, Buddha remains a symbol of home, endowed with the richness of love, that is unselfish, redemptive and timeless.

Priyadarshi Patnaik, a young poet from Orissa with two volumes of poetry so far, captures in his works the historical and religious significance of Khandagiri and Udaygiri. For Patnaik, Khandagiri and Udaygiri represent a living faith without which life in a difficult, materialistic world becomes meaningless. In *At Khandagiri*, Patnaik celebrates the enduring quality of Buddhism:

> Faithless I stood
> Before the rock hewn caves,
> That jagged yet rooted,
> Spoke of a faith
> That has lasted three thousand years.
>
> (*From the Shadows of the Sun 57*)

For Patnaik, Udaygiri remains a temple of the Almighty that brings in contentment. He writes:

> Many have come and gone
> And many more will come
> From far and wide
> And go away content.
>
> (*From the Shadows of the Sun 58*)

If for Patnaik rock edicts and caves at Khandagiri could emphatically epitomize a living faith, the temple at Udayagiri manifests the kind of contentment every mortal intends to achieve.

I.K. Sharma of Jaipur (Rajasthan), a very senior poet and academician, titled his volume as *Dharmasala and other poems* (1993). In this volume there are two very interesting poems on Dharmasala. The tone is satiric, the stance is very much ironic in order to show how the spiritual vacancy in men and women today has changed human hearts into iron shafts. It would be a mere pleonasm to say that the Buddha, the Enlightened One, is the point of reference as the epicentre of a living faith. Besides harping on the natural bounties of Dharmasala, Sharma calls the place as "the land of soft music and loud peaks/so near the sun and stars/ darkness does not settle upon your soul" (p. 11). He further depicts the ritualistic tradition of Dharmasala that has sanctified the hearts of the villagers:

> The villagers exchange their yarns
> To give you robes that neither wrinkle nor burn,

> The legendary Lama prays at your shrine
> For the safe return of the human voice (p. 11).

Sharma, therefore, views Dharmasala as the centre that can nurture not only what is divine or immortal but also what is essentially human. Sharma concludes the poem with a rewarding paradox:

> Dharmasala! Keep your crest always in sight!
> You will never miss the white sunshine.
> ....
> Here winter is forever warm
> Snow is never cold,
> Fields are always vibrant and green (p. 12).

The place assumes vibrancy, freshness, greenness and warmth because of the Buddha's spiritual influence and integrity. In the second poem, *Dharmasala 2,* Sharma celebrates the significance of Dharmasala as "Nature's meditation centre" (p. 26). Sharma, like Wordsworth, tries to unearth the mystical elements hidden in the store-house of nature.

He also suggests about the capacity of the place, as it is blessed and pure, to transform even the 'dogs' into 'mystics'. All animals and human beings maintain perfect silence, perhaps, the Buddha's meditative silence. The queer blending of naturalism and mysticism makes the poem significant. Sharma fuses the landscape with the personality of the Buddha with such exquisiteness, that the place embodies the Buddha's perpetual presence:

> The hooded Dholadhar stands straight and tall
> like Buddha blessing earthlings below.
> The trees stretch their arms, one above another,
> to get his benediction. Columns of colour
> fall from above and sit on heads of hills.
> Showers spray coolness along the urban nerves.
> Cycle of seasons shapes the interior, the hearts,
> and releases baser passions from its hold.
> Nothing here tampers with the Spirit, its autonomy.
> The green earth pleads for faith to many-tiered sky.

Dharmasala absorbs everyone; it disowns none, as if the place has imbibed this virtue from the Buddha's all-encompassing compassion and love:

Amazing, you, disown none.
Your spacious Eden in its home-spun harmony
owns both: the virtuous Lama and learned Margaret
not far from each other (p. 27).

Mary Ann Dasgupta's poem *Buddha Purnima* captures her agony of not being able to become as meditative as the Buddha. By showing her materialistic and love-sick attitude, Dasgupta has suggested the superiority of the Buddha's ways over our own:

Over the clover
and the sunshine and the grass,
over the tired earth below,
beyond mimosa and gardenia
sighing in the shadows
where monkeys rise and sway,
and green coke bottles pave the way
to rose's wing
or beetle's eye or mine.
I wish to pause and contemplate
but I've received the sign
of silk and satin petticoats,
mimosa and gardenia mate,
the woof and warf of evening wait;
with heavy breath
insinuating pleasantness,
I pass (*Hundred Indian Poets,* p. 78).

Rukmini Bhaya Nair in a recently published poem *Buddha,* characterizes Buddha's greatness as manifested in his silence. She tries to capture in her poem, the essence of the Buddha's redemptive powers with which he can transport mortals to the height of eternity:

A man who speaks
With his eyes
Hears with his hands ....
Lifts you effortless
To paradise! (Nair, p. 117)

S. Abid Husain in his book *The National Culture of India* (1994) maintains:

The Buddha showed the way to self-restraint instead of self-mortification, to right action instead of inactivity. What he specially emphasized was that giving up worldliness does not mean giving up the love and service of mankind. On the contrary, universal love is essential for attaining peace of mind. This law of love he enunciates in the following words: Hatred does not cease by meeting hatred with hatred but by meeting it with love. This is its nature. If one wants to live a happy life one should not hate one's enemies. Conquer resentment with love, evil with good, greed with generosity and falsehood with truth (p. 43).

Poets like Biswakesh Tripathy and late O.P. Bhatnagar have realized the significance of this universal love championed by the Buddha. Tripathy in his volume *Anticipations* (1990) celebrates this love:

> Love is the only hope of the living cell
> In the dying mass of human flesh,
> ....
> But for all of us
> Love is an illumination
> That lights up earth and heaven.
> Love is a light that lights other lamps (p. 42).

Similarly, late O.P. Bhatnagar in a poem *Restless Peace* published in a journal from Calcutta entitled *Bridge-in-Making* laid emphasis on peace, the need for peace, which as the Buddha opined, is the way of "higher wisdom, illumination and *nirvana*". Bhatnagar writes:

> We all need peace to begin with
> Not end with like desert after devastation:
> Not the one philosophers talk of
> With eyes fixed on space or down in dust
> But the one which soothes terror
> In the Japanese temple of silence
> Or in the jungles of staying repose (pp. 24-25).

The Indian poet in English, and for that matter, the creative artist is drawn towards Buddhism particularly because he or she discovers a viable connection between the act of meditation and the art of writing. Early in the canonical Buddhist text, *The Dhammapada*, we find a unique observation:

> Hard to hold down,
> nimble
> alighting wherever it likes:

the mind.
Its taming is good.
The mind well tamed
brings ease.

Any action is performed best and most beautifully when the actor practises what Buddhists call "mindfulness"; when he is wholly and selflessly aware of every nuance in the activity and immersed in it; when he gets the gossamer-thin illusion of the self out of the way and, in a delightful modulation of consciousness and temporality, experiences only the 'here' and the "now", with no concern at all for the unrecoverable past or a future that never comes.

I am sure of this fact that in a world which is becoming increasingly materialistic, increasingly terror-stricken, terrorism-ridden, and where higher values of life get constantly butchered by corruption, violence, selfishness, the Buddha as the living spirit and his messages as the salvaging panacea, would bring back peace and love and that the poets, writers and playwrights in the future years would draw their inspiration from the meditative silence of the blessed Buddha, to represent the world they live in, and to represent the air they breathe in.

REFERENCES

1. J. Parthasarathi (ed.), *Buddhist Themes in Modern Indian Literature*, Madras, Institute of Asian Studies, 1992.
2. Jawaharlal Nehru, *The Discovery of India*, Delhi, Asia Publishing House, 1981, pp. 131-32.
3. Quoted from S. Abid Hussain's *The National Culture of India*, Delhi, National Book Trust (1978), 1994, pp. 42-43.

BIBLIOGRAPHY

Bhatnagar, O.P., "Restless Peace", *Bridge in Making* (ed.), P. Majumber, April-September, 1995.

Dasgupta, Mary Ann., *Hundred Indian Poets* (ed), P. Bandyopadhy, Calcutta, United Writers, 1997.

Mahapatra, Jayanta, *Waiting Delhi*, Samketan Prakashan, 1979.

——, *Burden of Waves and Fruits*, Washington DC, Three Continents Press, 1988.

Nair, Rukmini Bhaya, "Buddha", *Journal of Literature and Aesthetics* (ed.), S. Sreenivasan, Vol. 1, No. 1, July–December, 2001, p. 117.

Padhi, Bibhu, *Going to the Temple*, Delhi, Indus Publishing Company, 1988.

Patnaik, Priyadarshi, *From the Shadows of the Sun*, Calcutta, Writers Workshop, 1991.

Sharma, I.K., *Dharmasala and Other Poems*, Aligarh, Skylark Publications, 1993.

22

मराठी साहित्य पर बौद्ध धम्म का प्रभाव

विमलकीर्ति

आधुनिक भारतीय साहित्य में मराठी साहित्य का अपना एक विशेष स्थान है। मराठी साहित्य की परम्परा काफी पुरानी मानी जाती है। मराठी साहित्य का सम्बन्ध मराठी सन्तों के साहित्य से जोड़ा जाता है और उसका प्रारम्भ सन्तों के साहित्य से ही माना जाता है। मराठी सन्तों का सम्बन्ध नाथपंथ के साथ जोड़ा जाता है और नाथपंथ का सम्बन्ध बौद्ध धम्म के साथ जोड़ा जाता है। बौद्ध धम्म में सरहपाद (ईसवी आठवीं सदी) का अपना एक महत्वपूर्ण स्थान है। उसी प्रकार सरहपाद का काल भारतवर्ष के इतिहास में कई दृष्टि से अत्यन्त महत्वपूर्ण है। इस महान बौद्ध विचारक, कवि और सन्त-सिद्ध के प्रादुर्भाव से एक नये युग की सूचना मिलती है। सरहपाद की सिद्ध परम्परा में ८४ सिद्धों के नाम मिलते हैं। यह परम्परा आठवीं सदी से ग्यारहवीं सदी ईसवी तक मिलती है। इसमें गोरखनाथ, जिनका पंथ अब भी सारे भारत में फैला हुआ है, सरहपाद शिष्य-परम्परा में थे। महाराष्ट्र के संत ज्ञानेश्वर भी सरह की परम्परा के ही थे। जैसे, आदिनाथ (जलंधर), मत्स्येंद्रनाथ, गोरखनाथ, गोहनीनाथ, निवृत्तिनाथ, ज्ञानेश्वर। ज्ञानेश्वर और गोरखनाथ के बीच की कुछ पीढ़ियां छूटी हुई मालूम देती हैं क्योंकि गोरखनाथ राजा देवपाल (ईसवीं ८१५-८५४) के समकालीन थे। सरहपाद का साहित्य अपभ्रंश भाषा का अत्यंत महत्वपूर्ण साहित्य है।

भारतवर्ष में सन्तों के प्रादुर्भाव का काल भी यही है। सन्तों ने जो साहित्य लिखा उसको सत्य साहित्य के नाम से जाना जाता है। इन सन्तों में कुछ सन्त हमें ब्राह्मणवादी परम्परा को माननेवाले दिखायी देते हैं और कुछ गैरब्राह्मण परम्परा को माननेवाले दिखायी देते हैं। उसी प्रकार ब्राह्मणी परम्परा को माननेवाले सन्त संस्कृत भाषा से प्रभावित दिखायी देते हैं, तो गैरब्राह्मणी परम्परा को माननेवाले संत जनभाषा (अपभ्रंश) का इस्तेमाल करते हैं। ब्राह्मणवादी परम्परा को माननेवाले जातिवाद, ब्राह्मण श्रेष्ठत्व को, वेदों के श्रेष्ठत्व को मानते हैं और गैरब्राह्मणी परम्परा को माननेवाले संत जातिवाद, ब्राह्मण श्रेष्ठत्व, वेदों के श्रेष्ठत्व को नकारते हैं।

सरहपाद विद्रोही कवि, संत और चिन्तक थे। वे विचारों की दुनिया के विद्रोही और कितने अंशों में सामाजिक विद्रोही भी थे। उन्होंने अपने 'दोहाकोश चर्यागीति' के पहले १२ दोहों में अपने समय के धार्मिक सम्प्रदायों और उनके विचारों का खण्डन किया है। 'यदि नग्न रहने

से मुक्ति हो, तो कुत्ते और सियार भी मुक्त हो जायेंगे। मोर-पंख ग्रहण करने से यदि मोक्ष हो तो मोर और चमर भी मुक्त हो जायेंगे। शीला चुगकर खाने से यदि ज्ञान हो जाए तो करि और तुरंग भी ज्ञानी हो जायेंगे। इन्हीं भावों को और करीब-करीब सरहपाद के ही शब्दों में, छह शताब्दियों बाद कबीर ने कहा-

का नांगे का बाधे चाम। जौ नहीं चीन्हसि आतम राम।
नांगे फिरे जोग जे होई। बनका मृग मुकति गया कोई।
मुंड-मुंडाये जौ सिधि होई। स्वर्गहि भीड़ न पहुंची कोई।

अपने समय के कितने ही मूढ़ विश्वासों का-जिनमें से बहुतेरे बारह सदियों बाद आज भी उसी तरह प्रबल हैं-जैसे सरह ने खण्डन किया है, उसके नमूने देखिए—-

मंत्र-तंत्र खंडन-

किन्तहि दीपे किं णेवेज्जे। किन्तइ किज्जई मन्तह भावें। (१२)
मन्त ण तन्त ण छेअ ण धारण। सब्बवि रे बढ़ विबभमकारण। (३४)

सरहपाद ने (धर्मशास्त्र) को मरुस्थल कहा है जिसकी भूल-भुलैया में पड़कर आदमी निकल नहीं सकता:

गुरू-वअण-अमिअ-रस, धवडि ण पिबिअड जेहिं।
बहुसातात्थ-मरीत्थलेहिं, तिसिह मरिबबो तेहिं॥ (४४)

और पंडितों की खबर लेते हुए सरहपाद कहते हैं:

पंडिअ सअल सत्थ बक्खाणअ। देहहि बुद्ध वसन्त ण जाणअ। (७४)

छूत-छात और भक्षाभक्ष्य के कठोर नियमों की निस्सारता बताते हुए सरहपाद कहते हैं:

यदि प्रमादे विधिवस, मूढ लहेऊ भेद।
जई चण्डालघरे भुंजइ, तअवि ण लग्गई लेड। (११२)

उसी प्रकार ब्राह्मणों के कर्मकाण्डों का मज़ाक उड़ाते हुए सरहपाद कहते हैं कि-

जिमि ब्राह्मणों धृत-तंडुल, ज्वलित अग्नि में होम कहै।
आकाश रस द्रव्य से उत्पन्न यह, सोई मुक्ति कहै॥

वर्ण-भेद का खण्डन करते हुए सरहपाद कहते है कि-

वर्ण भेद से बंधन न जीर्ण कहै, मूढ रत्न-परीक्षा व जानै।
वह पीतल सोने के ख्याल से, अनुभव से परमार्थ सधै॥

इस प्रकार सरहपाद ने जातिवाद और वर्णभेद का विरोध किया है। उसी प्रकार सरहपाद को ब्राह्मण वर्ण की जन्म और जाति के आधार पर श्रेष्ठता मान्य नहीं थी। ब्राह्मण वरण के श्रेष्ठत्व का खण्डन करते हुए कहते हैं कि,

ब्राह्मण न जानते भेद। यो ही पडे थे चारो वेद॥
मट्टी पानी कुश लेई पढन्त। घरही बैठी अग्नि होमन्त ॥
काज विना ही हुतवत होमे। आंख जलावें कडुये धूऐ ॥
एकदंडी त्रिदंडी भागवा भेसे। ज्ञानी होंके हंस उपदेसै॥
मिथ्येही जग बहा भूलैं। धर्म-अधर्म न जाना तुल्यै॥

सरहपाद पण्डितवाद पर कटाक्ष करते हैं-

पंडित सकल शास्त्र बक्खानै। देहहि बुद्ध वसंत न जानै।
अवनागवन न एकउ खंडित। तऊ निलज्ज भनै हम पंडित॥

ब्राह्मण किसे कहा जाये, इसके बारे में सरहपाद करते हैं कि,

जब्बें मण अत्थमण जाइ, तनु तुट्टई बन्धण ॥
तब्बे समरस सहजे वज्जइ, णउ सुददण बह्मण॥

इस प्रकार सरहपाद और उनके सहजयान बौद्ध पंथ की विचारधारा थी। सरहपाद की चौरासी सिद्धों की परम्परा है। जिस समय भारत से बौद्धधर्म लुप्त होने जा रहा था उस समय भी सिद्ध लोक कवि होते थे और जनजीवन पर, सामान्य लोगों पर उनकी विचारधारा का प्रभाव था। मतलब ईसा की चौदहवीं सदी तक भारत के जन-जीवन पर बौद्ध धर्म का प्रभाव था। इसलिए मराठी भाषी सन्तों पर भी बौद्ध धर्म का पभाव दिखायी देता है। संत ज्ञानेश्वर ईसा की चौदहवीं सदी में हुए। वे नाथ पंथ को मानने वाले थे। इसी समय महाराष्ट्र में वारकरी पंथ की स्थापना हुई। इसमें नामदेव, तुकाराम, गोरा कुंभार, संत जोखामेला, बहिणाबाई, संत कर्ममेला आदि संतों का कार्य बड़ा महत्वपूर्ण है। नाथ पंथ का दूसरा रूप वारकरी पंथ है। इस वारकरी पंथ पर स्पष्ट रूप से बौद्ध विचारधारा का प्रभाव दिखायी देता है। वास्तव में सरहपाद की बौद्ध विचारधारा का प्रभाव दिखायी देता है।

बौद्ध धर्म और मराठी संत साहित्य

महाराष्ट्र में मराठी सन्तों का और उनके साहित्य का काल ईसा की चौदहवीं सदी से प्रारम्भ होता है। इस समय दक्षिण भारत में महायान बौद्ध धर्म था और धीरे-धीरे समाप्त होने की प्रक्रिया में था। इस समय दक्षिण भारत में बौद्ध धर्म को राजाश्रय या किसी भी प्रकार की सत्ता का आश्रय नहीं था। उस समय यहां के राज-शासक ब्राह्मण धर्मिय थे और ब्राह्मणधर्म को, ब्राह्मण पण्डित-पुरोहितों को मदद कर रहे थे। फिर भी जनसामान्य में बौद्ध धर्म के प्रति

आस्था थी। जनसामान्य से जो संत कवि आते थे वे बौद्ध विचारधारा को अलग-अलग रूपों में, प्रत्यक्ष या परोक्ष रूप में जन सामान्य के सामने रखते थे। इसलिए हम देखते है कि मराठी सन्तों में जनसामान्य से जो संत आए हैं उनकी रचनाओं में स्पष्ट रूप से बौद्ध धर्म का प्रभाव दिखायी देता है। जैसे संत ज्ञानेश्वर की ज्ञानेश्वरी में बौद्ध धर्म का, बौद्ध विचारधारा का जितना प्रभाव दिखायी नहीं देगा उतना प्रभाव संत तुकाराम और संत नामदेव आदि के अभंगों में दिखायी देता है। मराठी संत बहिणाबाई (ई. स. १६२८) ने तो वर्णवादका खंडन करने वाले वज्रसूचीकोपनिषद का मराठी में अनुवाद किया था।

जाति की दृष्टि से विचार किया जाए तो मराठी सन्तों में उच्च वर्णिय (ब्राह्मण) और निम्न वर्णिय (गैर ब्राह्मणी) दोनों प्रकार के संत हुए हैं। उच्च वर्णी मराठी संतो ने अपने साहित्य में ब्राह्मणवाद की विचारधारा का, ब्राह्मण श्रेष्ठत्व का, वर्णवाद-जातिवाद का, कर्मसिद्धान्त का, यज्ञयाग आदि का और वेदों की सर्वश्रेष्ठता का समर्थन किया है और निम्न जाति के सन्तों ने ईश्वर भक्ति के साथ अपने-अपने समाज के दु:खों का भी वर्णन किया है। उन्होंने अपने काल की जातिभेद की स्थिति का और उसका निम्न जातियों पर हों रहे दुष्परिणामों का भी वर्णन किया है। उसी प्रकार उन्होंने उस काल के धार्मिक पाखण्डों की भी आलोचना की है। संत ज्ञानेश्वर और संत रामदास दोनों उच्च वर्णी हैं, ब्राह्मण जाति से हैं। दोनों सन्तों के साहित्य में जातिवाद का, जातिभेद का समर्थन है। उसी प्रकार उनके साहित्य में किसी में भी वैज्ञानिक और मानवी दृष्टि का अभाव है। किन्तु गैर-ब्राह्मण सन्तों के साहित्य में ईश्वरवाद के अलावा मानवी दृष्टि भी है। वे अपने-अपने समाज के लोंगों के दु:खों का अनुभव कर रहे थे और ईश्वर से अपनी पीड़ा, अपनी दु:ख भरी दास्तान कह रहे थे। सन्तों ने उस समय सम्पूर्ण समाज में समता की बात तो नहीं कही किन्तु ईश्वर के सामने परमार्थ में सभी की बराबरी की, ईश्वर भक्ति में सभी के बराबर होने की बात कही है।

महाराष्ट्र में बौद्ध धर्म के लुप्त होने के साथ ही मराठी सन्तों का उदय होता है। सन्तों का उदय भी एक तरह से बौद्ध धर्म का विरोध करने के लिए ही हुआ है अर्थात् बौद्ध धर्म के विरोध में एक प्रतिक्रिया के रूप में सन्तों का उदय हुआ और इन सन्तों को तत्कालीन बौद्ध विरोधी शक्तियों ने काफी समर्थन दिया। इसलिए संतों के साहित्य में ईश्वरवाद का, यथास्थितिवाद का, भक्तिवाद का, ब्राह्मणी कर्म काण्डों का काफी समर्थन है। जिस समय मराठी में संत अपने साहित्य की रचना कर रहे थे उस समय मराठी में बौद्ध धर्म तथा दर्शन पर कोई ग्रंथ उपलब्ध नहीं था। उसी प्रकार किसी संत ने किसी बौद्ध विषय पर उस समय किसी ग्रंथ की रचना नहीं की। मराठी सन्तों के साहित्य के विषय हिन्दू धर्म, ब्राह्मणधर्म से संबधित थे और उनका अधिकांश साहित्य किसी मूल ग्रंथ की रचना नहीं है बल्कि प्राचीन ब्राह्मणी विचारधारा के ग्रंथों पर भाष्य मात्र है या भक्ति का महत्व वर्णन करना मात्र है। संतों से पहले जो आचार्य हुए जिनमें आदिशंकराचार्य आदि हैं, उन्होंने बौद्ध धर्म का जबर्दस्त विरोध किया, वर्णभेद, जातिभेद का समर्थन किया, ब्राह्मणवाद का समर्थन किया, उसी परम्परा को सन्तों ने आगे बढ़ाया। बौद्ध नाथ परम्परा से या सरहपाद की चौरासी सिद्धों की परम्परा से

मराठी सन्तों का नाम मात्र का रिश्ता रह गया था। इसलिए मराठी संतों के काल में मराठी भाषा में किसी बौद्ध विषय पर कोई ग्रंथ लिखा गया हो ऐसा कोई प्रमाण हमारे पास उपलब्ध नहीं है। इसलिए मराठी सन्तों पर और उनके साहित्य पर बौद्ध धर्म का प्रभाव स्पष्ट रूप से कहीं दिखायी नहीं देता। मराठी संतों ने ब्राह्मण धर्म ग्रंथों पर, ब्राह्मण विषयों पर ही अपने काव्य की, अभंगों की, ग्रंथों की रचना की है। मराठी में संत ज्ञानेश्वर से लेकर संत रामदास तक सभी संतों का साहित्य हिन्दू धर्म की पुन:स्थापना के लिये, वर्णाश्रम धर्म के रक्षण और समर्थन के लिए, वेद और वेदांतों की मान्यताओं के समर्थन के लिए लिखा गया है। इसके लिए सन्तों ने भक्ति का जो मार्ग अपनाया है वह सामन्तवाद का और धार्मिक पाखण्डवाद का प्रतीक है।

संत ज्ञानेश्वर (ई.स. १२७१-१२९६) वैदिक ब्राह्मणी परम्परा के समर्थक थे, जब कि उनका संबंध बौद्ध नाथ परम्परा से था। संत ज्ञानेश्वर कहते है:

> सांधौ शूद्रगृही आघवी। जर्‌ही पक्वान्नें आतिथि करवीं।
> तिये द्विजे केवि सेवावी। दुबका जर्‌है॥ (ज्ञाने. ३-२१६)

मतलब यदि शूद्र के घर में मेहमानी के तौर पर कितने भी अच्छे पदार्थ बनाएँ हों, ब्राह्मण गरीब होने पर भी उन्हें उसने क्यों ग्रहण करना चाहिए? यह कहकर ज्ञानेश्वरजी वर्णवाद का जातपांत का समर्थन करते है। वे आगे कहते है:

> पैद्विजसेवे परौते, धावणें नाहिं शुद्राते ।
> चातुर्वर्ण्याची उचितें दाविली कर्मे।। (ज्ञाने. 18-80)

इसमें उन्होंने चातुर्वर्ण्य का सीधा-सीधा समर्थन किया है। संत ज्ञानेश्वर के साहित्य पर प्रत्यक्ष रूप में बौद्ध धर्म का कोई प्रभाव नहीं है। संत रामदास (ईस. 1657 से 1700) तो पूरी तरह से ब्राह्मणवादी है, वे वर्णवाद, जातिवाद के जर्बदस्त समर्थक हैं। वे कहते है-

> जही ब्राह्मण मूठमती तरी तो जगदवंध। (दा. द. स. ओ.)

यह कहकर वे ब्राह्मण वर्ण की श्रेष्ठता को स्वीकार करते है। संत रामदास अछूतों के बारे में कहते है-

> अंत्यज शब्दज्ञाता बरवा। परि तो नेऊन कामे करावा।
> बाह्मणा सनिद्ध पूजावा। हे तो न घडे की (दा.द.स.ओ. ४.१.१६)
> नीच प्राणी गुरूत्व पावला। तेथे आचारचि बुडाला।
> वेद शास्त्र ब्राह्मणाला कोण पुसे (दा.द.स.ओ. १४.७.१९)

संत रामदास जातिवाद का खुलकर समर्थन करते थे। वे वेदों की श्रेष्ठता को स्वीकार करते थे। उन्होंने जो भी लिखा है सब वैदिक और ब्राह्मणवादी विषयों पर ही लिखा है। यदि संत

समत्वभाव के होते तो कोई न कोई बौद्ध विषय पर वे जरूर लिखते। संतों ने परमार्थ में समता की बात कही है। किन्तु वास्तविक जगत में समता का समर्थन करने का साहस उनमें नहीं था। वे परोक्ष रूप से बौद्ध धर्म की कुछ बातों को स्वीकार करते हैं और वे उनके साहित्य में तथा जीवन में आयी हैं।

पण्डिती साहित्य और बौद्धधर्म

संत साहित्य की तरह मराठी में पण्डिती साहित्य भी है। पण्डिती मराठी साहित्य का प्रारंभिक संत साहित्य के बाद का है। पण्डिती साहित्य का मतलब सीधा-सीधा ब्राह्मण पण्डितों द्वारा लिखा गया साहित्य। यह साहित्य पूरी तरह वैदिक विचारधारा से प्रभावित और प्रेरित साहित्य है। पण्डिती साहित्य के विषय भी वैदिक परम्परा से संबंधित हैं। इसलिए पण्डिती मराठी साहित्य पर बौद्ध धर्म के प्रभाव की कल्पना ही नहीं की जा सकती। इस काल में भी मराठी में किसी विषय पर कोई ग्रंथ या काव्य नहीं लिखा गया और न मराठी भाषा में इस तरह का कोई ग्रंथ उपलब्ध था।

संत काल के बाद पंडिती साहित्य का काल आया। पण्डिती साहित्य का काल ई.स. १६०० से १९०० तक माना जाता है जिसमें वामन पंडित, रघुनाथ पण्डित, पोरोपंत आदि का विशेष उल्लेख किया जा सकता है। इस मराठी-पंडिती साहित्य का विषय और उद्देश्य था संतचरित्र लिखना, उसी प्रकार सन्तों द्वारा समर्थित अध्यात्म-ईश्वर या ईश्वर महिमा। मोक्षप्राप्ति, स्तोत्रगायन और स्तवन आदि के द्वारा लोगों में ब्राह्मणवाद के मूल्यों की रक्षा करना। उन्होंने संस्कृत प्रचुर मराठी में साहित्य रचना की और लोगों में संतों की भाँति अध्यात्मवाद, ईश्वर प्राप्ति, मोक्षप्रप्ति के विचारों का प्रचार किया। बुद्ध का दर्शन, अनात्मवादी, अनित्यवादी अनिश्वरवादी, समतावादी, मानवतावादी होने के कारण कोई भी बौद्ध विषय पण्डिती साहित्य का विषय नहीं हो सका।

मराठी में बौद्ध ग्रंथों का प्रारम्भ

आधुनिक भारत में बौद्ध धर्म की दृष्टि से उन्नीसवीं शताब्दीं का बड़ा महत्व है। मराठी भाषा में उन्नीसवीं शताब्दी के प्रारम्भ से बौद्ध धर्म की चर्चा प्रारम्भ होती है। ब्रिटिशपूर्व काल में या मध्य काल के मराठी साहित्य पर और मराठी आचार-विचारों पर पूरी तरह से ब्राह्मणवाद का प्रभाव दिखायी देता है। मराठी संत जो अपने विचारों की अभिव्यक्ति के लिए जन भाषा मराठी का इस्तेमाल करते हैं वे ब्राह्मण धर्म के आचार्यों द्वारा स्थापित मार्ग का ही अनुगमन करते हैं। संत ज्ञानेश्वर, एकनाथ, रामदास आदि संत आद्य शंकराचार्य की ही राह पर चलते दिखायी देते हैं। इस सम्बन्ध में विट्ठल रामजी शिन्दे (ई.स. १८७६-१९४४) ने अपने एक निबन्ध 'मराठी वाङ्मय तत्वज्ञान आणि समाजशास्त्र' में कहा है कि, 'पहले के आचार्यों

ने ही ऐसा किया इसलिए उसके बाद के संस्कृत आचार्यों को और जनभाषा मराठी में ग्रंथ लिखनेवाले ज्ञानेश्वर, एकनाथ आदि संतों को अपनी साहित्य रचना में यही सामान्य रास्ता अपनाना पड़ा। आगे आगे तो गीता के कोल्हू के पीछे-पीछे मराठी के सभी वैचारिक विचारचक्र घूमने लगे। ज्ञानेश्वर की भावार्थ गीता (ज्ञानेश्वरी) में भक्ति का महत्व वर्णन किया गया है। वामन पंडित भी अपने 'यथार्थ दीपिका' में अव्यभिचारित कृष्ण भक्ति के बाहर स्वतंत्र ज्ञान का मार्ग नहीं खोज सके। उसके बाद लोकमान्य तिलक ने कर्मयोग अपनाया, लेकिन वही गीता के जाल में फंसकर। मतलब परम्परागत मराठी साहित्य में न तो कोई स्वतंत्र विचारधारा थी और न कोई चिन्तन था, परंपरागत मराठी साहित्य भक्ति का जाल में फँसा हुआ था। परंपरगत मराठी साहित्य एक तरह से जातिवाद, भक्तिवाद, ईश्वरवाद, सामंतवाद, ब्राह्मणवाद के जाल में फँसा हुआ था।

जब चौदहवीं सदी में यूरोप में ग्रीक विद्या का पुनरुत्थान हो रहा था और वहां के लोगों को जब नये ज्ञान-विज्ञान की संजीवनी प्राप्त हो रही थी, नई दृष्टि, नया सोच, नया समाजचिन्तन, नये जीवन मूल्य प्राप्त हो रहे थे उस समय उत्तर भारत में ज्ञान, समाज चिंतन और धर्म के क्षेत्र में पूरी तरह से अंधेरा छाया हुआ था। इस काल में जब यूरोप में धर्मसत्ता का विरोध हो रहा था, उस समय भारत में धर्मवाद का, धर्मान्धिता का बड़ा प्रभाव था। सन्तों को और उनके साहित्य को बड़ी प्रतिष्ठा थी। समाज में भयंकर जातिवाद, अछूतपन, शोषण, उत्पीड़न का बोलबाला था। यहाँ धर्म के विरोध में बोलने का किसी में साहस नहीं था। ऐसी स्थिति में महाराष्ट्र में और मराठी साहित्य में समाज परिवर्तनवादी, प्रगतिशील, मानवतावादी और व्यक्ति की स्वतंत्रता, सामाजिक न्याय, व्यक्ति के मूल्य को महत्व देने वाले अनीश्वरवादी, अनात्मवादी विचारों के साहित्य के निर्माण की बात कल्पना से परे थी।

किन्तु सत्रहवीं सदी में ब्रिटिश सत्ता भारत में कायम हुई। यूरोप के भौतिक ज्ञान-विज्ञान का भारत में प्रचार हुआ। यूरोप के वैज्ञानिक खोजों का आधुनिक ज्ञान-विज्ञान की प्रगति का यूरोप की तरह भारत की धार्मिक मान्यताओं पर प्रभाव पड़ा। महाराष्ट्र की विचारधारा पर भी प्रभाव पड़ा। मुंबई विश्वविद्यालय की स्थापना सन. १८५६ में हुई और मराठी लेखकों को हर्बर्ट स्पेन्सर (ईस. १८२०-१९०२), डार्विन जैसे कई लेखकों, चिन्तकों, साहित्कारों के साहित्य का परिचय हुआ। इस सम्बन्ध में विट्ठल रामजी शिंदे (ई.स. १८७३-१९४४) कहते है कि, 'हम सब लोगों के कॉलेज में प्रवेश पाने से पहले ही मराठी साहित्यकार इन न्यूनतम पश्चिमी विचारों का अनुवाद और रूपान्तर के द्वारा इतना प्रभाव दिखायी दिया कि उतना प्रभाव ब्रह्मसूत्र, शांकरभाष्य और गीता-भागवत आदि संस्कृत ग्रंथों का भी महाराष्ट्र के पाठक वर्ग पर कम से कम संत एकनाथ के समय भी नहीं था। इसका मतलब यह है कि, अंग्रेजी शिक्षा और पश्चिमी विचारों का प्रभाव मराठी मानस और मराठी साहित्य पर पड़ने लगा था।

महाराष्ट्र में मुंबई विश्वविद्यालय की स्थापना ई.स. १८५६ के दरम्यान हुई। किन्तु महाराष्ट्र में सामाजिक, धार्मिक सुधार का आन्दोलन इस से बीस साल पहले ही शुरू हो गया था।

किन्तु इस आन्दोलन का लाभ मराठी भाषी आम आदमी को नहीं हो रहा था क्योंकि वह तब भी शिक्षा से काफी दूर था। इसका लाभ मराठी समाज के तथाकथित उच्च वर्ण और उच्च वर्ग और उच्च जातियों के ही लोगों को हो रहा था, वे लोग जागृत हो रहे थे। अपनी समाज व्यवस्था सदोष है। इसके बारे में इनमें जागृति आ रही थी। उनको यह महसूस हो रहा था कि अपने में कई अमानवीय मान्यताएँ, रिवाज और परम्पराएँ हैं और उससे समाज का नुकसान हो रहा है। समाज कमजोर हो रहा है इसलिए पश्चिमी शिक्षा, ज्ञान-विज्ञान, उदारवादी, बुर्ज्वा सुधारवादी विचारों से प्रेरणा लेकर महाराष्ट्र के उच्चवर्णीय लोगों में से कुछ पढ़े-लिखे लोगों ने समाज सुधार, धार्मिक सुधार और सामाजिक प्रबोधन, सामाजिक पुनर्जारण के कार्य को शुरू किया। पंडित ईश्वरचन्द्र विद्यासागर कलकत्ता के महर्षि देवेन्द्रनाथ के तत्वबोधिनी सभा के सदस्य थे। उनका मुंबई के परमहंस मंडल में ब्रह्म समाज के बारे में व्याख्यान हुआ। उससे प्रेरित होकर सन. १८४० के दरम्यान मुंबई में परमहंस मंडल की स्थापना हुई। लेकिन इस मंडल का कार्य भी कुछ लोगों तक ही सीमित रहा। बाद में ईस. १८६० में परमहंस मंडल बंद हो गया और ईस. १८६७ में मुंबई में प्रार्थना समाज की स्थापना हुई। इस समाज के सामाजिक सुधार की नींव धार्मिक सुधार थी। लेकिन कुछ लोगों को धर्म के मामले में हस्तक्षेप करना अच्छा नहीं लगा और लोकहित देशमुख, राजारामशास्त्री भागवत और कृष्णशास्त्री चिपलुनकर जैसे तत्कालीन सफेदपोश उच्चवर्णी लोगों के नेताओं ने धर्म को और श्रद्धा को छुए वगैर केवल सामाजिक मान्यताओं में सुधार करने के लिए साहित्य निर्माण का आन्दोलन चलाया। लेकिन उनका यह आन्दोलन कुछ शहरों तक और वह भी तथाकथित उच्च वर्णिय लोगों तक ही सीमित रहा। समाज के आम आदमी से इसका कोई सम्बन्ध नहीं रहा। इस आन्दोलन ने गांव-देहातों को भी नहीं छुआ था। महाराष्ट्र में सन. १८४० से शुरू हुआ प्रबोधन आंदोलन प्रारम्भ में केवल मुंबई, पूना जैसे शहरों तक ही और तथाकथित उच्चवर्णीय समाज तथा उनके सवालों तक ही सिमटकर रह गया था।

महाराष्ट्र में तथाकथित उच्च वर्ण के पढ़े-लिखे लोगों द्वारा जो सामाजिक और धार्मिक सुधार का कार्य हो रहा था उससे महाराष्ट्र के आम मराठी भाषी को कोई लाभ नहीं था, उससे आम मराठी मनुष्य का कोई सरोकार नहीं था। इसलिए जोतिराव गोविंदराव फुले ने बहुजन समाज में और अछूत समाज में जागृति पैदा करने के लिए स्वतंत्र रूप से प्रयास किया और उन्होंने इसके लिए सामान्य लोगों की मराठी भाषा का इस्तेमाल किया। उन्होंने आम लोगों की मराठी में महत्वपूर्ण ग्रंथों की रचना की। उन्होंने सन. १८७३ में सत्यशोधक समाज की स्थापना की और महाराष्ट्र के बहुजन तथा दलित समाज में सामाजिक, धार्मिक, सांस्कृतिक तथा वैचारिक क्रांन्ति का सूत्रपात किया जिसका प्रभाव महाराष्ट्र के महानगरों से लेकर ग्रामीण अंचल तक फैला और आज भी जोतिबा फुले के विचारों से सारे भारत वर्ष का दलित-बहुजन समाज प्रभावित है, आन्दोलित है।

जब महाराष्ट्र में सामाजिक प्रबोधन का आन्दोलन आगे बढ़ रहा था उस समय महाराष्ट्र

में बौद्ध धर्म पर मराठी भाषा में कोई ग्रंथ या किताब उपलब्ध नहीं थी। तथाकथित उच्च वर्णियों का सामाजिक और धार्मिक सुधार का आन्दोलन पूरी तरह पश्चिमी विचारों से, पश्चिमी शिक्षा से प्रभावित था। इसलिए तत्कालीन मराठी साहित्य पर भी, पश्चिमी विचार, शिक्षा और धार्मिक विचारों का प्रभाव दिखायी देता है। महात्मा जोतिबा फुले के साहित्य पर भी, उनके विचारों पर भी पश्चिमी विचारों का प्रभाव दिखायी देता है। महात्मा जोतिबा फुले के जीवनी लेखक और महात्मा फुले:समग्र वाङ्मय (मराठी संस्करण) के सम्पादक डॉ धनंजय कीर ने कहा है कि, ब्रिटिश राजसत्ता के साथ भारत में जो नया ज्ञान आया, बुद्धिवाद आया, यंत्र-तंत्र का युग आया और विज्ञान आया उसकी रोशनी में ब्राह्मणी धर्म की पुराने पोथी-पुराणों की, सनातन धर्मग्रंथों की और उनके द्वारा स्थापित सामाजिक मूल्यों की परीक्षा करने के लिए उन्नीसवीं शताब्दी के मध्य में जो चिन्तक आगे आए, उनमें जोतिराव फुले को सब से श्रेष्ठ स्थान देना स्वाभाविक ही है। टॉमस पेन नाम के महान क्रांतिकारी चिन्तक के 'मनुष्य के अधिकार' (rights of man) ग्रंथ का बहुत बड़ा परिणाम जोतिराव फुले के मन पर छात्र जीवन में ही हो गया था। और वहीं से उनके जीवन कार्य की दिशा तय हुई। उन्होंने अपना सारा जीवन मानवी स्वतंत्रता के लिए समर्पित किया। इसी मानवी स्वतंत्रता और मानवी अधिकार की रोशनी में उन्होंने भारतीय जाति व्यवस्था का विश्लेषण किया और इस व्यवस्था को उन्होंने गुलामगीरी (slavery) की संज्ञा दी। भारत की जाति व्यवस्था के दुष्परिणामों से भारत के शूद्र, अतिशूद्र (पिछड़ी जातियाँ और अछूत जातियाँ) तथा नारी का जो शोषण और उत्पीड़न हुआ है उसका विश्लेषण करते हुए उनका ध्यान भारत के बौद्ध इतिहास की ओर गया। महात्मा फुले कहते है, 'किन्तु उनमें से कई शेष कुतर्की ब्राह्मण कर्नाटक में भाग जाने के बाद इन लोगों में शंकराचार्य नाम का एक प्रकार से दुष्ट विद्या जानने वाला महापण्डित पैदा हो गया। उनको अपने ब्राह्मण जाति के दुष्ट कार्यों की हर जगह जो फजीहत और आलोचना हो रही थी और बुद्ध धर्म का जो प्रचार हो रहा था वह बर्दास्त नहीं हो रहा था। उसने जब देखा कि अपने लोगों के पेटपानी का धंधा ठीक नहीं चल रहा है इसलिए जिन दुष्ट कर्मों के कारण अपने वेदों सहित सभी ग्रंथों का बौद्ध लोगों ने निषेध और पराभव किया था, उनमें से गोमांस खाना और शराब पीना बंद करके अपने सभी ग्रंथों में परिवर्तन करके एक नये नास्तिकमत की स्थापना की। इसी को आज कल वेदान्त का ज्ञानमार्ग कहते है। बाद में उनसे शिवलिंग की स्थापना करके इस देश में जो तुर्क बनकर रहे थे उनको हिन्दू जाति के क्षत्रिय बनाकर उनकी मदद से, मुस्लिम लोगों की तरह तलवार के बल पर बुद्ध लोगों को पराजित कर पुन: उसने उस अपने शेष जादू मंत्र विद्या से और भागवत की भाकड़ दंत कथाओं से अज्ञानी शूद्रों को अपने जाल में फंसाया। शंकराचार्य के इस आक्रमण में उसके कई लोगों ने कई बुद्ध धर्मी लोगों को तेल की चक्की में पीसकर मारा और उनके अधिकांश अच्छे-अच्छे ग्रंथ जलाकर राख कर दिये। इस से पता चलता है कि महात्मा फुले भारत में बौद्ध धर्म के इतिहास से परिचित हो गए थे और मराठी साहित्य में बौद्ध धर्म के कार्य के

बारे में इस तरह के विचार सब से पहले महात्मा फुले के साहित्य में ही मिलते हैं। महात्मा फुले के समय का अन्य मराठी लेखक बौद्ध धर्म से शायद परिचित नहीं था या बौद्ध धर्म को जानने की उसमें कोई इच्छा नहीं थी। महात्मा फुले के समग्र साहित्य से पता चलता है कि उनके साहित्य पर, उनके विचारों पर बौद्ध धर्म का प्रभाव निश्चित रूप से था क्योंकि बौद्धधर्म जिस क्रान्तिकारी समाज परिवर्त्तन के सोच को लेकर, ब्राह्मण धर्म, वैदिक धर्म के विरोध में आगे आया वही सोच महात्मा फुले के सम्पूर्ण साहित्य में और कार्य में भी है। फिर भी उस समय तक मराठी भाषा में बुद्ध धर्म पर कोई स्वतंत्र ग्रंथ या किताब नहीं थी। लेकिन मराठी साहित्य में बौद्ध धर्म की चर्चा शुरू हो गई थी।

महात्मा जोतिराव फुले के कारण आज से १४०-१५० साल पहले मराठी भाषा में हिन्दू धर्म की समीक्षा प्रारंभ हुई। उसी प्रकार हिन्दू धर्म, दर्शन, साहित्य, ब्राह्मण वर्ण वर्चस्व जातिभेद, अछूतपन, यज्ञयाग आदि का खण्डन और विरोध करना प्रारंभ हो गया था। उन्हीं की प्रेरणा से तुकाराम तात्या पडवल नाम के भंडारी जाति के एक विद्वान व्यक्ति ने 'जातिभेद विवेक सार' नाम का एक जातिभेद का खण्डन करनेवाला, महत्वपूर्ण ग्रंथ लिखा था। वे महात्मा फुले के सत्यशोधकों में से एक थे और उनका मुंबई के परमहंस तथा प्रार्थना समाज, थिआँसाँफिकल सोसायटी आदि संस्थाओं से करीब का सम्बन्ध था। उनके 'जातिभेद विवेकसार' (पहला संस्करण १८६१) ग्रंथ का प्रकाशन भी फुले ने किया था। इस ग्रंथ की प्रस्तावना से पता चलता है कि लेखक को बौद्ध आचार्य अश्वघोष के 'वज्रसूची' ग्रंथ की जानकारी थी और उन्होंने जातिभेद विवेकसार ग्रंथ के साथ 'वज्रसूची' का मराठी अनुवाद भी छपवाया था। आधुनिक मराठी साहित्य में अनूदित बौद्ध धर्म का यह पहला ग्रंथ था। लेकिन उस समय 'वज्रसूची' का यह मराठी अनुवाद स्वतंत्र किताब के रूप में नहीं छपा था। बहिणाबाई (ई.स. १६२८) के 'वज्रसूचीकोपनिषद भाष्य' का तो किसी को पता नहीं था। लेकिन पता चलता हे कि महात्मा फुले के साहित्य, चिन्तन और कार्य के कारण सत्यशोधक समाज का बहुजन समाज का बुद्धिजीवी वर्ग बौद्ध दर्शन से तथा बुद्ध के सामाजिक विचारों से प्रेरित और प्रभावित था।

उसके बाद मराठी की पत्र-पत्रिकाओं में बुद्ध के बारे में लेख प्रकाशित होने लगे। मराठी पाठकों की बौद्ध धर्म को जानने के प्रति रुचि बढ़ने लगी। महात्मा फुले के ही सत्यशोधक आन्दोलन से प्रेरित होकर महान सत्यशोधक कृष्णराव अर्जुन केलुसकर (ई.स. १८६०-१९३४) ने मराठी में 'गौतम बुद्धाचे चरित्र' नाम का महत्वपूर्ण ग्रंथ लिखा। और यह ग्रंथ १८९८ में प्रकाशित हुआ। मराठी साहित्य में भगवान बुद्ध के जीवन तथा दर्शन पर यह महत्वपूर्ण ग्रंथ है।इस ग्रंथ के बारे में डॉ बाबासाहेब आम्बेडकर कहते है कि, 'दादा केलुसकर द्वारा दिये गए ग्रंथ के कारण मैं बुद्ध से प्रभावित हुआ। इस छोटी उम्र में भी मैं बगैर सोचे समझे बुद्ध के पास नहीं गया। मुझे पृष्ठभूमि थी और बुद्ध के जीवन के बारे में किताबें पढ़ते हुए तुलना और भेद करता था। बुद्ध और उनके धम्म के प्रति लगाव बढ़ने की यह मेरी शुरूआत

थी।' इस किताब के बारे में डॉ. आम्बेडकर के ये विचार बड़ा महत्व रखते हैं और बहुत कुछ कह जाते हैं। स्वयं केलूसकर (गुरूजी) जी ने अपने यह किताब डॉ आम्बेडकर को उनके मेट्रिक की परीक्षा में सफलता (ई.स. १९०७) प्राप्त करने के उपलक्ष में अपने हाथों भेंट की थी। इस किताब का प्रारंभिक मराठी बौद्ध साहित्य में अपना एक स्थान है। इस किताब ने मराठी साहित्य में बौद्ध धर्म के अध्ययन का एक रास्ता बना दिया, इसमें कोई सन्देह नहीं।

मराठी भाषी क्षेत्र के नवजागरण आन्दोलन के कारण और महात्मा फुले के सत्यशोधक आन्दोलन के कारण मराठी भाषा में बौद्ध धर्म तथा बौद्ध विषयों से संबंधित ग्रंथ लेखन की परम्परा शुरू हो गई। सन. १८८३ में मराठी में बौद्ध धर्म पर पहला ग्रंथ वासुदेव लक्ष्मण आठवले का 'बौद्ध धर्माचे संस्थापक शाक्यमुनि गौतम यांचे चरित्र', दूसरा ग्रंथ गोविंद नारायण काणे का 'श्रीजगदगुरु गौतम बुद्ध चरित्र' अथवा 'महाभिनिष्क्रमण' (१८९४) प्रकाशित हुए थे। सन १८९९ में वा.गो. आप्टे ने 'अशोक चरित्र' किताब रूप में प्रकाशित किया। उसको पढ़कर न्यायमूर्ति रानडे ने संतोष प्रदर्शित किया और उन्होंने लेखक को बौद्ध धर्म का इतिहास लिखने की सलाह दी और उन्होंने ईस. १९०९-१० में बौद्धपर्व अर्थात् 'बौद्ध धर्माचा साधना इतिहास' नामक किताब प्रकाशित की। इस ग्रंथ की भी डॉ. आम्बेडकर ने बड़ी प्रशंसा की थी और उन्होंने भारतीय बौद्ध महासभा द्वारा सन. १९५७ और १९५८ में इस ग्रंथ के दो संस्करण प्रकाशित करवाए थे। उस समय मराठी भाषा में बौद्ध विषयों पर ग्रंथों का इतना अभाव था कि लेखक के बौद्ध धर्म संबंधी कुछ विचारों से असहमत होने के बावजूद भी डॉ. आम्बेडकर ने इस ग्रंथ के दो संस्करण प्रकाशित करवाए थे।

डॉ बाबासाहेब आम्बेडकर से पूर्व मराठी साहित्य को जिन लेखकों ने प्रभावित किया उनमें कृष्णराव अर्जुन केलुसकर (गुरूजी) और वा. गो. आप्टे और धर्मानन्द कोसम्बी (ई.स. १९७६-१९४७) का नाम और उनकी रचनाएँ विशेष उल्लेखनीय है उसमें भी मराठी साहित्य में धर्मानन्द कोसम्बी का साहित्य विशेष महत्वपूर्ण है। धर्मानन्द के प्रयासों से ही पूना के फर्ग्युसन कॉलेज में ईसवीं सन. १९१२ में पालि भाषा की पढ़ाई शुरू हुई। धर्मानन्द कोसम्बीजी के बुद्ध धर्म से प्रभावित होने के बारे में काकासाहेब कालेलकर लिखते है कि 'धर्मानन्द कोसम्बी सन. १८७६ में गोवा के एक छोटे से गांव में पैदा हुए थे। गोवा में सरकार की ओर से शिक्षा का प्रबन्ध कुछ भी नहीं था। इसलिए उन्होंने निजी तौर पर कुछ संस्कृत और मराठी सीख ली, ... इसी अरसे में उन्होंने 'बालबोध' नामक बच्चों के एक मराठी मासिक में बुद्ध भगवान का जीवन-चरित्र पढ़ा, उससे वे इतने प्रभावित हुए कि उन्होंने और सब बातें छोड़कर बौद्ध धर्म का ज्ञान सम्पादित करने का निश्चय किया। अपने जीवन चरित्र में वे लिखते है कि, 'मुझे ऐसा लगने लगा कि, कितने कितने ही संकट क्यों न आएं, कितनी ही विपत्तियाँ क्यों न झेलनी पड़ें, लेकिन मुझे बुद्धोपदेश का ज्ञान हो जाए तो मेरा जीवन सफल हो जायेगा।' धर्मानन्द कोसम्बीजीने २२ वर्ष की उम्र में घर छोड़ दिया और उन्होंने मुंबई में प्रार्थना-समाज के कार्यालय में रहकर कुछ अध्ययन किया। वे नेपाल गए, श्रीलंका गए और बौद्ध धर्म का अध्ययन किया। उन्हीं के प्रयास से और डॉ. भंडारकर की मदद से मुंबई

विश्वविद्यालय में पालि-भाषा के अध्ययन को स्थान मिला। उन्होंने मराठी में महत्वपूर्ण ग्रंथों की रचना की। बौद्ध लोग अपने हर मंगल कार्य के प्रारंभ में 'शरण-त्रय' को ग्रहण करते हैं। इसी को लेकर धर्मानन्दजी ने सबसे पहले बुद्ध, धर्म और संघ दोनों के बारे में कुछ व्याख्यान दिए थे और उनकी एक छोटी सी किताब 'बुद्ध धर्म आणि संघ (सन. १९१०) नाम से सबसे पहले प्रकाशित हुई।

इसके बाद पालि-परम्परा के अनुसार उन्होंने भगवान बुद्ध की कुछ जातक कथाएँ, गौतम बुद्ध की विस्तृत जीवनी और उनके धर्मोपदेश का सार तीनों एकत्र करके 'बुद्धलीलासारसंग्रह' (१९१४) नामक अत्यन्त रोचक और सुबोध ग्रंथ लिखा। इस ग्रंथ ने घर-घर में पहुंचकर लोगों को बौद्ध धर्म के बारे में उत्साह के साथ काफी जानकारी प्रदान की। भगवान बुद्ध का धर्म बहुजन हिताय-बहुजन सुखाय है। इसके लिए उन्होंने भिक्षु संघ की स्थापना की और उनके लिए कुछ विनय-नियम भी बनाएँ जो विनयपिटक में संग्रहित है। उसका सारांश उन्होंने 'बौद्ध संघाचा परिचय' (१९२६) नामक ग्रंथ में दिया। भगवान बुद्ध के कुछ चुनिंदा उपदेश काव्यरूप में पालि धम्मपद और सुत्तनिपात में हैं। इन पालि ग्रंथों में कई विषयों पर भगवान बुद्ध के विचार संग्रहित है। इन ग्रंथों में मन की परिभाषा है, अनीश्वरवाद है, अनात्मवाद है, उसी प्रकार इन ग्रंथों में जातिवाद का खण्डन है, ब्राह्मण वर्णश्रेष्ठत्व का खंडन है। उनका मराठी अनुवाद उन्होंने किया जिसके कारण मराठी पाठकों को मूल बौद्ध धर्म का ज्ञान प्राप्त हो सका। उन्होंने विसुद्धिमग्ग का मराठी सार 'समाधि मार्ग' (१९२५) के नाम से लिखा है। उसी प्रकार उन्होंने 'भगवान बुद्ध' (१९४०) नाम से भगवान बुद्ध की एक विस्तृत जीवनी मराठी में लिखी है। भगवान बुद्ध ने गृह-त्याग क्यों किया, इसकी अपनी मीमांसा और उसके प्रमाण व्यवस्थित ढंग से लोगों के सामने रखने के लिए उन्होंने एक छोटा सा नाटक लिखा जो बोधिसत्व नाटक (१९४९) के नाम से मराठी में प्रकाशित हुआ। उसी प्रकार बौद्ध धर्म के ऐतिहासिक योगदान को समझाने के लिए उन्होंने 'हिन्दी संस्कृति आणि अहिंसा' (१९३५) नाम का एक महत्वपूर्ण ग्रंथ मराठी में लिखा। उनका 'जातक कथा' भाग एक और 'निवेदन' (१९२४) भी महत्वपूर्ण है।

बौद्ध धर्म की दृष्टि से धर्मानन्द कोसम्बी और राजाराम शास्त्री भागवत के बीच का पत्र व्यवहार बड़ा महत्वपूर्ण है। उसी प्रकार मराठी के उदारवादी और सुधारवादी लेखकों ने नवभारत ग्रंथ माला का जो प्रकाशन शुरू किया था उसमें भी धर्मानन्द जी का बौद्ध धर्म की दृष्टि से बड़ा योगदान रहा है। धर्मानन्द कोसम्बीजी के पहले मतलब सन १९१० के पहले मराठी में बुद्ध तथा बौद्ध धर्म का परिचय देने वाले तीन ही ग्रंथ थे। उसमें भी गो. वि. काणे का ग्रंथ एडविन आरनोल्ड द्वारा रचित 'लाईट ऑफ एशिया' के आधार पर लिखा था। आरनोल्ड का अंग्रेजी ग्रंथ और उसके आधार पर गो. वि. काणे द्वारा लिखे गये ग्रंथ के बारे में डॉ. भंडारकर ने धर्मानन्द कोसम्बीजी के पास कहा था कि 'मूल में जैसा है उसका एक चौथाई उसमें आया नहीं और अंग्रेजी के एक चौथाई मराठी में आया नहीं।' शेष दो ग्रंथों

के बारे में प्रसिद्ध भाषाशास्त्री डॉ. पां. दा. गुणे ने धर्मानन्द कोसम्बीजी के एक ग्रंथ पर लिखे अभिप्राय में कहा था कि, 'बुद्ध के बारे में हमारे लोगों को बुद्ध के सामने और वह अनिश्वरवादी था, उसके आगे ज्यादा जानकारी नहीं होती है'। इस से पता चलता है कि धर्मानन्द कोसम्बीजी ने बौद्ध धर्म पर अपना लेखन कार्य प्रारम्भ किया, उस समय भाषा और साहित्य में बौद्ध धर्म के बारे में क्या स्थिति थी। यह बात सच है कि सन. १९१० से पहले मराठी में बुद्ध के जीवन पर तथा बौद्ध धर्म पर विशेष महत्वपूर्ण या विशेष जानकारी पूर्ण साहित्य नहीं था। इसलिए इस काल के मराठी साहित्य पर बौद्ध धर्म के विशेष प्रभाव की बात करना उचित नही है। किन्तु मराठी में महात्मा जोतिराव फुले से जो समाज परिवर्तन का आन्दोलन शुरू होता है उसमें निश्चित तौर पर बौद्ध धर्म का प्रभाव दिखायी देता है। इतना ही नहीं तो महात्मा फुले की प्रेरणा से मराठी में जो साहित्य लिखा गया है उस पर स्पष्ट रूप से बौद्ध धर्म का प्रभाव दिखाई देता है। महाराष्ट्र का समाज परिवर्तनवादी, प्रगतिशील साहित्य, जीवनवादी साहित्य बौद्ध धर्म से प्रभावित है इसमें कोई सन्देह नही है।

विठ्ठल रामजी शिंदे के साहित्य पर और विचारों पर बौद्ध धर्म का प्रभाव है। जेधे-जवलकर के साहित्य पर बौद्ध धम्म का प्रभाव है, प्रबोधनकार ठाकरे और खंडेराव बागल के साहित्य पर बौद्ध धर्म का प्रभाव है। प्रसिद्ध मराठी कवि कुसुमाग्रज के साहित्य पर बौद्ध धर्म का प्रभाव है। कवि केशवसुत की कुछ रचनाओं मे बुद्ध धर्म का प्रभाव दिखायी देता है। बा. सी. मर्ढेकर की कुछ कविताओं पर विचारधारा का प्रभाव दिखायी देता है। मर्ढेकर कहते है- 'धम्मं सरणं' कुणी बोलिले। पाषाणातील बुद्ध भिषाने।

आज का मराठी साहित्य और बौद्ध प्रभाव

आधुनिक मराठी साहित्य में कई प्रकार की विचारधाराएँ मिलती हैं। 'कला के लिए कला' इस तरह की सोच रखने वाले साहित्यकारों, लेखकों का एक वर्ग मराठी साहित्य में था और आज भी है। उसी प्रकार सनातनी हिन्दुत्ववादी, ब्राह्मणवादी सोच रखनेवाले साहित्यकारों, लेखकों का एक वर्ग मराठी साहित्य में था और आज भी है। समाज परिवर्तन के लिए, जातिभेद और अछूतपन के विरोध में हिन्दू सनातनी और ब्राह्मणवादी मूल्यों तथा मान्यताओं के विरोधों में जन प्रबोधन की बात करने वाला, दलित तथा पिछड़ी जातियों में स्वाभिमान, अस्मिता और अस्तित्व की पहचान करा देने वाले चिन्तकों, समाज प्रबोधकों, लेखकों, साहित्कारों का भी एक वर्ग था और आज भी है। मराठी साहित्य में दलित साहित्य-आम्बेडकरवादी साहित्य की धारा है, मार्क्सवादी-जनवादी-प्रगतिशील साहित्य की धारा है, ग्रामीण साहित्य है, आदिवासी साहित्य है, मुस्लिम मराठी साहित्य, खिस्ती मराठी साहित्य, बहुजन मराठी साहित्य, विद्रोही साहित्य है। मराठी साहित्य में कभी एक सोच एक मान्यता नहीं ही है। संत साहित्य में भी ब्राह्मणवादी और ब्राह्मणवाद विरोधी दो धाराएँ रही है।

आधुनिक महाराष्ट्र में मराठी साहित्य में कई विचारधाराएँ कार्यरत हैं और इन विचारधाराओं को मोटे तौर पर हम दो भागों में बाँट सकते है, एक सनातन हिन्दू व्यवस्थावादी विचारधारा, जातिवाद समर्थक विचारधारा और दूसरी समतावादी, जातिवाद विरोधी, हिन्दुत्ववाद, ब्राह्मणवाद विरोधी विचारधारा। आज का मराठी साहित्य इन दोनों प्रकार की विचारधाराओं से प्रभावित है, इसमें कोई सन्देह नहीं।

आज का मराठी साहित्य आम्बेडकर विचारधारा से, बौद्ध विचारधारा से प्रभावित है। आज वो मराठी साहित्य में सनातनवाद के विरोध के स्वर है, जातिवाद विरोध के स्वर हैं, व्यवस्था परिवर्तन की बात हो रही है, सामाजिक समता और सामाजिक न्याय की बात कही जा रही है। सभी मनुष्य बराबर हैं की बात कही जा रही है। सामान्य आदमी पर कविता लिखी जा रही है। सामान्य दलित-शोषित, मजदूर, महिला, गांव का किसान, आदिवासी की स्थिति पर कविताएँ, कहानियाँ उपन्यास, लेख लिखे जा रहे हैं जो पहले कभी साहित्य के विषय नही होते थे। डॉ आम्बेडकर की विचारधारा के कारण, बुद्ध के विचारों के प्रसार और प्रचार के कारण मराठी साहित्य में आम आदमी साहित्य का विषय बना है। बौद्ध विषय मराठी साहित्य के विषय हुए हैं। बुद्ध पर कविताएँ लिखी जा रही हैं। पालि जातक कथाओं का मराठी में अनुवाद हुआ है। पालि ग्रंथों का मराठी में अनुवाद हुआ है। आधुनिक मराठी साहित्य का जो वैचारिक और निबंध साहित्य है उस पर बौद्ध धर्म और दर्शन का बड़ा प्रभाव है। महाराष्ट्र के सामाजिक परिवर्तन के आन्दोलन में मराठी के वैचारिक साहित्य अर्थात् लेखों और निबंधों की बड़ी महत्वपूर्ण भूमिका रही है। महात्मा फुले, न्यायमूर्ति महादेव गोविंद रानाडे, आगरकर, लोकहितवादी, गोपालबाबा वलंगकर, शिवराम जानबा कांबले, विठ्ठल रामजी शिंदे, खण्डेराव बागल, बॅ. सावरकर, धर्मानन्द कोसम्बी, दादा धर्माधिकारी, माधवराव बागल, गं. बा. सरदार, श्री. म. माटे, डॉ. पु. ग. सहस्त्रबुद्धे, तर्कतीर्थ लक्ष्मणशास्त्री जोशी आदि के वैचारिक साहित्य पर, लेखों तथा निबंधों पर स्पष्ट रूप से बौद्ध धर्म का प्रभाव दिखायी देता है। मराठी के अधिकांश निबन्धकारों ने समाज परिवर्तन की दृष्टि से सामाजिक क्रांति का, जातिभेद निर्मूलन का, सभी मनुष्यों में समानता का, मानवी मूल्यों की स्थापना का समर्थन किया है और ब्राह्मण वर्ण वर्चस्ववाद का, जातिवाद का खण्डन किया है। महाराष्ट्र में मराठी निबंधों की सवा सौ ड़ेढ सौ साल की परम्परा है। स्वंय बॅ. वि. दा. सावरकर ने 'सहा सोनेरी पाने' में भारत के पतन के लिए बौद्ध धर्म को जिम्मेदार माना। किन्तु उन्होंने अपने 'जात्युच्छेदक निबंध' में स्पष्ट रूप से कहा है कि हिन्दुस्तान का पतन जन्मनिष्ठ जातिभेद से हुआ है। जन्म पर आधारित किसी भी सामाजिक विषमता का विरोध तो बौद्ध धर्म की बुनियाद है। बॅ. सावरकर के साहित्य के आधार पर हम उन्हें आदिशंकराचार्य की तरह प्रछन्न बौद्ध कह सकते है।

डॉ. बाबासाहेब आम्बेडकर को मराठी साहित्य के निबन्धकारों में एक श्रेष्ठ निबन्धकार के रूप में ऊँचा स्थान है। वास्तव में डॉ. आम्बेडकर एक सामाजिक क्रान्तिकारी थे। वे दलित

जातियों और पिछड़ी जातियों के, तथा सम्पूर्ण नारी समाज की आजादी की लड़ाई लड़ रहे थे। उनका सारा लेखन और चिन्तन भी इसी दृष्टि से है। डॉ. आम्बेडकर अपने छात्र-जीवन से ही बौद्ध धर्म तथा बुद्ध के जीवन-चिन्तन से प्रभावित थे। उन्होंने ३१ मई १९३६ में मुंबई में आयोजित दलित परिषद में अपने भाषण में बौद्ध धर्म की चर्चा की थी। वे दलितों के सम्बोधित करते हुए कहते है कि, 'मुझे जो भी कहना आवश्यक था वह कह दिया है। सिद्धार्थ गौतम 'बुद्ध' के जीवन से सम्बन्धित एक प्रसंग मुझे याद आ रहा है। प्रसंग बुद्ध के महापरिनिर्वाण के पहले का है। बुद्ध के शिष्य भदन्त आनंद जब उनके पास जाते है और कहते है कि, 'आप अपने महापरिनिर्वाण के पहले संघ को कुछ मार्गदर्शन करें।' तब बुद्ध 'आनन्द से कहते है, आनन्द! संघ को बुद्ध से क्या चाहिए? मैनें जो कुछ जाना है वह सब मैंने संघ के सामने रख दिया है। बुद्ध रहस्यवादी नहीं है। आनन्द! आप स्वयं अपने दीप बनो। स्वयं प्रकाशित बनो। खुद पर भरोसा रखो। स्वयं की सरण में जावो। सच्चाई पर अटल रहो।' मैं बुद्ध के इन वचनों की याद दिलाकर अन्त में यही कहना चाहता हूँ कि आप स्वयं अपना आधार बनों। आप अपनी बुद्धि सरण जावो। अन्य किसी के बहकावे में मत जाओ। सत्य के आधार पर ही चलो। सत्य की ही सरण जावों। बुद्ध का यह मार्गदर्शन आप सभी को प्रेरक सिद्ध होगा और यदि आप लोगों ने बुद्ध के ही वचनों को ध्यान में रखा तो मुझे इस बात का पूरा यकीन है कि आप लोग जो भी निश्चय करोगे वह गलत नहीं होगा। डॉ. आम्बेडकर के सन. १९५६ के बौद्ध धम्म स्वीकार करने से और आधुनिक भारत में वह बौद्ध धर्म के पुनरुज्जीवन से इस व्याख्यान का बड़ा सम्बन्ध है।

दलित साहित्य और बौद्ध धर्म

मराठी साहित्य में दलित साहित्य का अपना एक स्थान है, अपनी एक पहचान है। इस साहित्य की प्रेरणा डॉ. बाबासाहेब आम्बेडकर का सामाजिक समानता, सामाजिक क्रान्ति और मानवतावाद का दर्शन-चिन्तन और आन्दोलन है। इस देश में डॉ. आम्बेडकर ने सन. १९२० से अर्थात् मूक नायक के सम्पादन तथा प्रकाशन से अपना सामाजिक क्रान्ति का आन्दोलन शुरू किया। उन्होंने मूक नायक के सम्पादकियों में, लेखों में, निबन्धों में हिन्दूधर्म की, जातिभेद की, अछूतपन की, हिन्दू धर्मग्रंथों की समीक्षा करना शुरू कर दिया था। डॉ. आम्बेडकर ने सन. १९-२० मार्च, १९२७ में महाराष्ट्र के महाड़ नाम के एक गांव में चवदार तलाब पर अछूतों को अपना मानवी हक मतलब उस सार्वजनिक तालाब का पानी पीने का हक मिलना चाहिए इसके लिए आन्दोलन किया था। उसी महाड़ में उन्होंने २५ दिसं. १९२७ को विषमतावादी, मानवता विरोधी कानूनों की जननी मनुस्मृति का दहन कर दफनाया था। उन्होंने नासिक में कालाराम मंदिर प्रवेश का सत्याग्रह किया, पूना के पार्वती मंदिर प्रवेश का सत्याग्रह किया, अमरावती के अंबादेवी मंदिर प्रवेश का सत्याग्रह (१९२७) किया था।

उन्होंने सन. १९२९ में सायमन कमीशन के सामने दलितों-अछूतों के राजनीतिक प्रतिनिधित्व तथा राजनीतिक अधिकारों की बात रखी थी। वे सन. १९३० से १९३२ तक इंग्लैंड में हुए राउण्ड टेबल कॉन्फरेन्स में अछूतों के राजनीतिक अधिकारों के लिए, उनके मानवी अधिकारों के लिये लड़ते रहे। उन्होंने १३ अक्टूबर १९३५ को महाराष्ट्र के येवले गांव में एक दलित परिषद में हिन्दू धर्म का त्याग और धिक्कार करने की घोषणा की और उस परिषद में उन्होंने कहा था कि, 'मैं हिन्दू होकर पैदा हुआ हूँ, यह मेरे बस की बात नहीं थी। किन्तु अब मैं हिन्दू होकर मरूँगा नहीं।' उसके बाद उन्होंने १९४२ में महाराष्ट्र के नागपुर शहर में अखिल भारतीय दलित वर्गीय परिषद का आयोजन किया था और उन्होंने १४ अक्टूबर १९५६ को नागपुर में ही बौद्ध धर्म को अपनाया। सन. १९२० से सन १९५६ के दरम्यान महाराष्ट्र में डॉ. आम्बेडकर ने सामाजिक क्रान्ति का एक तूफान खड़ा कर दिया जिसके कारण हिन्दुत्व की धरती डगमगाने लगी थी, थरथराने लगी थी। उनके आन्दोलन के कारण ब्राह्मणवाद, पण्डितवाद, वेद और वेदान्त, ईश्वरवाद आदि के खिलाफ मराठी साहित्य में साहित्य लिखा जाने लगा। मराठी साहित्य में बहुत बड़ी मात्रा में हिन्दू धर्म, हिन्दू धर्मशास्त्रों, हिन्दू देवी-देवताओं की समीक्षा होने लगी, आलोचना होने लगी। डॉ. आम्बेडकर द्वारा संपादित, प्रकाशित बहिष्कृत-भारत के दि. १५ मार्च १९२९ के अंक में 'पूर्व बंगाल्यातील अस्पृश्य वर्गाट्या उच्च शिक्षाणाची प्रगति' विषय पर वि. रा. शिंदे का लेख प्रकाशित हुआ। उसी प्रकार दि. ३१ मई १९२९ के अंक में त. वि. प्रधान का 'वणश्रिमाची मिमांसा' लेख प्रकाशित हुआ। इन दोनों लेखों में बौद्ध धर्म की विशेषता वर्णन की गई है।

डॉ. आम्बेडकर की इस सामाजिक क्रान्ति के आन्दोलन का मराठी साहित्य पर जबर्दस्त प्रभाव पड़ा है। उनके उस आन्दोलन का प्रस्थापित वर्ग के लेखकों, साहित्यकारों पर भी प्रभाव पड़ा और दलित, बहुजन समाज के लेखकों, साहित्यकारों, कवियों को प्रेरणा मिली और उन्होंने लिखना शुरू किया। डॉ आम्बेडकर का सारा आन्दोलन जातिव्यवस्था, जातिभेद और अछूतपन को समाप्त करने के लिए था। उनका आंदोलन समतावादी, मानवतावादी, लोकतांत्रिक तथा समतावादी मूल्यों तथा सिद्धान्तों पर भारतीय समाज के निर्माण के लिए था। यह कार्य हिन्दू बने रहकर, हिन्दू धर्म के आधार पर, वेद और वेदान्त के आधार पर सम्भव नही है यह डॉ. आम्बेडकर की मान्यता थी। उन्होंने सन. १९२० से १९५६ तक हिन्दू धर्म की समीक्षा पर कई ग्रंथों की रचना की। उन्होंने हिन्दू धर्म, दर्शन, जातिवाद, जातिभेद, अछूतपन, अछूतों की स्थिति, दलितों के मानवी अधिकार आदि पर सैकड़ों लेख, निबंध लिखे और व्याख्यान दिए। वे महाराष्ट्र के शहरों, नगरों और गांवों में गए। उन्होंने कई सभाओं, सम्मेलनों और परिषदों को सम्बोधित किया। उन्होंने महिला परिषदों में व्याख्यान दिए और उनमें परिवर्तन की चेतना जगाई। इसी के परिणामस्वरूप मराठी में दलित वर्ग से लेखक साहित्यकार, कवि, नाटककार तैयार हुए। सभी लोग डॉ. आम्बेडकर की प्रेरणा से लिखने लगे। डॉ. आम्बेडकर के विचारों को पढ़ने लगे महात्मा फुले के विचारों को पढ़ने लगे। मार्क्सवाद को पढ़ने लगे। दलित समाज से लिखने वाले ज्यादातर लेखक, साहित्यकार, कवि

सामाजिक परिवर्तन के आन्दोलन से जुड़े हुए थे। इसी तरह डॉ. आम्बेडकर से प्रेरणा लेकर साहित्य लिखा जा रहा है। यही प्रारम्भ में दलित साहित्य के नाम से जाना गया। आज उस साहित्य को आम्बेडकरवादी साहित्य के नाम से भी जाना जाता है, आम्बेडकरवादी बौद्ध साहित्य के नाम से भी जाना जाता है, दलित अस्मिता के साहित्य के नाम से भी जाना जाता है।

डॉ. आम्बेडकर ने अपने चिन्तन, दर्शन और कार्य का प्रारम्भ जातिवाद, जातिभेद, अछूतपन के विनाश के लिए तथा सामाजिक समानता और मानवता की स्थापना के लिए किया है। इसलिए उनकी प्रेरणा से जो मराठी साहित्य लिखा गया और लिखा जा रहा है उसमें भी इनकी बातों को ज्यादा महत्व दिया गया है। दलित साहित्य पर बौद्ध विचारधारा के प्रभाव के लिए १४ अक्टूबर १९५६ को नागपुर में सात लाख दलित लोगों द्वारा बौद्ध धर्म को स्वीकार करना, १६ अक्टूबर को १९५६ को चन्द्रपुर (महाराष्ट्र) में दो लाख लोगों द्वारा बौद्ध धर्म को स्वीकार करना और उसके बाद सम्पूर्ण महाराष्ट्र में बौद्ध धम्म दीक्षा समारोह का आयोजन होना, उनके द्वारा नवदीक्षित बौद्धों को बाईस धम्म-प्रतिज्ञाएँ कहलवाना तथा हर बौद्ध को अपने दैनिक जीवन में उन प्रतिज्ञाओं का पालन करना आदि घटनाएँ बौद्ध प्रभाव के लिए बड़ी उपयोगी सिद्ध हुई हैं। डॉ. आम्बेडकर द्वारा लिखित 'द बुद्ध एण्ड हिज धम्म' (भगवान बुद्ध और उनका धम्म) तो दलित साहित्यकारों का प्रेरणाग्रंथ बन गया। इस ग्रंथ से दलित साहित्य को एक दर्शन मिल गया। इस ग्रंथ के अध्ययन के और बाईस धम्म प्रतिज्ञाओं से दलित लेखकों, साहित्यकारों की वैचारिकता की नींव मजबूत हो गई। इसलिए दलित साहित्यकारों ने केवल जातिभेद, अछूतपन, सामाजिक उत्पीड़न, शोषण आदि बातों को ही अपने साहित्य का विषय नहीं बनाया बल्कि उन्होंने वर्णवाद, कर्मवाद, पुनर्जन्म, पूर्वजन्म, ईश्वरवाद, देव-दैववाद, वेद-वेदांत, कर्मकाण्ड. धार्मिक पाखण्ड, धर्मग्रंथ प्रमाण, शब्द प्रमाण, पुरोहितवाद, धर्मान्धता, आत्मवाद, परमात्मवाद आदि मान्यताओं का भी जबर्दस्त खण्डन किया है। डॉ. आम्बेडकर की बाईस धम्म प्रतिज्ञाएँ एक तरह से मराठी दलित साहित्य का ही नहीं बल्कि सम्पूर्ण भारत के दलित साहित्य का और परिवर्तनवादी साहित्य का घोषणा पत्र बन गया। इससे महाराष्ट्र में एक नई बौद्ध संस्कृति का निर्माण हो गया।

दलित साहित्य पूरी तरह से आम्बेडकरवादी प्रेरणा का साहित्य है इसमें कोई सन्देह नहीं। उसी प्रकार दलित साहित्य का दार्शनिक आधार भी बुद्ध का दर्शन ही है। आज हर दलित लेखक पर, परिवर्तनवादी लेखक पर डॉ. आम्बेडकर के 'बुद्ध और उनका धम्म' ग्रंथ का जबर्दस्त प्रभाव है। आज हर दलित लेखक, साहित्यकार बुद्ध और डॉ. आम्बेडकर से प्रेरित है। इसलिए बाबूराव बागलू जैसे मराठी दलित लेखक ने दलित साहित्य को आज क्रान्ति विज्ञान कहा है। वास्तव में दलित साहित्य बुद्ध के दर्शन के कारण क्रान्ति के चेतना का साहित्य बन गया है। इस बात को मराठी दलित साहित्य के महान आलोचक प्रा. रा. ग. जाधव भी स्वीकार करते हैं। आज मराठी दलित साहित्य पर ही नहीं बल्कि सम्पूर्ण मराठी साहित्य

पर बौद्ध धर्म का प्रभाव है। पिछले छह-सात दशकों में मराठी में पालि के कुछ बौद्ध ग्रंथों का, संस्कृत के कुछ बौद्ध ग्रंथों का मराठी में अनुवाद हुआ है और प्रकाशित हुआ है। महाराष्ट्र में स्कूलों, महाविद्यालयों और विश्वविद्यालयों में पालि तथा बौद्ध धर्म-दर्शन के अध्ययन-अध्यापन की भी व्यवस्था हुई है। कुछ बौद्ध विषयों पर भी स्वतंत्र ग्रंथ की रचना हुई है, संशोधन हो रहा है। बौद्ध विषय लेखकों, कवियों, साहित्यकारों, उपन्यासकारों की रचनाओं के विषय हो रहे हैं। बौद्ध विषय समाजचिन्तकों के चिन्तन और लेखन के विषय हो रहे हैं। लोग हिन्दुत्व का त्याग कर बौद्ध धम्म के स्वीकार कर रहे है। मराठी साहित्य में जातिभेद, अछूतपन, जातिवाद, धर्मान्धता, धार्मिक कर्मकाण्ड, ब्राह्मणवर्ग श्रेष्ठत्व, जाति-उत्पीड़न के खिलाफ काफी कुछ लिखा गया है, लिखा जा रहा है। जिस प्रकार दलित साहित्य में जातिवाद, जातिभेद, ब्राह्मणवाद आदि के खिलाफ, उसके कुप्रभाव के खिलाफ लिखा जा रहा है, ब्राह्मणवादी व्यवस्था के खिलाफ आक्रोश व्यक्त किया जा रहा है, ब्राह्मणी व्यवस्था के खिलाफ विद्रोह की बात की जा रही है। उसी प्रकार सम्पूर्ण मराठी साहित्य में भी जातिवाद, जातिभेद, अछूतपन, ब्राह्मणवाद, धर्मान्धता, धार्मिक पाखण्ड के खिलाफ लिखा गया है और लिखा जा रहा है और यह सब डॉ. बाबासाहेब आम्बेडकर प्रणीत बौद्ध धर्म के कारण ही मराठी साहित्य बौद्ध धर्म से प्रभावित हैं।

डॉ० आम्बेडकर के महापरिनिर्वाण के बाद मराठी के प्रसिद्ध दलित साहित्यकार कवि अण्णभाऊ साठे कहते हैं-

जग बदल घालुनी घाव सांगुन गेले मला भीमराव।
गुलामगिरीच्या या चिखलात। रूतून बतला का ऐरावत।
अंग झाडुनी निघ बाहेरी। घे बिनीवरती घाव॥
धनवंतांनी अखंड पिव्ठले धर्मान्धांनी तसेच छव्ठले।
मगराने जणु माणिक गिव्ठिले। चोर जाहले साव॥
ठरवुन आम्हा हीन कलंकित। जन्मोजन्मी करूनी अंकित।
जिणे लादुनी वर अवमानित। निर्मून हा भेदभाव॥
एकजुटीच्या या रथावरती। आरूढ होऊनी चल बा पुढती।
नव महाराष्ट्र निर्मून जगती। करी प्रकट निज गाव॥

इसमें उन्होंने डॉ. आम्बेडकर का संदेश बताया है और दलितों का किस प्रकार से दमन हो रहा है इस बात को भी बताया है और दलितों को दुनिया बदल देने का आह्वान किया है।

दलित कवि दया पवार अछूतपन की व्यवस्था और जातिभेद के खिलाफ अपना आक्रोश व्यक्त करते हुए भारत देश की तथाकथित 'महान' संस्कृति के असली रूप के बारे में कहते है-

हे महान देशा, किती दिवस चालणार तुक्षा पंक्तिप्रपंच.
आम्ही गावा बाहेर रहातो, यात आमचा दोष काय ?...
आमची पंगत नेहमी उशिरा बसते
तीही उकिरडयावर
वैष्णव जन तो तेने कहिये जो प्रीत पराई जाने रे ... (कोंडवाडा)

उन्होंने इस में भारतीय संस्कृति जो वसुधैवकुटुम्बकम् की बात करती है और वैष्णव वह है जो दूसरों को अपना समझता है के दोहरे चरित्र पर जबर्दस्त प्रहार किया है।

दुःखाने गदगदतांना हे झाड मी पाहिलेले
तशी याची मुव्ळे खोलवर बोधिवृक्षासारखी
बोधिवृक्षाला फुले तरी आली
हे झाड साया रूतूत कोव्ळपून गेलेले
धमनीधमनीत फुटू पाहणाया यातना
दुःखाने गदगदतांना हे झाड मी पाहिले। (कोंडवाडा)

इन पंक्तियों में दया पवार ने हिन्दुत्व को एक ऐसा वृक्ष कहा है जिसने आम आदमी के जीवन में दुख के अलावा कुछ नहीं दिया और बोधिवृक्ष है जो इस देश में फूला और सभी के लिए सुखद छाया दे गया।

कवि केशव मेश्राम ईश्वर की निर्लज्जता पर अपना गुस्सा व्यक्त करते हैं–

एक दिवस मी परमेश्ववाराला आईवरून शिवी दिली
तो लेकाचा फक्कन हसला ...
साल्या तुकडाभर भाकरीसाठी गाडीभर लाकडं फोडशील काय ? (उत्खनन)

कवि यशवंत मनोहर–हिन्दुत्वादी दर्शन के बारे में कहते है–

भारतीय परमात्यांने डिक्लेअर केलेल्या गुलामीसारखी
जीवनाची सर्व षंढ तत्वज्ञाने पुसावी लागतील
सर्वच बेरजा कशा होऊ शकतात
कडू भागाकारही करावे लागतील (उत्थान गुंफा)

कवि त्र्यंबक सपकाले अपनी कविता में कहते है–

नागडा आलो, पण इथेही नागवला गेलो,
समाज पुरूषाच्या अहंकाराने, हे संस्कृतिप्रिय देशा
माझा नागडेपणा तुला कधी झाकताच आला नाही.
रेडा इथला। वेदान्ती झाला।

मैलोगणती दूर ठेवले।
अक्षरशत्रू बनवून आम्हाला-(सुरंग, काव्यसंग्रह)

कवि ज. वि. पवार कहते है-

जाव्ठायजे म्हणतोय संस्कृतीचे मढे
शतकानुशतके तिरडीवर पडून आहे
ज्याला तुम्ही घाबरत आलायत
शेतातल्या बुजगावण्याला माकडाने भ्यावे तसे. (नाकेबंदी)

नामदेव ढसाल ने एक कविता में कहा है

'मी तुला शिव्यादेतो, तुझ्या ग्रंथाला शिव्या देतो,
तुझ्या संस्कृतीला शिव्या देतो, तुझ्या पाखंडीपणाला शिव्या देतो-
मी हे सारं काही बोलणार नव्हतो पण माझे हात जागे झालेत ....'
बेंबीचा देठ ओला होणाया वयात. (गोलपिठा, काव्यसंग्रह)

दलित कविता के मूल में जिस प्रकार डॉ. आम्बेडकर की प्रेरणा है कि उसी प्रकार बुद्ध की भी है। लेकिन उनके सामने बुद्ध एक अवतार के रूप में नहीं है बल्कि वह समग्र क्रान्ति का संदेश देने वाले के रूप में है। इसलिए दया पवार कहते है-

तुला मी असे कधीच पाहात नाही जेतवनात
डोव्ळे मिटून बसलेला, ध्यानस्थ पद्मासनातला
अथवा अजंठा वेरूव्ळच्या लेण्यात
दगडी ओठ शिवलेला, शेवटी निद्रा घेत असलेला
मी तुला पाहतो, चालता बोलता,
दीन दुबव्ळयां दुक्खावर फुंकर घालणारा
जीवघेण्या काव्ळोखात. हाती मशाल घेत
झोपडी झोपडीकडे जाणारा, संसर्गजन्य रोग्यासारखा
नरडीचा घोट घेणाया
दुक्खाचे नवे अर्थ सांगणारा (कोंडवाडा)

इस प्रकार मराठी दलित कविता जतिभेद, अछूतपन और मानवीय शोषण तथा उत्पीड़न की व्यवस्था को पैदा करने वाले हिन्दू धर्म को, उसके शास्त्रों को और इसकी मान्यताओं को नकारती है, उसके खिलाफ अपना आक्रोश व्यक्त करती है।

मराठी दलित साहित्य का आन्दोलन डॉ. आम्बेडकर के आन्दोलन से पैदा हुआ है। डॉ. आम्बेडकर ने अपने आंदोलन को बुद्ध के दर्शन का आधार दिया है। इसलिए दलित साहित्य का दार्शनिक तथा वैचारिक आधार भी बौद्ध दर्शन ही है इसमें कोई संदेह नहीं है। बौद्ध दर्शन

के कारण ही दलित साहित्य ने मराठी साहित्य में अपनी एक स्वतंत्र पहचान, अपना एक स्वतंत्र स्थान बना लिया है। मराठी दलित साहित्य में ब्राह्मणी व्यवस्था के प्रति विद्रोह, आक्रोश, घृणा और नफरत तो है ही। दलित साहित्य केवल विद्रोह का साहित्य नहीं है। बल्कि दलित साहित्य एक नवसमाज, समतावादी समाज, मानवतावादी मूल्यों पर आधारित समाज, धार्मिक पाखण्डों, कर्मकाण्डों और पुरोहितवाद से मुक्त समाज चाहता है। इसलिए मराठी दलित साहित्य ने डॉ. आम्बेडकर प्रणीत बुद्ध के दर्शन को अपना वैचारिक आधार स्वीकार किया है। कुल मिलाकर यह कहा जा सकता है कि आधुनिक मराठी साहित्य पर चाहे साहित्य की कोई भी विधा हो उस पर बौद्ध धर्म का प्रभाव निश्चित रूप से है।